INTO THE LOOP

Into the Loop

An Ethnography of Compulsive Repetition

SAMUELE
COLLU

Duke University Press   *Durham and London*   2026

Project Editor: Bird Williams
Designed by Courtney Leigh Richardson
Typeset in Garamond Premier Pro by Copperline Book Services

Library of Congress Cataloging-in-Publication Data
Names: Collu, Samuele, [date] author.
Title: Into the loop : an ethnography of compulsive repetition /
Samuele Collu.
Description: Durham : Duke University Press, 2026. | Includes
bibliographical references and index.
Identifiers: LCCN 2025025468 (print)
LCCN 2025025469 (ebook)
ISBN 9781478032946 (paperback)
ISBN 9781478029519 (hardcover)
ISBN 9781478061700 (ebook)
Subjects: LCSH: Visual anthropology. | Systemic therapy (Family
therapy)—Argentina. | Relationship quality—Psychological aspects. |
Psychotherapy—Argentina. | Hypnotism.
Classification: LCC GN347 . C65 2026 (print)
LCC GN347 (ebook)
DDC 301.01—dc23/eng/2025062
LC record available at https://lccn.loc.gov/2025025468
LC ebook record available at https://lccn.loc.gov/2025025469

Cover art: Background courtesy Adobe Stock/Uuganbayar.

To my first love,

Contents

Acknowledgments   ix

Introduction   1

1   SEEING YOURSELF BEING SEEN   15

2   ATMOSPHERIC CRISIS   47

3   COMPULSIVE REPETITIONS   79

4   OSCILLATIONS   111

Outro   133

Notes   135

Bibliography   177

Index   197

Acknowledgments

When someone I care about—for whichever reason and in whichever way—doesn't mention me in their acknowledgments or when they seem to have forgotten, or repressed, in their own writing the impact of my contributions to their conceptual life, it hurts. I feel the opening of a narcissistic wound pulsing in a tiny spot right where a breathing psyche encounters my ruminating stomach. Then I breathe through the wound and allow myself to remember that nothing is really mine, that I never had a single idea that wasn't refracting someone else's idea, and that, in fact, there has never been a *single* author in the first place. But still, it hurts. This is to say that I am sorry if you thought you should be named in what follows but you aren't. If the next time we meet you feel like telling me you wanted to be in this book, but you aren't . . . drinks are on me, I promise.

My ethnographic research would not have been possible without the openness of the many psychotherapists and patients in Buenos Aires who allowed me to observe live sessions of couple therapy behind the one-way mirror. Observing couples undergoing their own therapy sessions has deeply impacted my psycho-affective life, and I have an immense gratitude for all the couples who agreed to be observed while processing intimate impasses, wounds, and ongoing transformations. I hope that, if they were to read this book, they could see the passion with which I followed their therapeutic journeys. This book re-presents only refracted fragments of their emotional life.

In Buenos Aires, a particular group of therapists folded me into their midst with the warmth of an adoptive family. Almibar, Clara, Micol, and Wanda, as I call you in this book, I really hope I was able to capture your insightful wit, therapeutic generosity, and care-full sharpness toward your patients, your colleagues, and your anthropologist-in-residence. Thinking about your work over and over again healed more than one wound (and, who knows, maybe even opened a few new ones). While we watched ongoing therapy sessions together, you also accepted with ironic generosity temporarily acting as my therapists, gifting me with innumerable insights to tackle my own personal struggles. Thank you.

Sofía, your motherly care throughout our sessions of hypnotherapy kept me grounded as I drifted across an oceanic confusion—thank you for teaching me how to reconnect with the creative force of my imagistic unconscious and to learn how to embrace the pulsing movement of an absent presence.

Asado after *asado, fernet* after *fernet, mate* after *mate,* my friends in Cordoba and Buenos Aires introduced me to Argentina's joyful melancholy, as we laughed at this and that walking back home at sunrise after a night of this and that. I will never forget my time there, also because it took me years to burn the extra ten kilos I gained. Cordoba, my ex-partner's hometown, conquered my heart in more ways than one. Rodrigo and Ema, *gracias boludos de mi corazón*! Wanda, Pocha, Conejo, Mechu, Presi, Romi, Plinio, Graciela, thank you for offering material and affective shelter in different phases of the research. In Buenos Aires, I am deeply grateful for generative conversations with Mariano Plotkin, Nicolás Viotti, and Sergio Visacovsky about my ongoing research and Argentina's *mundopsi*. I am also grateful for a quick glass of wine I had with a minimalist tango dancer who told me that, after all, to dance tango is to glide over a radical absence and that tango itself is, or should be, like walking over nothing. I might have tried to do this in the book, somehow—to dance and glide through my thoughts, finding my balance over a constellation of losses, absences, and departures.

At UC Berkeley, my dear mentors played a fundamental role in shaping, orienting, and nourishing my conceptual life. Thinking with Lawrence Cohen is like running at the speed of light through the baroque infinity of a conversation diagramming the intimate exteriorities of a Möbius strip. His impact on my thinking is difficult to pin down, and it runs throughout the entirety of this work. With her poetic approach to thinking, Stefania Pandolfo created an enchanted world where my thoughts could thrive. Stefania gave me the courage to dance with, and summon, an *outside*, one which animates the movement of thinking beyond the disciplinary genres of academic institutionality. Maybe this work can be read as the result of an internal debate I have been having with my introjected Stefania—it's about therapeutics, vitalism, and the death drive. Ian Whitmarsh has been a mentor and a friend in more than one way. Ian taught me how to embrace the radical ambivalence at the core of my libidinal investments—I will never forget our conversations about the twists and turns of our conceptual and not-so-conceptual existence. Niklaus Largier's welcoming curiosity toward the crazy anthropologist who believed that medieval mysticism, ethnographic genres of presence, and couple therapy could be brought together offered a much-appreciated intellectual harbor outside the Anthropology Department. At UC San Francisco, Vincanne Adams challenged my thinking in graceful, generative, and insightful ways, and I am deeply thankful for her mentorship.

I applied to Berkeley because of an email from Nancy Scheper-Hughes I received in the middle of the night. I am so grateful to Nancy; her unstoppable energy set an unbeatable example for me ten years ago, when I was still working on my dissertation and she was advising me to "never stop writing with your Italian accent!" Liu Xin has been an important interlocutor and a figure I will always look up to. He taught me the humbling pleasure of reading thousands of pages in a very short time, and then reading them again, and then again. Widely, my graduate experience in Berkeley was characterized by a deeply conceptual atmosphere, and walking by the doors and chatting with so many amazing thinkers has been a quotidian source of insights. Mariane Ferme, Saba Mahmood, Cori Hayden, Bill Hanks, Charles Briggs, and Paul Rabinow's intellectual projects have accompanied me throughout.

Friends and fellow graduate students at Berkeley kept me somewhat grounded while journeying across a wide range of hermeneutic frames. For the joyfulness of thinking-with, thank you to Miguél Perez Ahumada, Nishant Bagadia, Hector Beltrán, Emily Chua, Gabriel Coren, Joshua Craze, Michael D'Arcy, Antonello De Lucia, Ned Dostaler, Sam Dubal, Dylan Fagan, Lyle Fearnley, Emiliano Frignani, Giacomo Frignani, Drew Halley, Cole Hansen, Leila Juzam, Kevin Kenjar, Noémie Merleau-Ponty, Rachel Niehuus, Milad Odabaei, Jayshree Patel, Amedeo Policante, Raphaëlle Rabanes, Bruno Reinhardt, Antonia Rivas, Kamala Russell, Tomáš Ryška, Cheryl Smith, Jeremy Soh, William Stafford, Anthony Stavrianakis, and Marlee Tichenor.

Special gratitude across my graduate years to Mila Djordjevic for the support, careful feedback, and joyous fun. Jason Price, I can't thank you enough for the endless inspiration and feedback on my dissertation and the book, and the shared conversations we had with Yahsuan Huang too, in that beautiful family-form Berkeley-concept type of house. Thank you.

I can't find the poetic words I would like to use now to say how lucky and grateful I feel to have landed in the Anthropology Department at McGill University and, more widely, in the city of Montreal, a city that taught me how to fall in love over and over again—to fall in love even, or especially, when it's so cold your eyelids are freezing shut and the flickering lights of the soul are all that is left to see. I couldn't have found the writerly ambition animating this book's form without feeling fully supported by the excitement and affection of my wonderful friends, students, and colleagues in Montreal.

In the logic of a book about the couple form, I am first of all grateful to the many dyads that folded Haley and me within their midst with the generosity of a table full of the most delicious delicacies, copious drinks, and an intellectual commitment that never stops nourishing my soul. As I write these sentences, I am thinking about sitting at the table with Diana Allan, Curtis Brown, Claudia Fabbricatore, Eduardo Kohn, Setrag Manoukian, and Lisa Stevenson—and their brilliant kids Benjamin, Freya, Leila, Milo, and Vahagn. And now that I think of it, this Montreal culinary and conceptual bonanza keeps expanding in my head, and I imagine myself eating, drinking, jumping in a lake in the middle of the night, and sharing ideas with so many Montrealers who helped the writing of this book with their anticipatory enthusiasms: Francesco Amodio, Jean-Philippe Bombay, Gillian Chilibeck, Nicola di Croce, Julian Flavin, Kiara Flavin, Micah Flavin, Alessandro Garino, Michael Lifshitz, Kate Moore, Isabelle Ouellet-Chong, Claudia Picard-Deland, Jasmine Pisapia, Les Sabiston, Elisa Scaraggi, and Eli Sheiner. Helena Deland, you are my ideal reader, and thank you for all your effervescent support and the music (and also for listening to some of the postmasculinity Italian indie pop that accompanied the writing of the book).

If you ask my neighbors, I have been writing this book since forever, and I am grateful for all the times they let me rant about it, like that time with a bag of trash in my hands on a Monday evening: Thank you Hugo, Isa, Jennifer, Leo, Marylin, and Maxime.

In the Department of Anthropology, I am grateful for the generous support of my colleagues Kristin Norget, Setrag Manoukian, Sandra Hyde, Diana Allan, Katherine Lemons, Les Sabiston, Alyssa Bader, Lisa Stevenson, Peter Johansen, Eduardo Kohn, Lisa Overholtzer, Nicole Couture, Ismael Vaccaro, Hillary Kaell, Colin Scott, John Galaty, Todd Meyers, and Sahar Sadjadi. At McGill my thinking has been deeply impacted by the interdisciplinary vibrancy of the Transcultural Psychiatry Division. I am grateful for the ongoing generative conversations and excited for all the collaborations to come, with Laurence Kirmayer, Michael Lifshitz, Ana Gomez-Carrillo, Elizaveta Solomonova, Samuel Veissiére, Guillaume Dumas, Vincent Laliberté, Maxwell Ramstead, and Jonas Mago.

I wrote this book hoping it could be read and enjoyed by my amazing graduate and undergraduate students, and I am so grateful for their help, inspiration, and support. The s/Lab team kept me excited about my work in the past years: Elliot Durkee, Lauren Frasca, Karuna Hill, Livia Ion, Megan Lauener, Neal Lonergan, Mina Mahdi, Zahara Mustin, and Angela Nelson. Graduate students in different moments read, commented, edited, and overall improved this manuscript with their brilliance: Amy Donovan. Livia Filotico, Jordan Hodgins, Naïm Jeanbart, Ramzi Nimr, Jeremiah Scalia, Eli Sheiner, Amélie Ward, and Sara Wishloff. Daisy Couture and Leo Stillinger's enthusiastic, sharp, and timely interventions on the full manuscript literally made this book possible; I can't thank you enough for your hard work, conceptual dedication, and willingness to push me beyond what I thought I could pull off.

At Duke University Press, I am grateful to Ken Wissoker for supporting this project without hesitation and for offering his wise and brilliant supervision. Thank you also to Kate Mullen's enthusiasm and editorial help. The two anonymous reviewers of the book have been truly generous and generative— your comments and suggestions made this book deeper, sharper, and tighter. Thank you.

Across the years, a wide range of academic friends and colleagues helped me think through the book with their own intellectual projects, invitations to share my work in progress, or with the warm curiosity one needs to bump into to gather some new energy and just keep writing despite all sorts of professional and personal funks. Among others, I am thinking about Felicity Aulino, Robert Desjarlais, William Mazzarella, Todd Meyers, Jason Throop, Sylvia Tidey, and Jarrett Zigon.

Ongoing conversations with Aidan Seale-Feldman about psychic life have been an important source of inspiration and generative thinking-with during the writing of this book. Eric Taggart, my dear friend, you keep injecting vitality into my thinking, and I am so grateful for our friendship; thank you for thinking with me and all the adrenalinic warmth. Emily Ng, thank you for being my friend throughout this all, from the academic to the frivolous, from the vitality of an oceanic wave to a contemplative silence letting the negative do its work. I can't imagine surviving the psychic pressures of academia without being able to talk to you.

My Italian friends, thank you for folding me within your life-forms every time I come back to pick up the fragments of an always already lost home— sometimes I fall asleep thinking about the crisp smell of a Genovese focaccia fading into the salty scent of the sea and we are there laughing like in high school: Emilia Davi, Luca Falomi, Enrico Nardi, Marco Parodi, and Chiara Zingaretti. I am grateful for all the family love I keep receiving from my family: Davide, Giacomo, Lorena, and Tiziana—thank you for all the Christmas-like warmth. Julie, thank you for the sisterly love and breaking through the fog of impasses, violence, and sadness together with me. My interest in systemic therapy was initially sparked through a book that my brilliant brother-in-law Giacomo Crivellaro gifted me—thank you for all the conversations about psychotherapy, methods, and approaches.

Yanina Gori, I most definitely wouldn't have ended up in Argentina without you. The majestic psycho-geographic adventures we embraced together flicker throughout the book. Part of my thinking will always be tethered to the images of thought we articulated together in our romantic bubble.

Haley Baird, you have animated with beauty and grace the joyful melancholia texturing the rhythm of the book—thank you for reading the whole manuscript multiple times and gifting me with so many concepts and ideas. There are no words to express my love and gratitude.

Françoise and Gianpiero, *maman* and *papà*, now that you morphed into spirit images, thank you for visiting me in my dreams and holding me tight with the strength of a warm bright light.

I am a resonating chamber of the movements that emerged between us.

INTRODUCTION

Buenos Aires, Argentina. August 2013. I'm sitting in a room with three psycho-therapists looking at a screen in contemplative silence. The screen is connected to a closed-circuit television system live streaming a session of couple therapy taking place in the room next door. The two patients in therapy, Paula and Thiago, are talking to Wanda, their therapist. Their voices cut through the walls.

"We went to see a therapist two years ago, but he gave up," Paula says to Wanda.

"I didn't give up!" Thiago replies loudly. "You were so miserable after those sessions! No?"

"What? The therapist asked *you* to leave during our last session!"

"It wasn't working!" Thiago replies. "You talked and talked but nothing changed, like when you went to that Lacanian psychoanalyst. . . . Nothing changed! Nothing! Nothing changes."

"So . . . you want *me* to change? That's it? You come to therapy so that *I* can change?"

"I meant the relationship!" Thiago explains to Wanda. "The relationship didn't change."

"So that's it! You just wanted me to change. You wanted to leave me alone with the therapist!"

"I said the relationship! And the therapist didn't ask me to leave, she just didn't leave me any—"

"So, you thought that *I* was the one who had to change?"

Waiting for a reply, Paula looks at Wanda and then straight into the camera. "Do you see? *Do you see?* That's what I have to deal with!"

"I said the relationship!" Thiago screams at the camera.

. . .

Ten minutes earlier. The video camera is running. Paula is waiting for Thiago to arrive and looks nervously at the screen of her phone. After a couple of minutes, Thiago hurries into the room and sits down. Paula is about to tell him something, but Wanda enters. She sits down and explains that she is using the video camera to allow a team of therapists and one anthropologist to observe the session in another room. "Yes, Dr. Almibar told us. It's okay," Paula says smiling. Thiago nods silently.

"So, what brings you here to this space?" Wanda asks.

Paula and Thiago glance at each other. Paula gently shakes her head while looking down.

"What do you want me to say?" Thiago says. "I can only offer the final words of someone who's drowning. . . ."

"Do you think you're drowning?" Wanda asks.

Thiago looks quickly into the eye of the camera. "No, no, I think we've already drowned. We're doing bad, bad, bad. . . . We've drowned already. . . . We are drowning."

On the other side of the wall, I am fully absorbed in the screen live streaming the session. The screen displays what the camera is recording, and it feels like Thiago is looking right at me. I stare at the screen, looking back at him. We are both looking at each other without really seeing the other. We are separated by a screen monitor, a wall, and a video camera. I suddenly feel tired, drained, and stuck.

The three psychotherapists close to me are nodding pensively while jotting down some notes. In a moment of suspended silence, the echoes of Thiago's words reverberate across the two rooms. *We're drowning. We're drowning. We've drowned already.* I take out my notebook to write something and discharge a rising anxiety, but nothing comes to my mind. I draw a rectangle.

. . .

Into the Loop is based on ethnographic research I conducted in Buenos Aires, Argentina, where I immersed myself in the theory and practice of systemic couple therapy. Over the course of 2013–14, different teams of systemic psychotherapists allowed me, as an anthropologist, to follow their work and observe over two hundred hours of couple therapy from behind a one-way mirror, a closed-circuit television, or both at once.[1] During this time in Argentina, I also pursued a research project on the use of hypnosis in a therapeutic context. This led me, among other things, to undergo hypnotherapy as a patient and to film my own sessions.

The couple therapy sessions I observed, together with my hypnotherapy recordings, constitute the empirical ground of the book; but as I was writing it, a lot of other things slipped in.

. . .

Systemic psychotherapists use visual devices, such as the one-way mirror or closed-circuit television, to observe or supervise live sessions of therapy. In a systemic therapy setting, you have a group of therapists in an observing room—usually there are therapists in training among them—while another therapist is conducting the session in the therapy room. The one-way mirror is built into the wall separating the two rooms, allowing the therapists to observe the session without being seen. If there is no one-way mirror, therapists use a closed-circuit television system that broadcasts the live session into the observing room through a video camera installed in the therapy room. In some settings, you can have both the one-way mirror and the closed-circuit television system.

One of the primary concerns of systemic couple therapy is to explore how romantic partners get caught in loops of interaction that can thwart therapeutic transformation or make it difficult to end potentially harmful or abusive relationships. When partners are caught in a loop, they repeat a series of actions, affective habits, and communicative practices that keep their relational problems in place despite recursive attempts to break away from or interrupt what can be experienced as an endless circularity. When partners are stuck in a loop, they barely know who or what started the loop, and, more importantly, they rarely know how to interrupt its circular repetitions.

Yesterday we promised we'd stop fighting over it. How are we back here again?

. . .

A *loop* is a structure, series, or process, the end of which is connected to the beginning—think about a feedback loop. A loop is also an endless strip of tape or film allowing continuous repetition, or a complete circuit for an electric current. In computing, a loop is a programmed sequence of instructions that is repeated until or while a particular condition is satisfied.

To loop is to coil, wind, twist, spiral, make circles with; but it's also to fasten, tie, join, connect, bind, and tether.[2]

. . .

You are coming back home, and the last thing you want is to spend the next hours in a screaming match with your partner. You bought a nice bottle of red wine, you are happy thinking that you will be home soon, and your partner just texted you that they can't wait to see you. But as soon as you get in the house, things scale up faster than a slap of wind. You say something, your partner replies, you add something, they add something too. You are not there yet but, after a few exchanges, you can feel it already—your body is getting warmer, your heart is pounding.

You could try to do something to interrupt the escalation—run to the bathroom and wash your face with cold water or grab a pillow and scream into it—but instead you open your mouth and say *that* thing, the one which opens the door to a five-hour-long fight. You don't want it to happen, but it's already happening. And now you are screaming words that, as soon as they leave your body, you wish you didn't say.

. . .

"*I* didn't give up! *You* were so miserable after those sessions! No?"

"*What? The therapist asked* you *to leave!*"

. . .

Systemic therapy moves away from linear causality and privileges circular causality. Instead of focusing on how A causes B, this therapeutic model considers A's action as a reaction to B's input, which, in turn, incorporates A's feedback. This circular perspective comes from cybernetics, an interdisciplinary approach that developed mostly in the United States after World War II.

Cybernetics focuses on the capacity of human and nonhuman systems to self-regulate through feedback loops—you have a feedback loop when the output is fed back into the system as input. This implies that the individual is always plugged into a broader system of relations—a choreographic composition of elements that both exceeds and shapes the individual.

During the cybernetic era of the 1950s and '60s, a wide range of disciplines, from military engineering to psychology, embraced the focus on circular exchanges of information between humans, machines, and their environment.[3] In this same period, different traditions of experimental psychology employed visual technologies such as the one-way mirror to pursue a "naturalistic observation" of the interactive loops within families and couples in therapy.[4]

The anthropologist Gregory Bateson (1904–80) substantially impacted the development of the systemic therapy model. Bateson drew from anthropology, ethology, psychology, and cybernetics to show how societies, families, and romantic couples were parts of wider relational systems.[5]

. . .

One of Gregory Bateson's central arguments in favor of the systemic epistemology is that it troubles the Western tendency to understand the human self as separated from the very systems that, in fact, generate it.[6] The self, Bateson writes, is only a small part of a larger system, a "false reification of an improperly delimited part of this much larger field of interlocking processes."[7]

A systemic approach, according to Bateson, supports the idea that the self alone, as an autonomous center of willpower, cannot interrupt a relational loop. To interrupt a loop, you need, first of all, to give in to the possibility that no matter what you think you are, there is a loop that precedes and exceeds you.[8] A loop "whose boundaries do not at all coincide with the boundaries either of the body or of what is popularly called the 'self' or 'consciousness.'"[9]

Bateson explores the therapeutic impact of a systemic perspective in a provocative essay about Alcoholics Anonymous (AA), where he describes how in the first two steps of the Twelve-Step Program, the alcoholic needs to acknowledge their powerlessness over alcohol and surrender to a wider force, a "higher power" that can interrupt the compulsive repetition of the loop. This higher power, according to Bateson, is the emergent property of a system, one bigger than the sum of its parts.

Bateson suggests that the AA approach works because it challenges the alcoholic's reliance on individual willpower and promotes a deeper understanding of how the self's actions are folded within, and impacted by, nonindividual forces and systems.[10] The point here is that whatever the problem, it might be generated and sustained through processes that are happening beneath, beyond, and even despite you.[11]

. . .

"So . . . you want *me* to change? You come to therapy so that *I* can change?"

"I said the relationship!"

. . .

The focus on systems and feedback loops, together with the development of information theory, has laid the ground for all sorts of technologies and intellectual traditions that can be traced back to basic cybernetic principles—computers, the internet, military weapons, the Gaia hypothesis, Silvan Tomkins's affect theory, Gregory Bateson's ecological anthropology, climate change research, screaming at your partner, and compulsively checking your phone.

It can all be looped back to the loopy logic of loops.[12]

. . .

Into the Loop draws from affect theory, psychoanalysis, and phenomenology to address the psychosocial forces that compel people to repeat, interrupt, or drift aside from relational loops. I wrote this book compulsively returning to a small set of refrains, haunting questions that will never find a final answer: Why do people keep returning to relationships that are draining their vitality? How can we interrupt the repetitions that define us, even if just for a second?

The book is also a minor experiment in form or, rather, in rhythm. To drift aside from my own writing loops, I organized *Into the Loop* as a somewhat eclectic choreography of short sections—ranging in length from a few paragraphs to one-liners. These short sections or fragments are written in aspirational resonance with a wide range of authors who develop poetic, literary, and imagistic approaches in anthropology and beyond—and sometimes in a short-form genre too.[13]

. . .

The book's fragments are animated, if not haunted, by different voices—the academic, the personal, and their uncanny in-betweens. This allows me to play with, and ventriloquize, different propositions—conceptual, therapeutic, anthropological, psychoanalytic, or intimate. But there is also some nano-ranting, self-addressed pep talks, mildly surrealist exercises, and the joyful indexing of ephemeral afterimages.

The voicing can be jarring at times. I just like to slap my own thinking out of a looping track with things coming out of nowhere. I also love to repeat repetitions until they catch fire—or at least spark some sparkles in between us. In its quasi-aphoristic undertone, *Into the Loop* nudges the writer and the reader in and out of a series of loops—sometimes we hold hands, sometimes I forget.

. . .

"What? The therapist asked *you* to leave during our last session!"

"It wasn't working! You talked and talked but nothing changed, like when you went to that Lacanian psychoanalyst.... Nothing *changed!* Nothing! Nothing *changes.*"

. . .

Thinking and writing through short scenes is also a way to re-present what I've learned about couples by watching live therapy sessions from behind a one-way mirror. The rectangular surface of the one-way mirror led me to think about coupled forms of life as a composition of scenes, a collage of quasi-cinematic moments that are acted out by partners. Therapy sessions can follow a linear narrative, loop onto themselves repeating over and over the same refrains, or be led astray by something completely unexpected.

Scenes emerge and take shape in the therapeutic space, just like scenes emerge and take shape in the ordinariness of coupled intimacy. Some scenes evaporate in the daily repetitions that shape the quotidian. Some scenes acquire force and will be revisited over and over and over again. *That time, that time you said that thing that changed everything. That time.* We build a frame around these moments, and we hang them on the walls we build to separate ourselves from our own becoming.[14]

. . .

Cristina is reading a book on the couch. Hernan is screaming at her. She keeps reading. He keeps screaming. He gives up and goes to the kitchen to pour himself another drink. She picks up her half-full wineglass and contemplates it for a few seconds. She looks at a tiny spot on the edge of the glass where she can see the imprint of her lips. She looks at the white wall in front of her. She screams. The wineglass cuts through the air and breaks into at least seventy-five tiny fragments as it hits the wall. Hernan runs back into the living room. He distractedly contemplates the star-shaped stain of red Malbec on the wall.

"The therapist called," Cristina says. "Our first session of systemic therapy is Friday at 9 a.m."

"What the fuck is systemic therapy? With you it always ends up being some New Age bullshit!"

"That has nothing to do with anything, like always, that's not at all . . . oh, fuck you, Hernan."

. . .

Things went completely astray sometimes. One time it was like five in the morning, and we were walking on the opposite side of the street fighting as if there was no tomorrow. A couple form of the night, screaming drunk and angry things. You *just* wanted to be held tight in our floating couple-bubble, and I *just* wanted the same. A hug could have changed things. We *just*—but I think we also loved the idea of screaming at each other, with an empty street in between us. Theatrical beauty, romance as spectacle. Love was pumping through our veins like a motherfucker. And we loved returning to that scene.

. . .

"I just want to put couples in touch with their own becoming, the present of their encounter, not the past or the future. Their becoming. That's where a surprising amount of curiosity and love and novelty can come their way. Couples are stuck because they are resisting their becoming."
—*interview with Dr. Marina, sixty-five, (Deleuzian) couples therapist, Buenos Aires*

. . .

My angle of arrival to the question of how to interrupt a loop, or drift aside from it, was deeply personal. As a graduate student in anthropology, I began reading about cybernetics and systemic couple therapy during a period of my life when I was interested in finding a way to improve, reconfigure, or interrupt the loops haunting my own romantic relationship. With a degree of ambitious arrogance, I convinced myself that studying and researching couple therapy, instead of just going to couple therapy, could help even more.

I know, I know—watching so many sessions of live couple therapy probably jammed my psycho-affective life for at least a decade. But when I initially chose to focus on couple therapy, it sounded like a potentially reparative doctoral project, a kind of research that could help me figure something out about my life. When I decided to do my research in Buenos Aires, I was floating through a foggy confusion. I didn't know what to do with my life, and Argentina seemed an easy enough choice considering my partner's family ties there.

Drifting through the haze of an existential disorientation, I landed in Argentina tethering myself to an obsessive question: *How do you interrupt a loop a loop a loop?*[15]

. . .

So I ended up in Argentina because I didn't know what else to do, what else to ask, or how else to do it—I mean interrupting a loop a loop a loop. But Argentina, it turns out, was kind of the perfect place to be lost, to drift through the folds of an open question, to wander in a sleepless crisis mode bouncing from one *asado* to another at 6 a.m., to stumble upon all sorts of technicians, magicians, and artists of the psyche.

. . .

Indeed, Argentina is a unique context for the study of psychotherapeutic treatments, being the country with the highest number of therapeutic practitioners per capita in the world.[16] Argentina has long been known to scholars of the psychological disciplines for its exceptional relationship with psychoanalysis in particular.[17] For heterogeneous historical reasons, which could be connected to migratory flows as well as the insertion of psychoanalysis into the public health system in the 1960s, in Argentina psychoanalytic culture permeates political discourse, everyday conversations, and the media sphere.[18] Especially in Buenos Aires, you could end up talking about psychoanalysis with your taxi driver, or hear a politician use psychoanalytic language to address national issues, or talk to a friend who started psychoanalysis because they just got pregnant and don't want to pass their traumas on to the baby.[19]

. . .

In Buenos Aires, I used to live with my partner in a part of the city informally called Villa Freud, owing to the number of therapists who moved to that area in the 1960s. Six months into my fieldwork, I found myself in the kitchen of our tiny apartment in Villa Freud talking to the plumber about a broken pipe. Without knowing how, I suddenly found myself in a heated debate about the therapeutic efficacy of hypnosis versus Lacanian psychoanalysis. The plumber was a hardcore Lacanian.[20]

. . .

Argentina's distinctive psychoanalytic culture is also entangled with an important tradition of social psychology—whose most representative figure was the psychoanalyst Enrique Pichon-Rivière.[21] In 1958 Pichon-Rivière headed the famous Operación Rosario, where he tried to turn the whole city of Rosario into a therapeutic project through the creation of small therapeutic groups open to the public and which included all sorts of people—from academics to therapists to boxers. Pichon-Rivière's idea was to provoke social change through psychosocial interventions outside the private space of the clinic.[22]

In Buenos Aires, therapy was also literally brought to the streets during the devastating Argentinean economic crisis of 2001–2, where psychotherapists emerged from their private offices to offer free therapy on street corners. During the crisis, psychotherapy was considered an essential public good that people should be able to access freely.[23] Even today, if you are into it, you could find yourself in Buenos Aires participating in a collective session of psychoanalysis where analysts and analysands come together to engage in an experimental form of group analysis.[24]

These are just a few examples of how Argentina's therapeutic culture keeps challenging our assumptions about therapy as a private and intimate process happening behind closed doors. While systemic therapy isn't particularly widespread in Argentina, this model's use of visual technologies seems to further blur the lines between the private and the public space of therapy.

Where does therapy start, and where does it end?

. . .

Buenos Aires, Argentina. May 2013. I enter the dark room following Amalia. The therapy session has already started. I nod to the three therapists in training who are observing the session through the one-way mirror; they are all taking notes. Hesitantly, I walk toward the one-way mirror and stand a few feet away from it. I can see the back of the therapist in the other room. In front of him, facing the mirror, a woman is crying—she is talking about someone named Mateo. Is Mateo her son? Sitting close to her on the couch, a man looks out the window. Is he Mateo? The man says something I can't catch. The woman close to him stops crying.

He says he can't take it anymore; she responds that she is tired of this situation. She looks around for a tissue, but there are no tissues in the therapy room. The therapist on the other side of the mirror looks around and realizes that the tissue box is empty. He apologizes and looks for a tissue in his own backpack. I look around, searching for a tissue.

A few seconds later, I realize that I wouldn't be able to offer it to her anyway because I am on the other side of the one-way mirror. I am caught off guard by this detail. I am so far away and so close to the patients I am observing; I didn't even get their names, but here I am, right in the middle of their intimacy.

I'm watching the session without understanding much, maybe because the surface of the one-way mirror partially reflects my own image and keeps distracting me. In the mirror's reflection, I see the pupils of my eyes. Amalia—the psychotherapist who invited me to my first session behind the mirror—looks at me and says something I don't understand. What did Amalia just say about Mateo's school counselor? Ah, okay, so Mateo is the woman's son. No, he's the man's son. Okay, got it.

. . .

What does it mean not to be able to take it anymore?

. . .

A few minutes later, Amalia taps my shoulder to get my attention. I look at her while she picks up an intercom handset hanging on the right side of the mirror. She presses the button to buzz into the other room. When the phone rings on the other side of the mirror, I emit a nervous whisper. The therapist in the other room picks up the phone: "Yes? Yes, yes . . . yes. Okay."

Amalia puts down the phone. My heart is racing—the call to the other room broke the spell and revealed our presence behind the mirror. I feel suddenly self-aware when I glimpse at the video camera recording the session. The camera is standing on a tripod inside the therapist's room, to the right side of the therapist. I notice that the man on the couch is looking right into the eye of the camera, so I instinctively bring my attention to the monitor on my left side.

A sudden blush reveals my embarrassment at being able to see him without being seen.

. . .

The first time I watched a therapy session from behind the one-way mirror with Amalia and the three therapists in training, I was so overwhelmed by the intimacy with the patients on the other side of the mirror that I partially dissociated from the therapy session. The visual infrastructure that surrounded the session kept reorienting my attention. It was like falling under a spell cast by a play of surfaces—the TV monitors, the video camera, the big rectangular one-way mirror.

I had initially imagined that the visual technologies used during systemic therapy would simply be the means through which I would access live couple therapy—a way to observe what really happens during therapy. But visual technologies, cannot, in fact, be disentangled from this type of therapy.[25] To begin with, the observing audience behind the screen or the mirror is not a passive or invisible eye but can actually participate in the sessions by calling into the therapy room or providing feedback to the lead therapists during a break that usually splits the session in two parts. At the same time, the consciousness of being observed deeply impacts, if not determines, the experience of patients in therapy.

I will write about this extensively, but for now let me say that in the systemic setting of therapy, visual technologies are not only transparent media that allow for a naturalistic observation, but also active presences that generate a rather peculiar therapeutic atmosphere, a relational system that enfolds the couple's loops, creating a broader loop.[26]

. . .

I didn't simply watch therapy through screens: The therapy itself was happening through, with, and sometimes because of the screen. Therapy itself became its own kind of screen.

Or screens their own kind of therapy.

. . .

Into the Loop describes how the systemic setting facilitates therapeutic experiences through the creation of a system that includes visual technologies, armchairs, patients, more than one therapist, and sometimes even an anthropologist.[27] Whatever works, if and when it does, seems to work because of what this setting generates, sometimes even regardless of the specific therapeutic technique employed.

In the pages of this book, the systemic setting of therapy is a quasi-theatrical space where patients and therapists alike act out and externalize affective and psychic processes that are central to the constitution of both the individual and the couple. In the four chapters of this book, I focus on identification (chapter 1), affective transmission (chapter 2), and compulsive repetition (chapter 3); acting out my own psycho-imagistic processes, I then turn to hypnotic experience (chapter 4).

Throughout these chapters, I suggest that these psychic processes—identification, affective transmission, compulsive repetition, and hypnosis—are the pulsing beat of relational loops. These processes are not, however, intrinsically good or bad—*they are just what happens when something that has nothing to do with you turns you into you.*

. . .

Paula looks straight into the camera. "Do you see? *Do you see?*"

"I said the relationship!" Thiago screams at the camera.

. . .

Due to the insistent presence of screens and visual devices that were connecting me to, and separating me from, the subjects and objects of my research, *Into the Loop* develops a *refractive anthropology*, one that is always already mediated by visual devices that transform, bend, and distort whatever comes into view through the rectangular space of the screen.[28]

. . .

In the years following my fieldwork, while teaching psychological anthropology courses to undergrads, I came to realize that the questions provoked by systemic couple therapy—questions of screens and mediations, loops and affective attachments—were, in a different way, defining the psychic life of an entire generation of college students. Hearing me rant about compulsive loops and one-way mirrors, they intuitively understood that I was also talking about another kind of one-way mirror: the flickering rectangle we carry everywhere in our pockets.

After I finished writing my dissertation, I thus realized that my research on the compulsive loops haunting the romantic dyad could offer insights on the user-screen dyad too. This is why *Into the Loop* keeps turning to the question of digital media and our compulsive returns to them—my students made me. The user's relationship with screens would, eventually, become the subject of my next research project; in this book I address it only laterally.[29] In a sense, however, the whole book could also be understood as an attempt to ask what screenified loops can do to, and for, our affective life.

. . .

You keep returning to your objects of attachment to sustain a loop that sustains you.

. . .

A caveat for the anthropology police: *Into the Loop* is not a book about Argentina, nor about systemic therapy. Without dismissing them, the book drifts aside from historicist and culturalist critique as the dominant mode of anthropological knowledge.[30] Maybe it also drifts away from critique altogether, but I am not sure. This is a book *from* Argentina and *from* the systemic model, a book that privileges thinking-with over thinking-against.[31]

. . .

Yes, but what's this book actually about? Frantically searching for an answer, I could end up babbling something like this: We get folded into the repetition of affective loops because they hold for us a set of identificatory ties that would imply our own dissolution if we let them go (chapters 1–3). Within a dyadic loop, we can end up identifying with our partner's projections (chapter 1), as well as becoming their go-to affective dump (chapter 2). In the contemporary condition, we are hypnotized by a very restricted range of affective attachments (chapters 3, 4). Our affective ties can drain as much as awaken our vitality (chapters 1–4). Whatever cosmology you are plugged into, ritually re-peated returns make you available to be possessed by the affective forces of that cosmology (chapter 3).

Repeated returns can hypnotize you into a looping immobility or make you available to be possessed by the forces moving across the nervous system of a different cosmology; This process might displace whatever it is you have iden-tified as *you* (chapters 3, 4).

Drifting aside from relational loops is fun, scary, and sometimes necessary (chapters 1–4).

Oh, yes, then there is that claim about projective identification and cannibal-ism (chapter 1), and the one about hypnosis and image work (chapter 4), and the one about the death drive and decompositional transformation (chapter 3), and the one about opening the windows (chapter 2); it's going to be a fun and loopy ride, I promise.

. . .

A crisis is a crisis in the reproduction of something.[32]

. . .

Into the Loop is not about a teleological and liberatory stepping out of the loop, but rather about a playful dance between liberation and capture.[33] The libera-tion phenomenology of the book, if there is one, lies in an oscillatory move-ment between the loops we are trapped within, the loops we move away from, the loops we choose, the loops we don't.

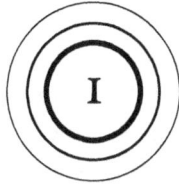

I

SEEING YOURSELF BEING SEEN

Buenos Aires, Argentina. February 2014. I am sitting in a small dark room with three couple therapists in training. We are all facing the one-way mirror that separates us from Brenda and Claudio, two patients in therapy. Scanning the therapy room through the one-way mirror, my gaze lands on the window inside the therapy room. It's pouring outside; the warmth of the room coats the window with a layer of steam. Brenda and Claudio have been together for five years, and Brenda says they have been fighting nonstop for the past year. Claudio says that she spends all her time on WhatsApp with her high school friends. She says he is jealous for no reason and that she would love to go out more, maybe even start dancing again, but she feels that Claudio is not interested in doing anything with her anymore.

"Do you remember how fun it was dancing in that salsa place?"

Claudio ignores Brenda's question and tells the therapist that Brenda dated one of her high school friends just a few weeks before dating him.

"Didn't you sleep with Matías?" he asks Brenda. "Right? I am not that crazy."

She says it meant nothing. He says it doesn't even matter. She says that's the problem; that he doesn't understand what she means. Heavy raindrops offer a rhythmic texture to the session, hitting the window of the therapy room with metallic precision. Sometimes heavy rain seems to anticipate an imminent and liberatory change; other times it just makes you feel stuck inside.

"I just want her to learn," Claudio says.

Marisa, the therapist in the room with them, looks at him with curiosity. "To learn what?"

"Not to be so stupid [*boluda*]!" Claudio bursts into a quick laugh.

"See?" Brenda cuts in and shakes her head. "What can I do with someone who says things like that! This is not a joke; do you even understand what we are doing here? We were talking about you being so jealous that I can't even write a fucking text message anymore! Are you even listening?"

Hearing thunder, Claudio looks distractedly out the window.

"I just . . . it's always like this. He says a stupid thing and then he checks out. He doesn't register me [*no me registra*]. He just doesn't. I don't think I can take this anymore, Claudio."

"What are you talking about? I don't check out. If you say stupid things, I don't respond."

"No, you check out, and you just think about your dumb soccer games with the only people you care about. C'mon man [*dale flaco*], you are always out drinking beers with the guys!"

"What? What? When? Tell me when I went out the last time!"

"Last Wednesday? Remember? You came home wasted? Do you even remember?"

Claudio stops talking. He looks at his shoes and then glances quickly at the therapist.

"Are you even interested in trying to make things work?" Brenda continues. "Are you even here?!"

Claudio stares again at his shoes as if searching for something. The rain's patter fills a moment of silence. Marisa nods at her patients for a few seconds, then suddenly turns her body around and looks toward the one-way mirror behind her. She knocks against the mirror four times.

Knock, knock, knock, knock.

The sound catches everyone on the other side by surprise, as if breaking us from a spell.

"Rodrigo, are you writing this down?" Marisa is talking through the mirror to a trainee sitting close to me. She can't see him because we are on the other side of the mirror. Rodrigo smiles but doesn't reply, knowing that Marisa knocked against the mirror to interrupt a loop that could have occupied the whole session without going anywhere. I look straight ahead.

The sound has suddenly redirected Brenda and Claudio's attention to the one-way mirror. They are now both looking at the reflecting surface of the mirror. I am behind the mirror and sitting next to Rodrigo. Brenda and Claudio can only see their own reflected figures in the mirror, but they seem to be looking beyond it. I see them *seeing themselves being seen*.[1]

We are suspended in a shared play of gazes that don't really meet.

Claudio stops looking at the mirror and goes back to his shoe-staring, while Brenda lingers on her own reflected image, as though trying to catch something behind the surface of the mirror.

"But ... look!" she says, still looking at the one-way mirror. "I hate this. Look at him, also you guys behind [the mirror] can see his face. . . . Look at him—he looks like a stray dog. He doesn't know what to say or do. He just checks out. It's so pitiful. . . . Look at him! Look at yourself, Claudio. You can't even reply to what I say—look at your stupid face! Now at least someone else can see it! Do you see? *Do you see?*"

. . .

In what follows you can expect some jumps, splits, folds, and cuts across an eclectic range of ideas in psychoanalysis, phenomenology, and media theory. The overall movement doesn't necessarily offer a coherent proposition; I have been stitching together different theories to see if they can suture some of my relational wounds and, who knows, maybe some of yours. A way to stay grounded without feeling that I took you for one too many spins is to latch onto the one-way mirror as one of the central allegories of the chapter—an allegory, however, that works more like a cliff hanging over a tumultuous ocean, a cliff we will need to jump off, so we get to splash together into the blind spots of our dyadic attachments. I can hold your hand for a short while as we jump, but I will loosen the grip when you would think it's way too early to do so.

As we fall, you might hear me screaming, seeing is eating!

. . .

The systemic therapists I worked with in Buenos Aires use visual technologies such as the one-way mirror to lead, supervise, or observe live therapy sessions.

"Through the one-way mirror," Marisa commented right before Brenda and Claudio's session, "you can observe how someone is sitting or how they dissociate when their partner is talking. From the perspective of systemic therapy, through the one-way mirror you can literally see a system in action, because interactive patterns are acted out right in front of our eyes. Watching live therapies through the one-way mirror allows us to see better, to learn to see better."[2]

According to Marisa, visual technologies like the one-way mirror thus allow for a naturalistic and nonintrusive observation of live therapy, letting the therapist see what actually happens during a session. On the observer's side of the mirror, one can indeed feel like a fly on the wall; or, better, like an invisible fly silently flapping its wings in the space between a patient's sigh and therapist's nod.

. . .

"What an honor and a waste! Five invisible therapists listening to our bullshit [*boludeces*]."
—*Stefano, a patient in therapy, looking at the one-way mirror while holding his partner's hands.*

. . .

Within systemic therapy sessions, the one-way mirror works like multiple visual devices at the same time. On the observer's side, the therapists use the mirror like a rectangular window on a wall that shows them the ongoing therapy session on the other side. These therapists often forget about the presence of the one-way mirror; as they focus on what's happening on the other side, the mirror itself disappears from their conscious awareness, becoming more like a transparent window. It's easy to imagine the observer's perspective if you think about the disappearance of the screen from your conscious awareness when you are streaming the season finale of your favorite TV show—from your viewpoint, the screen is transparent because you are looking through it but not looking at it.[3]

But this transparency is not perfect: The one-way mirror is darker than a normal window, and from the observer's side it can sometimes produce a blurred reflection of your own image, thus revealing itself to be something other than a transparent window. Many times, I found myself fully absorbed in a therapy session only to be suddenly distracted by a reflection of my own eyes on the surface of the one-way mirror; the reflection was often layered over what I could see of the patients on the other side (pretty trippy).[4]

On the observed side, within the therapy room, the one-way mirror works just like a normal mirror: You can see only your own reflection, and you are left imagining what's on the other side. But this depends on the lighting conditions: The one-way mirror only works if the observing room is darker than the room being observed. If the observer's room suddenly brightens, those on the observed side can see shadows appearing right behind their own reflected image (also pretty trippy). With an even more intense change of lighting, the mirroring effect vanishes altogether and transforms the one-way mirror into a two-way window: Observers and observed can finally see each other (less trippy but somewhat more disturbing).[5]

Thus, while mostly offering systemic therapists a clear view of the ongoing therapy session (when shielding their image from those in the therapy room), the one-way mirror also has the capacity to plunge observer and observed alike into an uncanny play of reflections and visions. Shifting from transparency to opacity and back again in strange and sudden ways, the one-way mirror feeds vision as much as the imagination. *One could say that a real one-way mirror doesn't exist.*

. . .

Since at least the Renaissance, vision has held an ontological and epistemological primacy in Western ways of knowing and relating to the world. Only that which can be seen or made visible is considered, most of the time, to be anything at all. The very word *phenomenon* comes from the Greek verb *phaínō*, which means "to appear, to cause to appear." The primacy of vision in Western cosmology is thus entangled with the phenomenal world down to its etymological roots: An empirically relevant phenomenon is usually something that can be seen, that shows itself to the viewer.

The philosopher Maurice Merleau-Ponty writes that the primacy accorded to the visual in Western modernity derives from the capacity of the sense of sight to create an experiential separation between subjects and objects, between the viewer and what is seen. Vision, according to Merleau-Ponty, has this ability to leave things exactly where they are, to leave them as if untouched and unaffected by the viewer—this makes vision the perfect sensory partner of scientific objectivism.[6]

The realm of vision, which for Merleau-Ponty includes both the sense of sight and visual technologies, has indeed supported for centuries the distinction between subjects and objects, real phenomena and imagined ones, science and superstition.[7] Think about when your doctor can't find anything visible to explain that strange headache that has been bothering you for months. They will probably tell you that it's just stress—which means that it's something psychological and that, whatever it is, it belongs to the realm of the imagined, the subjective, and the invisible.[8]

To be seen is to be real; to be real is to be seen.

. . .

But things are not that simple. Merleau-Ponty suggests that the capacity of vision to leave things untouched and separated from the viewer is, in fact, a feverish mystery—because vision is not as transparent as we perceive it to be.[9]

On the contrary, scholars in a wide range of disciplines have challenged the notion of vision as a straightforward sensory process whereby the outside world is transmitted as input through our optical nerves and becomes an objective visual representation of that input. From the philosophical investigations of Merleau-Ponty to neurophenomenological research on optical illusions, vision instead emerges as the result of predictive and imaginative processes that complete and piece together the sensory information registered through the retina.[10]

There are numerous optical illusions you might have already seen that show how easily you can be conditioned to see what you expect you are going to see.[11] Optical illusions can shock us because they reveal the fundamental arbitrariness of the imaginative and predictive processes underlying vision; they show that what you see could be otherwise. It's what I call the fundamental arbitrariness of perceived immediacy.

In this perspective, vision never really gives us access to something that is just out there in the world but is rather the result of processes of prediction, selection, and imagination that are as much part of our brain as part of the world outside us. To put it more bluntly, what you see is not an objective perception of a reality that exists independently from you, but rather an encounter—something midway between you and the world.[12]

. . .

I scroll through my feed and linger on that image of that person doing that thing. The mindless scrolling freezes—I hold my breath. I keep looking. I see her smiling—she seems happy; who is that guy? What is he laughing about? No but really, who is that guy? I click on his profile; I can't see much. I go back to the picture. She said she never wanted to go to that place. She seems happy though—her eyes are looking. . . . What are they looking at? I feel she is looking for something. Is she really smiling?

As my fingers scroll to the next image, my phone dies. I suddenly see myself reflected in the dark glass of my phone's screen: sitting in my room, alone, with the phone in my hands. I wasted a few hours now. My back hurts. What am I doing? After a moment of buzzing nothingness, my supercharged phone turns on again. I can't stop looking.

. . .

"When through the water's thickness I see the tiled bottom of the pool, I do not see it despite the water and the reflections; I see it through them and because of them," Merleau-Ponty writes.[13] What we see is the result of mediating processes that make the visible *visible*. There is always something in between us and the world we see.[14] This is because our perception keeps filling the gaps, clothing the visible with our imagination, bringing into the field of vision something hidden, latent.

Yet these processes disappear from our perception, thus becoming transparent and giving us the idea that what we see is unmediated, unfiltered, given.[15] But the fact is, Merleau-Ponty writes, that "there is no vision without the screen."[16]

. . .

Another way to put it: Just as there is a one-way mirror between Brenda and me—a reflective, transparent, and imaginative device—there is also a one-way mirror between you and the world available to your perception. A one-way mirror is planted right in the middle of your skull, slicing your brain in half. If you didn't already, it's amazing you never noticed it—it's so big! So big you can't see the world without it, so big if you try to take it out you might have a psychotic meltdown.

. . .

"From the perspective of systemic therapy, through the one-way mirror you can literally see *a system in action*, because interactive patterns are acted out right in front of our eyes. Watching live therapies through the one-way mirror allows us to see better, to learn to see better. In systemic therapy we talk about learning the *mirada* [gaze]."
—*Marisa*

. . .

There is something else about the realm of the visual, something important from a therapeutic perspective. In the realm of the visual, not only can we see, but we are also visible beings. This is what Merleau-Ponty calls the "reversibility" of vision: To see implies the reverse possibility of being seen.[17] We are both visual and visible creatures. While it is easier to understand this by picturing an actual person who is looking back at you when you are looking at them, this reversibility belongs to the imagination as well.[18] Think about the feeling that someone is looking at you even when you don't see anyone around—maybe this imagined presence looking at you becomes a feeling that spreads all over your skin or morphs into a cold shiver across your shoulders.[19]

Sometimes you might even notice how objects around you can look back at you, how you can sense their gaze. If this sounds too strange, maybe an easier starting point would be to look at the camera of your phone or laptop for a minute. As you stare into the camera's eye, you might begin to sense that something or someone behind the camera is, or could be, there. The camera is indeed one of the primary places where we can encounter the gaze of an anonymous, imagined, and invisible other.[20]

Where does this gaze come from?

. . .

When I write about the gaze, I mean something midway between vision and the imagination, midway between literally being seen and imagining being seen.[21] The philosopher Jean-Paul Sartre writes that when you hear someone's steps, their gaze is already sneaking into your consciousness.[22] The gaze is not really, or not only, about vision. Vision is not only, or not really, about vision.

. . .

Knock, knock, knock, knock

Do you see? Do you see?

. . .

A few weeks after returning from my fieldwork research in Argentina, I had a conversation with an anthropology professor at a party. As a side note, when professors and graduate students get together, they don't really have parties. It is more like a disjointed choreography of people in the business of class reproduction bathing in paranoid, insecure, obsessive, and narcissistic affects—but there is a lot of affection, brilliance, and friendship too. During the party, the professor, whom I'll call Professor Z., asked me where I had done my fieldwork, and I told her I had spent most of my time behind a one-way mirror in Argentina.

"I know, right? That's exactly how it feels sometimes!" she replied between sips of a tremendously sugary Californian chardonnay.

When Professor Z. learned that I had literally been behind a one-way mirror, she found that my ethnographic project was, in fact, not really ethnographic, and that the setting of systemic therapy was somewhat disturbing. "How can people agree to be watched by someone they can't see? That can't be therapeutic!" After gulping my third glass of sugar wine, I tried to convince Professor Z. that it was, in fact, therapeutic and that the one-way mirror could easily be used as a generative allegory—like she initially thought it was—for thinking about the role of the gaze in the contemporary condition.

"It's about the literal one-way mirror, but it is also about something else. It's an allegorical performance about vision and its imaginal depths. It's about *seeing and being seen* in our screenified present!" Professor Z. smiled cordially while drifting toward another conversation. I didn't convince her, not even a little bit; and for a few days after that conversation Professor Z. became my primary imagined audience. Every time I was thinking about my research, I felt her presence hovering over my shoulders. I could see her shaking her head while reading what I was writing.

. . .

In this very moment I am looking at the screen while also having a vague sense of my own self seen from above and from behind. I also feel looked back at by my own words appearing on the screen. Every word I type also contains you, too, and even if I don't really know who you are, I feel looked back at by you. You are in my words. I know, this all sounds a little paranoid, but there is a lot of transformative potential that can be unleashed through an awareness of this process.

. . .

Zoom meetings, Zoom cocktail parties, Zoom yoga sessions to help you reach Zoom enlightenment. Our everyday life has been Zoomified to such an extent that sometimes I just open the Zoom app, start a meeting with no participants, and look at myself being seen by my own self. Only in that moment can I experience an almost seamless absence of delay where I can finally *see myself seeing myself being seen by myself* #DigitalEcstasy #CyberneticErotics.[23]

. . .

When my imagined audience includes gazes like Professor Z.'s, writing and thinking become exhausting and often meaningless operations. These people, usually people who have structural power over me, find their way into my psychic life because their rejection poses a threat, a challenge to my existence.

The threat feels all the more present when I identify with what I write, when I am attached to my ideas as if they overlapped with my whole being. To obsessively defend and protect this attachment to my own self, I waste time writing against them.

This is the type of imagined gaze that pushes me to write as if being interrogated by the police—the internalized Anthropology Police. And when I write against the AnthroPoPo, my fingers freeze up, my ideas wither beneath their skeptical gaze, my sentences become defensive and overexplanatory, and my English grammar collapses onto itself, getting even clunkier than usual. Professor Z.'s gaze has slipped into my psyche and, in defending myself against it, I've identified with it.

. . .

Freud writes about identification as "the earliest expression of an emotional tie with another person," a tie that has the capacity to "mould a person's own Ego after the fashion of the one that has been taken as a model."[24] When we identify with something, we (mostly unconsciously) make space for it to occupy a portion of our ego. This portion of the ego, once we incorporate it, can be a good neighbor to the other parts of the ego or instead act like a neighbor who hammers on the wall at 3 a.m. to hang an impossibly large bookshelf.[25]

During a child's early development, identification usually happens with the parental figures. When a child identifies with his father, for example, he develops a desire to become like his father and progressively assumes some of his traits and characteristics.[26] The child's psychic makeup changes, absorbing and incorporating the traits of the person he is identifying with. When we identify with something, we become, at least partially, like the object of our identification.[27] In a psychoanalytic sense, this means "we" are never really "our" selves, but rather a composition of internalized external elements.[28] And among the many objects we may internalize is an imagined gaze directed at us.

. . .

Knock, knock, knock, knock

. . .

In the work of Jacques Lacan, the stage of early childhood identification with the gaze of the other is called the *mirror stage*. In the mirror stage, an infant develops mastery over her own sense of self when she sees her reflected image on the surface of the mirror and identifies with it. *That image is me!*[29] According to Lacan, in this quasi-mythical moment, the infant identifies with the reflected image she sees in the mirror; in this reflected image, the infant encounters a coherent whole that will hold together her sense of self.[30] The image gives form to the infant's ego.[31] "It suffices to understand the mirror stage," Lacan writes, "*as an identification*, in the full sense analysis gives to the term: namely, the transformation that takes place in the subject when he assumes an image."[32]

Lacan uses the mirror stage, which hypothetically happens when the infant is between six and eighteen months, as a "scene" to point out that the ego is formed through a fundamental misrecognition because the infant identifies with an image that doesn't actually come from her inner psychic life but is rather an external, and fundamentally alien, reflection.[33]

Lacan writes that the mirror stage is at "the threshold of the visible world," meaning that this stage is what allows the infant to access the realm of the visual but also that this process is as imaginative as it is visual. When identifying with her own image, the infant is indeed reaching toward a realm beyond the image itself, as if her look could pierce through the mirror and get caught in an imaginal realm on the other side of it.

The scene of Brenda looking at her own reflection while trying to look beyond it should be knocking at the doors of your allegorical faculties.

. . .

Through Lacan's mirror stage, Freud's notion of identification can thus be tied back to Merleau-Ponty's imaginal reversibility of vision. Because *to see* is *to be seen* and *to be seen* is always *to (potentially) identify with*. This is probably what Merleau-Ponty also meant when he wrote that there is "a fundamental narcissism of all vision."[34]

. . .

I = Eye

. . .

Professor Z. thus managed to impact my own sense of self-worth because I had identified with, and incorporated, the way I imagined her seeing me. This might have happened so easily for a whole series of reasons, from precarious dynamics between professors and students to my own psychic availability to latch onto any feedback that could confirm that I am a useless piece of nothing.[35] The point here is to start thinking about how other people's gazes can get to you, even or especially when you are just imagining them.

To be fair, however, Professor Z. probably liked me very much, and with her feedback she just wanted to help me clarify my project.[36] But things can get way more violent gaze-wise when the person holding more power actually projects a harmful gaze onto the other person, who doesn't have enough range of motion to refuse the identification with that gaze.

In psychoanalysis this identificatory dynamic is called "projective identification."[37] In a projective identification loop, you identify with my projections. I have a fantasy about you—say I have a projection about you being a distracted reader, and then you start feeling a sense of distraction in your own body. In this case, you act out my fantasy. You welcome my fantasy about you as if it was yours in the first place. Worried about being anxious or boring, I start seeing you as the anxious or boring one—which makes you start feeling anxious, or boring, or best of all, anxious about being boring.

Projective identification is like shooting someone with a psychic paintball, a stain of invisible paint spreading all over their ego.[38]

. . .

Frantz Fanon, in *Black Skin, White Masks*, offers a vivid description of how colonized people of color in the Antilles have identified with a white, racist gaze that haunts and distorts their own understanding of themselves.[39] To identify with a white gaze means to see yourself, as a person of color, through the degrading eyes of the colonizer; it means that there is no difference between how the colonizer sees you and the way you see yourself.

Fanon describes the shattering force of the colonizer's gaze in his experience in Paris as a French Martinican: As he moves through the city, white people look at him and move away from him in a way that reifies, fixes, and fragments Fanon's perception of his own body. Fanon's body becomes an "object among other objects" and, locked in a "suffocating reification," Fanon's bodily experience becomes intensely dysmorphic.[40]

To have a dysmorphic experience means to see your body through someone else's (imagined) perspective, to see it through a filter that makes it unrecognizable to you. An image has been projected onto you, and now you look at the mirror, and within, beneath, and through its reflections you can only see an abject object.[41]

. . .

So identity mirrors can be thrown at you, and if you are open enough—or pried open with all sorts of psychic or structural violence—the mirrors will slide right down into your guts and reflect back whichever "you" they please.

. . .

The mirror stage is not an exclusively visual experience. Imagine an infant looking at herself in front of the mirror while her m/other says something like, "There you are! Look at you—you look so *chubby*, or *sleepy*, or *like a princess*, or *skinny*, or *just like your father!*"[42] The mirror reflections we identify with come to us as a reflected image, but also a facial expression, a sentence, a sound, a silence, a slap.[43] The incorporation of a reflected image, then, includes all sorts of external feedback and injunctions that belong to the relational and historical context of the infant and are not only visual.

More widely, the gaze of the other, being both real and imagined, can be any type of feedback we receive from the external world. The breast(s) of my mother—ah, the repressed memories!—might have been the first gaze I have ever encountered; a social media notification can also be something that looks back at me with the force of a thrillingly unknown gaze; my leg feeling the vibration of the phone can work like a gaze too.[44] *Your buzzing pocket is looking at you.*

. . .

Together with critical race theory, feminist theory has widely explored how subaltern subjectivities are shaped by a dominant "male gaze" that produces violent forms of gendered subjectification.[45] Drawing from Iris Marion Young, the philosopher Alia Al-Saji describes how the incorporation of a male gaze prompts the feminine body to acquire a hesitantly self-conscious way of moving across space.[46] The incorporation of the male gaze shapes the feminine body schema and restricts the range of its embodied sense of possibility. *Think about a ride on the metro and the ways in which different positionalities occupy space differently— look at the bros with their legs and arms extended in space as if the train was empty.*[47] The male gaze freezes the feminine body, forcing upon it all sorts of destructively identificatory processes. It's like being trapped inside a box of mirrors where whatever reflection you see about yourself, *it can't be otherwise.*[48]

. . .

I've seen several TikTok videos where young teenagers look at themselves on their phone as they appear modified through a filter that deforms their faces. Many do so because they have heard that if they look at their disfigured face long enough, they will perceive themselves as prettier when they go back to #NoFilter. Now think about the possibility that your partner's gaze works like one of these disfiguring filters, but you don't know that the filter function is on, or you forgot that there is a filter at all—so that whatever the filter shows you is what you think you are without a filter.

. . .

We have been talking for several pages about vision, the gaze, and imaginative processes of identification with the gaze of the other, processes that shape your very self. In romantic relationships, and particularly in not-so-healthy relationships, these processes become very clear when the gaze of a partner completely takes over the way the other partner sees themselves, thus suffocating any other possible viewpoint on their being. If toxic processes of gaze identification happen across structural axes of power imbalance—from structural forms of violence across race and gender lines, to the kind of academic precarity embodied in the haunting gaze of Professor Z.—then the romantic couple form might be one of the places to observe this dynamic. For whose gaze do we become more vulnerable to, do we introject more deeply into our own soul, than that of our beloved partner?

. . .

"I can't see myself through his eyes anymore," says Simona during her fourth systemic couple therapy session with her husband Enrique. Simona bites her lips for a second, recalling how she used to see a sparkle in her partner's eyes, a glow that would animate his gaze when he was looking at her. His eyes, once the mirrors of her beauty-full soul, now reflect a dark absence, a judging disinterest.

"When I wake up and see him looking at me, it just makes me cry. *I cry imagining what he sees.* I don't know why. . . . I just cry looking at his eyes, the eyes I used to love. . . . " Simona takes a breath, looks down, and brushes something off her right leg.

. . .

In this chapter I wanted to throw at you a full-length mirror so you could see yourself, but you didn't catch it, so it shattered into a thousand fragments. Now we are both looking at the broken mirror fragments in between us.[49] Some of these fragments are about you, some about me, some about us, some about the couples in therapy I have observed. But I am not giving you too many details about the therapy sessions I have seen. After hundreds of hours watching therapy sessions behind the one-way mirror, I want to resist reproducing a type of voyeurism that doesn't teach us anything but gives us this pleasure, the pleasure of seeing without being seen, of scrolling through someone else's life.

Of course, I also do that, and this project is based on a form of anthropological voyeurism.[50] But I try to keep it to a minimum, and the only couple dramas you will get to know a bit better are the ones of Simona and Enrique in chapter 2, and Romina and Julio in chapter 3.

. . .

The couple form makes partners particularly available to a reciprocal incorporation of gazes, projections, and identifications.[51] Through a quotidian exposure to the presence of your partner, every single gesture you make can absorb their gaze. Especially in a context where one is open to identify with the other's projection—we called it projective identification—it can become quite difficult to distinguish who is seeing whom in which way.

. . .

Paula and Thiago (we briefly met them in the introduction) often explained their relational crisis as an impossibility to see themselves in the "eyes" of the other. Or better, what they saw of themselves through the gaze of the other was mostly a destructive distortion of their own identity. "I hate myself when I see myself through her gaze [*mirada*]," Thiago comments during his fifth session with Paula. "He sees me only as the mother of his kids. I can't stand seeing myself as this nagging unemployed mother," Paula replies.

Things can get confusing when, after thirty years, Paula has absorbed Thiago's gaze to such an extent that she can't distinguish any more what she thinks from what he thinks about herself. And this is true also for Thiago, who got used to thinking that he is just someone who forgets everything and who doesn't care, because that's how Paula sees him.[52] The more Paula identifies with Thiago's gaze, the more she becomes what he thinks he is seeing, the more Thiago really sees Paula that way, the more Paula really *really* thinks that that's who she is. . . .

. . .

In Gregory Bateson's terms, Paula and Thiago might be stuck in a "symmetrical" feedback loop. As Bateson proposed, in symmetrical feedback loops, the more A does something, the more B will do it too. And, being a loop, there is no point in trying to figure out exactly who started what and when. Bateson often referred to the "armaments races" or "keeping up with the Joneses" as examples of what he called a symmetrical loop.[53] Or consider Thiago embodying Paula's projections: The more Paula thinks he is in this or that way, the more he becomes it.[54]

For Bateson, symmetrical loops are opposed to, and alternate with, "complementary" feedback loops, where the reactive behaviors within the dyad—or "binary relationship," to use Bateson's terms—are dissimilar: The more A does something, the less B does it. Bateson, for example, referred to *dominance-submission* or *spectatorship-exhibitionism* as complementary relationships.[55] The more Paula screams, the less Thiago talks; the less he talks, the more she screams, the more he retreats.

Bateson suggested that both complementary and symmetrical feedback loops, if they keep feeding on their own reactivity, can escalate or spin out of control, progressively leading to detrimental escalations, and provoke violent if not pathological ruptures of the dyadic relation. Bateson called this process *schismogenesis*.[56]

. . .

"So, you thought that I was the one who had to change!?" Paula asks Thiago back in the opening scene of this book's introduction. Paula looks at Wanda and then looks straight into the eye of the video camera: "Do you see? Do you see? That's what I have to deal with!"

"I said the relationship!" Thiago screams at the camera.

. . .

Yeah, so you thought I *had to* change? *And what about* YOU?!

I said the relationship!

. . .

From a systemic perspective, the question of who must change might not be the most generative. Once partners are stuck in a loop, the properties of the loop exceed its individual parts.[57] The dyadic couple form is a system, and, for what concerns me in this chapter, it is a system that tends to foster projective identification loops tied to ways of seeing and incorporating the other. Where does *you* start, where does *you* end? The projective identification loop can have a choking grip, especially when you end up being eaten up by your partner's gaze.

. . .

I like to talk about eating within these dyadic loops in reference to a disturbingly generative connection that Freud makes between the oral phase of the infant and identification. Identification, Freud writes, "behaves like a derivative of the first, *oral* phase of the organization of the libido, in which the object that we long for and prize is assimilated by eating and is in that way annihilated as such."[58] This, according to Freud, also accounts for an intrinsic ambivalence of the identificatory process, which can turn into "an expression of tenderness as easily as a wish for someone's removal."[59] So to identify with something is also to eat it up and drop it down into your ego.[60]

And to love someone *a lot a lot* in this identificatory way might also mean to harbor a desire for that person's removal. So you can be (eat) them.[61]

. . .

We were so in love. We were wrapped within such a delightfully topological continuity of our souls that I once asked her if she would eat my ashes when I died. She said *yes*, the flowers of the desert humming in the back of her pupils.

. . .

A friend from my Tai Chi class, a superfit old lady who could kick my ass with a few kung fu moves, is telling me a story in a beautifully half-empty Chinese restaurant.

"The other day I read an article about romantic relationships that mentioned this old Chinese story about a young man who is sitting by a river, eating a fish he just caught. An old man approaches him and asks him why he is eating that fish. *Because I love it*, the younger man replies. *But if you love it, why did you take it out of its beloved river and kill it to eat it?*"

I laugh, telling her that's exactly what I am writing about in the first chapter of my book and then launch into a nano-lecture about identification, gazes, and the oral drive. The old-young lady smiles with nodding warmth.

"Relationships are hard," she replies.

. . .

Knock, knock, knock, knock

Marisa, the therapist, has just knocked four times on the one-way mirror, producing an interruption in Brenda and Claudio's interminable conversational loop. After a moment of silence, Brenda begins speaking again. She is looking directly at the one-way mirror.

"It's so pitiful. . . . Look at him!" Brenda is saying. "Look at yourself, Claudio— you can't even reply to what I say. Look at your stupid face! Now at least someone else can see it! Do you see? *Do you see?*"

After addressing the mirror, Brenda hesitates for a few seconds. The raindrops texturing the session's atmosphere sound heavier than before. Something shifts in Brenda's face. The therapist in front of her doesn't say anything. Then Brenda looks at Claudio and tells him with firm calm that she wants to break up. She wants to end their relationship.

"I can't take it anymore," she closes.

The moment hangs in the air. Claudio doesn't respond. He gets up from his chair, glances at the one-way mirror, and leaves.

. . .

"Do you see? Do you see?" Brenda's question in front of the mirror produced a small shift, a quick interruption that brought Brenda to a tipping point—to that moment when people draw a line or make a cut. A short choreography, acted out before our eyes through the one-way mirror, leading to the dissolution of a five-year relationship. But what did she want us to see?

At the end of the session between Brenda and Claudio, I walked back home, under the pouring rain, haunted by what I had just witnessed. The recursive conversational loops, the sound of Marisa knocking on the mirror, and above all Brenda's question, *Do you see? Do you see?* The refrains of Marisa's knocking and Brenda's question echoed through the streets, mixing with the sounds of traffic and rain.

Knock, knock, knock, knock

Do you see? Do you see?

This is it. It's over.

Cut.

I can't take it anymore. This is it. It's over.

. . .

A therapeutic event interrupts the repetition of a loop and makes people available to transformation. This can happen at different scales and have different durational impacts. Even the smallest interruption, the most insignificant event, can facilitate the interruption of repetition. Brenda suddenly looking at the mirror, a question that lands in the right spot and opens a new way of seeing— something that triggers something else.[62]

. . .

Thiago and Paula were having a heated argument about Thiago always coming home later than expected. Midway into a sentence, Thiago turned to the eye of the camera and screamed, "Do you see? *Do you see?* It's like this every day! Now at least someone can see! She just doesn't believe me!"

One session later, Thiago was saying that he had forgotten they had dinner plans because he had too much work and added that Paula never, ever understood what it meant to have to work—Paula interrupted him and looked straight into the eye of the camera: "Do you see this? What should I do with this guy? We talked about this last time. I mean, do you see?"[63]

. . .

Partners stuck in dyadic feedback loops can bump into, create, or look for decompression points that decrease, rebalance, or interrupt all sorts of loopy and detrimental escalations. Within systemic therapy, visual devices themselves can play such a role, providing decompressive possibilities.

During their sessions, for example, Paula and Thiago would often address their therapist or the invisible audience on the other side of the camera, asking them to act like referees on the sidelines of a match, ready to interrupt the game and whistle a fault. In the scenes I shared above, Paula and Thiago's arguments reach a climax when they both turn to the eye of the camera, sidestepping the therapist who is in the room with them.[64]

. . .

Many couples and therapists I have observed seemed to interact with the visual setting of systemic therapy not only to slow down the schismogenetic compulsion of feedback loops but also to summon an external, potentially more spacious, viewpoint on the dyad. This external gaze, as channeled through visual devices like the one-way mirror, acts like a third element sliding into the fissures of a tightly rehearsed dyadic loop.

Thirdness might indeed be what's needed to crack the dyadic loop open, even if just for a second. The psychoanalyst Jessica Benjamin, among others, has developed a therapeutic theory of thirdness suggesting that dyadic loops can be interrupted or at least rebalanced when partners manage to surrender to a third space, an idea, a gaze, or a frame that exists outside of the dyad.[65]

Different things can act like thirds; sometimes it's even just the possibility to understand one's own situation through a concept, a notion, a narrative frame, a displacement that mediates the way one sees oneself being seen. *Do you see?* Some thirds might be more easily accessible than others, and, within systemic therapy, the imaginal depths of visual devices like the one-way mirror or the camera seem to be particularly able to invite a potentially infinite thirdness within the tight spirals of twoness.

. . .

When Marisa knocks on the mirror, its reflective surface suddenly becomes an opaque surface of a depth, one hiding an invisible audience. Within Brenda and Claudio's dyadic gaze loop, this audience becomes a crucial third point *whose gaze can only be imagined*. Once Brenda's gaze is redirected toward the mirror, we are witness to an improvised reenactment of the mirror stage, one that potentially allows Brenda to interrupt or rearticulate her preexisting identifications, to reach new invisible depths beyond her own self-reflection.[66] The invisible third on the other side of the mirror offers a relatively spacious response to Brenda because it can't actually interact with her and is thus capable of becoming whatever Brenda is imagining.

This offers Brenda a crucial therapeutic possibility: to see herself being seen differently.

. . .

Even just talking about projective identification loops in your couple can be a way to start inserting thirdness into a dyadic loop. Here is a suggested couple-form activity: Sit down with your partner, have a few generous glasses of a super-dry and zesty white wine, and take turns guessing who projects what onto whom and who takes on whose projections. You could even try to identify a few of the loops you're relationally stuck in. Are they complementary or symmetrical?

It's going to be fun, I promise.

. . .

Buenos Aires, Argentina, c. 1984–85.[67] The screen flickers for a few seconds. The recording of the therapy session begins. At the center of the frame there are two chairs in front of a one-way mirror. Gala and Jorge enter the room and sit down; the therapist, Sánchez, is out of the frame, but we can see an opaque reflection of his figure on the one-way mirror behind Jorge and Gala. We don't know if there is anyone behind the one-way mirror. Jorge readjusts his jeans, and Gala sits down, commenting on a public protest happening close by. Gala and Jorge are probably in their early thirties. The therapy starts with a fast-paced rhythm.

"Did you get a new haircut, Jorge?" Sánchez asks.

"Yes—" Jorge starts responding.

"I prefer him like this, shorter!" interrupts Gala.

"Do you like it too, Jorge?"

"Yes, yes … it's more …"

"He looks so much better now!"

"Yes, Gala likes it more like this, it's true."

Sánchez pauses for a second. "But do you also like it, Jorge?"

"Yes, me too, it looks cleaner."

"So, how was your week? How did the couple do?"

"Well at the begin—"

"We did better, I think . . . less fights," Gala interrupts Jorge.

"Yes, less fights, I mean yesterday when I—"

"Yesterday we had a little fight about the trash. He really never ever takes it out!" Gala interjects.

"Yeah, and then I—"

"Then he just got offended and he didn't talk for two hours!"

"So, it's always like this? You talk over him while he talks to you and vice versa?" Sánchez asks.

"But I already know what he thinks! He doesn't need to explain it!"

"Yes, it's true that she already knows . . ." confirms Jorge.

For about five minutes Gala and Jorge perform a well-rehearsed dance of reciprocal interruptions. Jorge starts talking about Gala's intrusion into Jorge's relationships with his family. Gala interrupts him saying that she needs to know what the problem is. He says he owes so much to his uncle, and she interjects that nothing of what Jorge just said is true, and that she doesn't interfere in his relationship with his uncle. Gala is about to say something else, but Sánchez abruptly interrupts her.

"Gala, do you have a pocket mirror by any chance?"

. . .

Have you ever entered a state of mild hypnotic trance while looking at yourself in the mirror? I am talking about looking straight into your own eyes and entering into this circular state where you see your eyes looking at yourself and it all feels rather surreal—maybe you feel ejected from your ordinary sense of things while looking at yourself in a mirror. Try it. Spend three minutes looking at yourself. Just look at yourself straight in the eyes.

. . .

"Gala, do you have a pocket mirror by any chance?" Sánchez repeats.

"Yes . . . ?" Gala says hesitantly before reaching into her purse for a mirror.

Jorge is looking at the scene, amused and surprised. Gala looks more surprised than amused. Sánchez, whose face we see for the first time in the recording and only for a couple of seconds, leans toward Gala to take the mirror. Sánchez looks at himself in the mirror and then gives it back to Gala.

"Okay, now . . . Jorge, you can say whatever you want to say, and you, Gala, look at the mirror. Focus on your face reflected in the mirror and listen to what

Jorge is saying. Notice your reactions to what he says but don't say anything. I just want your dialogues to be monologues for now."

Gala is startled. Jorge looks up to the ceiling for a moment and then starts talking again about his uncle.

"But . . . so I have to look at myself in the mirror?" Gala interrupts.

Sánchez doesn't reply. Gala looks at herself in the mirror, moves her chair, and cleans the surface of the mirror with her shirt. Jorge is talking, but he is not looking at Gala, nor at the therapist. He seems to be talking to himself. His gaze wanders through the room until it lands on the eye of the camera. Gala seems fully absorbed in her own reflected image in the small mirror. She is looking at her reflected lips. Jorge starts talking straight into the eye of the camera.

. . .

Repetition: Thiago's "Now at least someone can see" and Paula's "Do you see this?" were directed at the eye of the camera, not at the therapist.

. . .

Jorge's gaze slowly moves away from the eye of the camera—he looks at Gala, as if waiting for a response. Gala glances nervously at him while trying to focus on the mirror. She looks at Jorge, then the mirror, then the therapist, then the mirror. Jorge seems lost as he jumps from one topic to another.

"It's also this type of therapy," Jorge says. "Sometimes I don't understand what's happening, and I did so much psychoanalysis, which helped me with my father, but now it is more about my uncle. I need to call him . . . but I am not sure I understand the method of this therapy."

Sánchez doesn't respond. Then, for the first time during the session, there are fifteen seconds of silence. Jorge and Gala's gazes intersect briefly. Twenty seconds of silence. The dance of interruptions is interrupted by the disruptive presence of the small mirror Gala is holding. Thirty seconds. Gala looks at herself in the mirror; she bites her lips. Thirty-five seconds. Jorge and Gala smile at each other as if about to perform a synchronized gesture. But they both stay still. After a deep breath, Jorge starts talking again but turning away from Gala. With the possibility to address her without being interrupted, he looks elsewhere, toward the camera.

"Talk to her when you talk!" Sánchez tells him. Jorge looks at Gala. She bites her lips struggling to keep silent. She glances at the therapist, at the mirror, and at Jorge as if asking how much longer she needs to be trapped by the mirror image of her own silence. She rubs her eyes; she coughs. Jorge says his uncle's wife doesn't interfere that much in their conjugal life; Gala bursts out in laughter, breaking the silence. She dramatically drops the mirror over her bag and says, "She doesn't interfere? She doesn't? What are you talking about!" Jorge quickly responds, "But she doesn't—"

The recording of this session breaks here. The DVD *is scratched beyond repair.*

. . .

I want your dialogues to be monologues. That's a suggestion that surprised me, especially paired with asking Gala to look at herself in the mirror to let Jorge talk. There is an evident gendered violence in the therapist's interruption. But there is also something generative in this idea, which creates an interruption of a conversational loop through the literal insertion of a "reflecting third." Echoing Marisa's interruption, Sánchez also summons a third through the interruption of the session's rhythm by way of a mirror, a reflecting visual device.

The difference with Brenda's scene is maybe that this intervention seems to further trap Gala into her own reflective loops rather than creating more space. After a brief moment of interruption—a moment that could have gone anywhere—Gala appears ready to hop back in the ring to beat Jorge, or maybe more precisely to be(eat) him—to be, eat, and beat him.[68]

Still, I am so fascinated by this theatrical therapeutic intervention that during my next couple-form argument, instead of reacting to my partner, I will be holding a mirror to myself while she talks. I will report back on the results of the experiment.

. . .

Knock, knock
  Who is there?
  The knocking sound.
  The knocking sound who?
  The knocking sound that summoned a third space to loosen up your dyadic loops.
  The knocking sound what?
  The sonic animation of the potentially reparative gaze you are imagining.
  Wait, what? Who is there?
  Knock, knock

. . .

Marisa's knocking turns the one-way mirror into a permeable boundary that brings to life multiple visual processes — from reflective to imaginative.[69] I would say that Marisa and Sánchez both use the one-way mirror in its capacity to be, more widely, a screen. Following Merleau-Ponty, I consider here the screen as a surface of contact between the visible and the invisible, the surface of an imaginal depth, a disappearing in-between that mediates whatever is coming the viewer's way. Think about the shadows projected on Plato's cave: A wall swallows its viewers to such an extent that they cannot see the wall is just a screen. In the myth of the cave, the screen is the real, and what's outside of the screen is just a myth.[70]

. . .

What is it about screens that lets them work so well as thirds?

. . .

The screen you imagine when you read the word *screen* is a surface that creates a separation between spaces, a cut that posits a boundary between a "here" and a "there," between the viewer and that which must be contemplated.[71] Through a short etymological detour, we can discover that there is a relationship between the rectangular space of the screen and the very action of cutting.

The Greek verb *témnō* (τέμνω), "to cut," is etymologically related to the word *temple*. The temple (*témenos*, τέμενος) in ancient Greece was the "sacred enclosure" created by the act of *cutting off* a specific area on the ground.[72] Related to the Greek *témnō*, the Latin *templum* was a square or rectangle that Roman haruspices (divinatory priests) drew in the sky to make their "observations in order to determine the future from the flight, cries, and eating habits of birds."[73] The rectangular space of the screen thus articulates a cut between realms. The screen cuts like a sharp knife from the spirit world and creates a boundary, one that prompts the viewer's desire toward what's beyond that boundary.[74]

This is not only a property of the digital devices in front of your nose. Just make a rectangle with your hands and look through it: The frame selects a privileged area in space; the space you see changes and acquires a force that comes from elsewhere; your gaze is invested in it in a different way; what you see starts looking back at you. Screens catalyze attention because there is something else that happens within the frame, within the space of the screen. Something that does not really belong to the screen itself.[75]

Screens are not only, or not really, about screens.

. . .

Oops, I just realized I have loosened my hand's grip.[76] I think I felt your hand sliding away from mine some time ago. Happy splash. And don't forget that *to see is to be seen is to identify is to eat is to be eaten*. Or, more concisely, *seeing is eating!*

. . .

When I talked before about the one-way mirror right in the middle of your brain, I was really talking about a screen—a massive screen, bigger than the sum of your neural networks. The screen is not only the literal screen in front of you. Lacan says some pretty wild things about screens, and I don't want to drag you down a Lacanian spiral, although maybe I already did. But to say just one thing about it, for Lacan, just like for Merleau-Ponty, the screen is what allows the subject to enter the field of vision, to become visible, and, in fact, to become anything at all. In *Seminar XI* Lacan refers to the screen as a "stain," an "envelope," a "mask," a "double," and a "thrown-off skin."[77]

. . .

I mentioned above that the eye of the camera can be a place where we encounter the gaze. The cinematic apparatus has indeed been a primary location for a specific type of gaze to propagate across the media sphere. Laura Mulvey has famously shown how cinema, and images more widely, reproduce a "male gaze," depicting passive and objectified females that prompt the viewer—of any gendered positionality—to identify with the male gaze.[78] In a wider sense, Kaja Silverman writes about the screen as a cultural repertoire that mediates the viewer's identifications.[79] If there is no vision without the screen and no screen without identification, then the question is really about what to identify with and through which culturally available screen.

. . .

Maybe what happens within the frame of the screen attracts us so much in our digital present because the screen holds captive the way we see ourselves being seen. We see something shimmering on the other side of the screen, and we get swallowed by it as we cross the threshold of its depths looking for a potentially infinite mirror. When did screens start mostly working like identity mirrors?

. . .

If you find yourself in front of a screen and during a new moon night, turn off the lights, close your eyes, sink your mind into your body, let your breath reach the lower part of your abdomen, and keep your awareness down there for a bit. When you feel ready, knock against the screen four times and make a wish.

. . .

"I see only from one point," Jacques Lacan writes, "but in my existence I am looked at from all sides."[80] Interestingly, for Lacan we can't really see the gaze that shapes us; in Joan Copjec's interpretation of Lacan, "it is what the subject does not see and not simply what it sees that founds it."[81]

You are thus shaped by *and* cut off from the gaze. You need a screen between you and the gaze to be able to face it, a screen that both connects and separates you from the gaze.[82]

A screen that cuts and stitches.

. . .

Well beyond Michel Foucault's disciplinary societies, our most intimate actions today are plugged into the tentacular surveillance of our Big Data Brother.[83] Most of us are not physically forced into this panopticon. We deliver ourselves to it because we love it, find pleasure in it, are addicted to it, get nervous and excited when we're about to log on to it, and even experience relational death when outside of its reach. We are subjectivized by the panopticon to the extent that we lose our minds when we feel no one is looking at us. The digital panopticon we are addicted to is a flickering house of mirrors.[84]

. . .

Look at me, doing this thing in this place. Look at me—I need to see myself being seen by you to feel real. Look at me, so I can be subjected to the gaze of a potentially infinite other. Look at me—I feel you scrolling through my feed-world. Look at me, your "I" has morphed into a screened and screening "eye."[85] Look at me—you are casting a spell on each fragment of me you can find. Look at me—your destructive gaze cuts through the screen, and I can feel its blade tinkering with my lungs. Look at me, available like a frozen flower to the cutting work of the screen.

[Don't] stop looking at me.

. . .

Social media has become the easiest way for me to explain the relationship between the gaze and witchcraft, which was famously described by the anthropologist E. E. Evans-Pritchard as a "psychic act."[86] Through the screen the witch-like force of the evil eye, a malevolent gaze sent your way, can stick to you like a tick and suck whatever lifeblood it finds. People literally have died because of this type of witchcraft across historical and cultural settings.[87] Projective identification certainly has some witchcraft force to it; and the screen can distribute gazes that have devastating effects on the user's vitality.

Maybe the gaze can get to users so seamlessly because of the affective porosity users develop when they are given over to screens. Users today are so porously tethered to the screen they have erased the screen's thirdness and become what they see. Users who fell inside the flickering rectangle and morphed into tweeting birds caged within a dyadic *eat or be eaten* spiral.[88]

Instead of an interrupting third, the screen has become the partner in a new dyad, the user-screen dyad, and a pretty suffocating dyad if you ask me. *To see is to eat is to . . .*

. . .

The dyadic loops of projective identification are thus not only about romantic couples. The anthropologist William Mazzarella, for example, proposes that we think about dyadic loops and cannibalistic identification to address a polarized political present that moves at the beat of an *eat or be eaten* dance. If we don't find ways to inject thirdness within the "trap of dyadic relation," we might spiral into a Freudian cannibalistic feast where it's either *me* or *you*, where we are either *pro* or *against*.[89] "Pure identification," Mazzarella writes, "has to be mediated by a third term—be it law, language, an analytic third space—in order not to end in universal cannibalism."[90]

This thirdness, Mazzarella writes, echoing Jessica Benjamin, can be encountered in the analytic and therapeutic space when the therapist allows the patient to act out their own libidinal investments without responding to them, without getting trapped in a dyadic feedback loop with the patient. This is possible when the therapist can "hold the frame" for the patient without getting sucked into "playing the game."[91]

Brenda's one-way mirror, Paula and Thiago's eye of the camera, or Gala's purse mirror seem to, rather literally, hold the frame for them and activate a third space that exceeds their dyadic dynamics, that interrupts their game—the loopy games of reciprocal interruption and projective identification. Mobilizing this therapeutic dynamic, Mazzarella suggests, could offer generative insights to rethink the way we engage with the present moment's rather polarized political bonanza. Widely, the question for the contemporary citizen/user/subject might be what type of frame the screen is holding for them, and which sorts of dyadic games they are getting trapped within.

. . .

In this chapter I have been writing about dyadic suffocation, but I also unapologetically keep addressing you, inviting you to what would seem a dyadic dance that sidesteps thirdness.[92] I know, it's a bit unfair because it draws you in, not so subtly asking you to identify with what I write. And maybe also to eat me up. But, you know, it feels lonely out here, and it's kind of cold on the empty dance floor of writerly exposure. I just wanted you to dance with me for a bit, tiptoeing around some broken fragments by our feet.

If you thought, however, this was a dance that had us facing each other in a dyadic embrace, then you will have to look more closely because there are multiple screens between us.[93] Come close to the screen, reach out to the fire on the other side of it, so that you can move away once it starts burning.

. . .

It takes (more than) two to tango.

. . .

Brenda's addressing an invisible gaze beyond her own reflected image shifted her position in the dyadic loop with Claudio ever so slightly, just enough that it prompted her to make a cut. Screens might thus not be evil eyes all the way down. One way to think about this is to remember that just as there is such a thing as the evil eye, there are also practices that summon a prophylactic and protective gaze.[94] Think about the southern Italian red horn or the widely circulated eye beads that are supposed to chase away or redirect evil gazes.[95] Screens can channel protective, reparative, or transformative gazes too.

. . .

When asked about their relationship with the one-way mirror, therapists often told me that the one-way mirror offered *contención*, a term that can be translated as "containment." "The one-way mirror offers me so much *contención*," Elsa told me. "When there is a mirror behind me, I am less afraid of my mistakes. I feel protected. . . . The team's gaze takes care of me. To be seen by them gives me a lot of *contención* . . ." Maria, another systemic therapist, commented during an interview. "The team behind the mirror limits and contains your mistakes, *you see?*" As she continued, she explained that when she realized that she was going in the wrong direction during a therapy session, she felt supported by the idea of being observed.[96] At the same time, she noticed how she was more present when she knew a team of therapists was (literally) behind her back.[97]

. . .

At least since the fifteenth century, the very word *screen* has indeed been used to indicate a protective surface, a covering and concealing device warding off, for example, the heat of fire.[98] One of the possible etymologies of the word *screen* is found in the verb *skirmjan*, which, in old Germanic language, meant "to cover, to protect."[99] So maybe the point is not so much about breaking, or moving away from, the screen but about animating different affordances, surrendering to a more reparative thirdness mediating the in-betweens of a dyad that would burn up in a flaming spiral unless screened.[100]

. . .

We are circling around a strange possibility: that a toxic loop of gazes can be interrupted by the properties of the screen itself; that the screen can mediate destructive gazes as well as reparative thirdness.

. . .

At the end of ten sessions of couple therapy, Simona, who was in treatment with her husband Enrique, looked straight into the camera and thanked the team for the support and *contención* provided throughout the sessions. She addressed the camera directly, but when the leading therapist asked if she wanted to meet the team, she did not take up the offer. Our screened anonymity had been providing an imaginative holding space that would have been broken had she lifted the protective screen of the mirror.[101]

. . .

Repetition: The therapeutics lies in understanding that what looks back at us can shape our self when we identify with it.[102] So to imagine different gazes is to imagine different selves.

. . .

Professor Z., however, had a point. Who would really want to be recorded during a fight with one's own (maybe soon to be ex) partner? Who would want to be seen by an anonymous audience? And even more importantly, how can this setting be therapeutic? In the context of psychotherapeutic treatments, therapeutic efficacy is a strange issue because it can be measured in very different ways, and according to the parameters we use, the same model can be considered more, or less, effective.

If you consult a brief strategic therapist to treat an intense paranoia—you think that you are being recorded and surveilled by invisible algorithms hiding inside your phone—and after ten sessions you are not cured, the treatment could be considered ineffective. If the goal of therapy is to eliminate your symptoms to make you more functional and productive, a cognitive behavioral therapist or a psychiatrist who likes to prescribe medications would not consider it effective to spend years exploring why you always feel abandoned by the people who love you.

If you are undergoing Lacanian psychoanalysis, your treatment will be complete when—if ever—you get in touch with your own fantasies and desires, which doesn't imply that your paranoid anxiety about being both surveilled and abandoned will be solved. And if the goal of therapy is to develop a different relationship with your symptoms and explore their individual, social, and historical conditions of emergence, all these approaches could be considered highly ineffective. But this doesn't answer the question about the therapeutic efficacy of the visual setup in systemic psychotherapy.[103]

. . .

Eager to perform the mirror-holding experiment during an argument with my partner, I ran to get it in the shower. The mirror slipped from my grip and fragmented into tiny pieces inside the bathtub.

. . .

As in Simona's case, none of the patients in therapy I have observed expressed the desire to meet face to face with the team or the ethnographer, even if the team behind the mirror was consistently addressed through the eye of the camera or the surface of the mirror. Maybe the comfort with such a setting can be related to the copious circulation of psychological treatments within the Argentinean milieu.[104] Even if patients weren't familiar with the systemic model, they were familiar with a wide range of therapeutic options, models, and approaches. But the mirror-plus-team structure adds something else.

The screen seems to provide patients with a third space that shows (while hiding) the anonymous gaze of therapists behind the mirror. I mentioned how therapists feel encouraged and protected by the feeling that there is a team of colleagues behind them—a team that can intervene in, help with, or witness the therapeutic process. This felt gaze protects them even as they cannot see the team itself.

In my observations, patients like Paula, Thiago, Brenda, or Simona interact with the invisible and anonymous gaze on the other side of the mirror in a similar way, mobilizing its therapeutic potential. Being seen by a potentially infinite gaze that finally sees them and sees what's going on in their coupled intimacy has a powerful impact on their therapeutic process. Whether a one-way mirror or another visual device (a camera, a purse mirror), the screen creates a cut between spaces that sustains the patient's imagination about what is beyond the cut. A process that shows how much reparative potential can be held by what we imagine is looking back at us.

. . .

Sometimes on my third hour of binge-scrolling I want to ask: When did screens stop protecting us from the heat of fire? When did they start feeding algorithms that burn us out instead? Then I remember Brenda and the mirror, and I think that a slightly more generative (and de-secularized) question would be: Which or whose spirits are on the other side of our screens?

. . .

Thinking about the therapeutic care provided by screens troubles a technophobic discourse about surveillance societies. The anonymous gaze can rebuild as much as it can destroy. Screens can protect us from fire as much as burn us out. The question is how to develop awareness about who we imagine is looking back at us. The imagined gaze of the other can produce a wide range of experiences— pathological, racialized, gendered, dysmorphic, therapeutic, liberatory, paranoid, mystical. Or all of the above at the same time.[105]

. . .

The thing is that the type of gaze you are looking for can't be fully delivered and held by your partner. You are looking for something that might be beyond the capacities of a single human gaze. And I am not talking about a religious entity. But there is something nonhuman about it. Understanding that what you are looking for in your partner is something that exceeds them can make for calmer dinners.

. . .

Sometimes I start writing and I feel this punch in the stomach. I can barely move my fingers and type a single word. I tell myself it's okay, that it always happens, that it's about staying grounded and slowly moving my fingertips. I write down sentences like, "Just keep moving the fingertips motherfucker, it doesn't even matter what you are writing." The imagined or anticipated audience gets to me, it gets hold of my stomach and paralyzes me. And it feels like what I am writing makes no sense and that it won't work. I imagine the scoffing face of that person who said this is not anthropology, that I am too self-referential, and that this is not rigorous scholarship.

Then the smiling face of a friend takes shape in front of me. They like how I write and what I am saying. I start feeling their loving gaze, and slowly my typing gains speed, precision, and intention. I feel a voice coming through my chest, and I stand by it. I get excited, I feel that this project is fun, and I love every aspect of it. Sentences start flowing, things make sense again. But that's because I am writing for that friend, the friend with the loving gaze that makes me flourish.

. . .

Knock, knock, knock, knock

Do you see? Do you see?

. . .

The power of the gaze to make "you into you" can morph into the power of re-making you. Therapeutic transformation within and without the couple form can start from optical practices of diversion that redirect the shaping force of the gaze.

Diffract abusive gazes, make them explode.

ATMOSPHERIC CRISIS

There is something heavily atmospheric in the everydayness of relational exhaustion. The following scenes and short sections depict gendered forms of drained vitality, recursive returns to never-fully-collapsing relationships, and the therapeutic role of holding spaces. There is something powerful when therapeutic environments absorb a cathartic discharge that pierces through the exhaustion and brings forth new forms of vitality.

. . .

Almibar, Wanda, Micol, and Clara are a team of systemic couple therapists who have been meeting weekly for about fifteen years in Buenos Aires.[1] Together they carry out live sessions of couple therapy—while one of the therapists leads the session, the others watch it on a screen.[2]

Differently from the therapeutic settings I described in the first chapter, which mostly use the one-way mirror, this team uses a video camera in the therapy room to broadcast the session on a screen in the observing room. In this chapter I focus on the sessions I observed with this team and thus only through the closed-circuit television screen. The absence of the one-way mirror makes the observer feel a bit less right in the middle of someone else's session, but this doesn't prevent the emergence of a rather unique therapeutic atmosphere.[3]

. . .

Buenos Aires, Argentina. November 2013. I am sitting with the team in the screening room during a session break.[4] Micol is leading the session today, but she is now standing in front of us, leaving the couple alone in the therapy room. Her right hand is shaking; she bites her lips while bringing a tissue to her face. I can see the two patients in the other room on the screen behind Micol. They are sitting silently, looking away from each other. Micol turns to the screen for a second and takes a long breath.

"What's going on? How are you, Micol?" Almibar asks.

Micol smiles at us with an absent look, glances at her watch, and dissolves into tears.

. . .

Forty-five minutes earlier. Almibar, Clara, Wanda, and I are in the screening room. Clara brought some sweet pastries, delicious *facturas*, and we are all eating quickly while positioning ourselves in front of the screen that will soon project the upcoming session. Almibar, the head of the team, looks at me: "Doing well, dear?" As I start responding, Micol arrives and peeks into our room to say hello. "I think I have an angle for today; I am going to explore the money problems that Simona mentioned the other time. Okay, see you later!" Micol enters the therapy room. She turns on the camera and adjusts the brightness.

After a few seconds, the camera transmits a clear image to the screening room. Simona and Enrique, the two patients in therapy, appear on the screen; they are sitting on two white armchairs facing Micol. It is their eighth session of systemic couple therapy. On the screen, we can see Micol's back as if we were watching over her shoulders. Clara, who is sitting close to me, picks up her notebook. "I am not sure about this couple. . . . Let's see what happens," she says.

In the therapy room, Simona smiles at Micol while Enrique is looking down at his shoes. He is wearing a crisp button-up blue shirt. Simona is wearing a red summer dress.

"How elegant!" says Micol to open the session. She finds a comfortable position in her armchair and continues, "Okay, so . . . how is the couple doing?"

Simona looks at Enrique with a sardonic grimace. "Hmm ... bad, very bad, very bad. No?"

"Yes, very bad, very bad," Enrique confirms.

Simona stares at Micol, as if hoping that this moment, this look, this session of therapy could vaporize their problems. "We did slightly better after our last session with you," she says, "but now we are back doing really bad. These past two weeks I felt really alone, sad.... I cried a lot ... out of nowhere, maybe it was coming from my anxiety problems. I don't know. I was alone, sad, tired.... I don't even remember why."

Simona tells Micol that every single interaction she has with Enrique ends with a fight—it doesn't even matter what he says or what she says. "The other day, I don't even remember how we got there, I had just asked him something about his work and he exploded." Fight after fight, Simona and Enrique's everyday life feels like an endless succession of missed encounters. "I don't know what to do. Every day I think things might be different but it's more of the same, more of the same, you know? More of the same." Simona is exhausted. She says that she can't take it anymore, that she can't find a way to escape the "more of the same" in which she feels stuck.

. . .

Enrique lost his job, and most of his savings, during the Argentinean economic crisis of 2001–2. Since then, he has struggled to find consistent work. He is angry and frustrated. Lately, Enrique comes home from work and feels alienated from family life. Simona wants to help him but feels he closes himself off and becomes "unreachable" when he gets angry. One of their three daughters still lives with them, and Enrique often gets into heated fights with her too. "In my home, in the house I built, I have no say, no life, nothing, in my home," he says.

Like other men I observed in therapy, Enrique symptomatizes his existential frustration by losing himself in the city.[5] He wanders around, comes home late, forgetting the habitual temporalities of the couple form. "I waited for him for hours.... Then he comes late, and he doesn't even know why he was late," says Simona in a whisper.[6]

"Where were you when Simona was waiting for you?" Micol asks, with a maternally irritated tone.

"I don't know. I was just ... I don't know, I was walking, then I forgot what time it was, you know. At work ... they are just driving me crazy."

Enrique wanders through Buenos Aires like a distracted passerby, just as he engages with the therapeutic space with a disengaged vagueness. "I don't know,

I don't know what I have to do," he says with resignation. Trapped in a job he is not trained for, frustrated by an object-less dissatisfaction, Enrique distractedly observes Simona's attempts to break through this crisis-scape and reach out to something else, someone else, anything else.

. . .

In these moments, when a cloudy confusion is wrapped around your body, in these moments you *just don't know*, and things are foggy and confusing, and you are exhausted, and drained, and lonely. And hopeless. And.

. . .

"I don't know what to do, I don't know." After the fifth time Enrique says the same sentence, Micol, Simona, and Enrique share a moment of silence. In the screening room, I feel a pressure around my chest. I don't know what's going on, but the air seems noticeably thicker as I breathe in the silence across the rooms. I glance at Almibar, who is jotting down some notes. Clara is sitting at my side, also writing. Wanda is pensively looking out the window. They are all silently absorbed, and they look worried. Almibar takes a deep breath. Clara emits a whispered "*uff. . .*"

I write down "thick, impasse, don't know" in my notebook.

. . .

During my ethnographic research an atmospheric sense of impasse took hold of me. Whether I was walking through the streets of the city, watching live sessions of therapy, or spending time with my friends, I felt folded within an underoxygenated atmosphere. As I was observing couples in therapy I was also going through a personal crisis, which included a crisis in my marriage, and this created a resonant amplification, if not an uncanny symmetry, between the ethnographer and his object of study, the dark irony of which wasn't lost on my panic and anxiety attacks. The inside and outside of the therapy room seemed to blur in a foggy stuckness. During these times, I often imagined therapists, patients, and myself as if all floating inside a bubble filled with a dense fog that tasted like we were heading nowhere. Despite the recursive attempts of partners to separate, despite their desires to find new ways of relating, despite all the therapeutic techniques, *despite it all . . .* nothing seemed to change.

Everybody's life seemed wrapped within Simona's *more of the same* and Enrique's *I don't know.*

. . .

Affective atmospheres possess us, they take hold.[7] Kathleen Stewart writes that affective atmospheres are not "inert contexts" but "force fields in which people find themselves."[8] Affective atmospheres, Ben Anderson suggests, "fill spaces like a gas"; a "certain tone of feeling," he continues, can fill the space "like a haze."[9] In Anderson's words, atmospheres are an "ill-defined" something that "exceeds rational explanation," even as "the affective qualities that are given to this something by those who feel it are remarkable for their singularity."[10]

. . .

Maybe you don't know what's going on, but your body knows how it feels—especially on those days when you feel an atmospheric pressure in the air around you and you *just* don't want to get out of bed, you *just* can't do it, not today (and people usually tell you to *just* get up, to *just* snap out of it). Atmospheric stuckness folds us into a frozen temporality, coating the world around with a layer of gray ice. We can't hear the vital murmurs of the waters of becoming running beneath the ice—we can only breathe in a glacial sense of impossibility.

Nothing changes, *more of the same.*[11]

. . .

Nothing, everybody—atmospheres clothe the world with a vagueness encapsulated in words that resist singularization while pointing at "something that feels like something."[12] *Nothing changes.* What does it even mean to say that nothing, like *nothing*, changes? We know that the world is in constant transformation, that every single repetition, that every single fraction of a second contains infinite changes. By the time I finish this sentence things will already be different than half a nanosecond ago.[13]

. . .

Affective atmospheres can get to us because our body is a porous interface that receives, leaks, holds onto, and transmits affects of all kinds.[14] Since the work of Baruch Spinoza, this porosity has been described as the body's capacity to affect and be affected. "A body affects other bodies, or is affected by other bodies," Gilles Deleuze writes, echoing Spinoza. "It is this capacity for affecting and being affected that also defines a body in its individuality."[15]

Across disciplines, from philosophy to neuroscience, the notion of affect clusters around itself a constellation of definitions and debates that can be contradictory and confusing. Affective neuroscience, for example, describes affect in relation to subcortical systems that universally underly human psychobiology, or as a state of arousal that precedes what we would generally call emotions.[16]

The critical theorist Brian Massumi, on the other hand, describes affect as a nonconscious intensity almost synonymous with potentiality.[17] Massumi echoes a range of authors in philosophy and critical theory who understand affect as a name for something that we can't quite pin down, a signpost for an ineffable something our linguistic traps will never quite capture. Affect, Ben Anderson writes, is "something that hesitates at the edge of the unsayable."[18] This is how I often end up justifying my like or dislike of songs, objects, or people— *I don't know, just a bad affect.*[19]

Call me an affect nerd, but I am deeply interested in all of the disciplinary variations of this term, even when, or precisely because, it's the same name given to seemingly different phenomena. Can what's called an affect of joy in facial expression recognition be the same thing as the affect of joy radiating from an artist's composition?[20] I have spent about fifteen years spiraling upward, downward, and sideways thinking and reading about affects, and I wrote and rewrote sections like the very section you are reading now one too many times.[21] So the very concept of affect can affect you (and me) in rather affective ways, and things get foggy and confusing and.

. . .

In this book, I draw mostly from philosophy and psychoanalysis to consider affects as psychic forces that are accumulated in, discharged from, and transmitted across bodies.[22]

Affects, as forces, have an impact on the affected body, an impact that is registered and retained to different degrees and scales—from conscious to nonconscious, from muscular to conceptual. This means that if we look at the affective impact that a video clip has on your body from a neurobiological perspective, we might be looking into your states of arousal or the up/down regulation of your nervous system.[23] From a cultural studies perspective, we might be describing how your way of being impacted by the video resonates with the historical "structure of feeling" of your generation.[24]

Through different scales we might see completely different things, which doesn't mean, however, that they are not somehow related. At least, affectively.

. . .

Imagine entering a room that feels so *lit* that in half a second your whole body is pervaded by a sense of euphoric optimism.[25] You realize you have been smiling since you got into that room only because your facial muscles are starting to hurt. Mostly unconsciously, your body has been affected by the room and the room's affective atmosphere. Or imagine entering a room where a romantic couple has just had a fight.[26] You cross the threshold of the door, and you immediately feel a heavy sense of silence and discomfort—*something is up*. This affectation is the body's reaction to a wide range of inputs coming from other bodies, objects, frequencies, or, more widely, the environment.

There is thus something intrinsically relational about affects because they are about the impact that bodies have on each other—human bodies bumping into other bodies, but also rooms, objects, concepts, atmospheres. Melissa Gregg and Gregory Seigworth write that affects are "forces of encounter."[27] And any *body* can affect *any* body.[28]

. . .

Following Baruch Spinoza's affect theory, we can make a distinction between the impact that affects, as forces, have on bodies—what Spinoza called *affectus*—and the trace or residue of this impact, that is to say what the body retains when it has been affected by a force—Spinoza called it *affectio*.[29]

Affective impact is mostly registered at a nonconscious level, and it can leave different types of traces: from autonomic bodily reactions that happen so fast that it's as if they didn't happen (think about the tensing up of your facial muscles), to a psychic dent so deep it becomes a traumatic memory that holds your body captive (think about an image you saw a long time ago that still haunts you).[30] Whatever the scale, affects alter your biochemical makeup as much as your thoughts and consequently shape, influence, and color your experience of the world.

. . .

Affect is the sound of an impact; sometimes you hear it, sometimes you don't. The impact leaves a trace, sometimes for a nanosecond, sometimes much, much, much longer.

. . .

The body has also the capacity *to affect*, which, conversely, is the capacity to impact other bodies, to transmit to them a psychic force.[31] When you are affecting the world around you, you are unleashing a force that radiates from you and hits other bodies, spaces, situations. So, in a somewhat circular motion, you can affect the world around you just like it can affect you. Both movements can happen at the same time in what could be understood as an affective loop.

Think again about entering the lit room I was mentioning. You entered the room, and a compositional orchestration of bodies, objects, and frequencies affects you—the world changes your body, which, in turn, changes your perception of the world. Maybe precisely because of the way the room is affecting you, you also start giving off an optimistic affect, you unleash into the environment a sense of joyful lightness. Your jokes are landing like mofos. You don't even really know why, but isn't tonight just so amazing? *I think if you keep surfing this affective vibe you are going to meet someone tonight....* [32]

. . .

Spinoza proposed that we think of affects as forces that have the capacity to increase or diminish the body's power of acting in the world.[33]

Think about that friend of yours who has the quasi-magical power to drain the hell out of you. Every time you spend some time with them, your thoughts get kind of jumbled, you lose your sharpness, and you feel so tired. An affect they radiate gets under your skin and takes up residence within your veins. You fall silent, you start nodding, you check out, but you can't find a way to get up from the chair and leave.[34] You are affected in such a way that your psycho-existential range of motion shrinks.

Now think about hanging out with a friend who energizes you. Every time you are together, the whole world is filled to the brim with possibilities, you are pervaded by a sense of joyful spaciousness, you realize how hilarious you can be, and your thoughts become sharp like arrows.[35]

Affect, Massumi writes, is the "felt reality of a relation."[36] And, in this case, affect is the felt difference between your two friends.

. . .

You can tackle your affective states from many different angles and scales. Sometimes forces just take over; other times, if you change your muscular tensions, your muscular intentions, you can make space for specific affective forces to take up residence in your body. You can activate affects from the muscular scale, which is most definitely not the only possible scale, but just one possibility.

I say this while thinking about affects and reading. To read a book with a smile stamped on your face changes things. Try to do it for the next minute or so, with this book or with another book. Smile and read. Maybe a renewed energy kicks in, maybe you cannot take seriously what you are reading anymore, maybe you like it more. Affects are forces that impact your perception. And it can start with a muscular change in your face. Like a smile.[37]

. . .

Dwell on this for a second: Affects, which diminish or increase our ability to move and act in the world, are mostly nonconscious psychic forces. Most of the time you are not aware of the affects that are shaping your experience of the world. Following Merleau-Ponty, we could say that our body is not only *in* the world, but it is also *of* the world, it belongs to it.[38] Our body belongs to the texture of a world that enfolds it, a world we are literally breathing in and out—when you are *in* an affective atmosphere, you are also *of* it (remember that lit room?). That's not a little thing, because you might spend years being drained by something without knowing what it is, something that has you, a force field you find yourself wrapped within.

. . .

"I come home, and I feel like a stranger. Alicia is there, talking to my daughter Maria, and I'm like a complete stranger. All I have to do is open the door. It's like a wave that hits me. What is it? I open the door and after a few steps I've already walked into a mess. Every day. Every fucking day. What is it?"

Emanuel is talking to the therapist. On the couch, his crossed right leg is touching Alicia's left knee. It's their second and last session.

. . .

If affects are forces traveling between bodies, then affective atmospheres are force fields composed and traversed by such forces.

Repetition: Affects are forces. Atmospheric force fields can hold you captive.

. . .

Simona and Enrique's everydayness is affected by an atmospheric crisis that *has* them: *I don't know, I don't know*, Enrique keeps saying. This atmosphere obstructs the emergence of something different, anything different, and it dissolves any attempt to make sense of it, to create a narrative about it. This atmosphere traps them in a shared impasse rendering narrativization impossible.[39]

I don't know, I don't know.

It's just more of the same, more of the same.

. . .

Impasse, Lauren Berlant writes, is "a stretch of time in which one moves around with a sense that the world is at once intensely present and enigmatic."[40] Stuck in an intensely enigmatic present that doesn't go away, Simona is taken by sadness without knowing what is happening to her—she cries almost every morning for a week, but she doesn't remember why. Enrique, in the meantime, gets lost in the city without knowing how to explain the reason for his urban drifts.

Sometimes it is also hard for the therapist to understand what's going on in the room with their patients. Talking about Simona and Enrique's sessions, Micol once told me, "We pick up the fragments of what patients tell us.... I know as much about Simona and Enrique as you do when you are watching the session in the other room."[41]

In the absence of clear explanations, we can imagine many things about Simona and Enrique: Maybe Enrique wanders the city because he has lost his job, maybe he has another lover, maybe he is having neurological troubles with memory—as he himself suggested during a session. Maybe Simona is sad because she is the one who has another lover and doesn't know what to do about it, maybe she is mourning the loss of a life she never had, or maybe she is exhausted by all the work she is doing in and out of the house. Maybe. Be that as it may, Simona and Enrique bring to the therapeutic space an overwhelming sense of disorientation, an affective atmosphere that doesn't let them see beyond the fog of their ever-present present.

More of the same is the name of this frozen present.

. . .

Yet they are still here, sitting close to each other, hoping things will change, at some point, somehow.

(Uff...)

. . .

A wide range of feminist and queer research has described how the modern couple form keeps sustaining the reproduction of patriarchal and heteronormative forms of power. At the core of modern genres of intimacy, the couple form has indeed been under critical examination for its complicit relationship with gendered forms of labor, consumption, and violence.[42]

But critical theories of romantic love, together with decades of sociopolitical struggles, have not seemed to displace the couple form's centrality in contemporary life.[43] Coupled romantic love continues to be a social magnet that attracts and orients global flows of desire—from the entertainment industry to dating apps.[44] Why do we keep returning to the romantic ideal? The sociologist Anthony Giddens suggests that modern love, differently from previous romantic structures of relation, is a "pure relationship"—a relationship we engage with because of the qualities of the relation itself—we want love for love's sake.[45]

However, it seems we keep turning to love not only because we "love being in love," but also because we desire what we imagine will come with it.[46] According to Lauren Berlant, we turn and return to romantic love in the name of the good life it promises. The good life is a cultural imaginary that clusters around itself shared ideals about what a good future should look like, which things, forms, and people we should be close to.[47] The good life is a promise we tend toward, a promise that condenses our desires for love, social recognition, upward mobility, a house, a family, a backyard, a dog, sharing patterns of consumption with someone, not dying alone.[48]

Thus one of the ways to understand the enchanting force of modern love is that the couple form clusters around itself a whole series of fantasies that are not exclusively related to the qualities of love itself. Romantic modern love is a phantasmatic tension toward a cluster of promises. And we are so pulled toward what it promises that we might keep turning and returning to the couple form despite its recurrent failures to deliver.

. . .

Sometimes you just need to close the door behind you and open another one to exit the atmospheric force field. Other times the atmosphere fills up every corner of your existence. It swallows a whole day, a year, a decade, a life. And, in the foggy darkness of your days, you can't seem to find a door, not even a window to crawl through.

. . .

Berlant defines the attachment to objects that don't deliver what they promise as a relation of cruel optimism. "A relation of cruel optimism," they write, "exists when something you desire is actually an obstacle to your flourishing."[49] In a relation of cruel optimism, we invest our psychic energy in objects of attachments that might be draining us, if not slowly killing us.[50] But we stick around in the hope that one day, soon enough, things will be different—we wait for that moment when the promises will be delivered. We wait to be finally closer to what we fantasize about—the good life. And there is always that object, that practice, that person, that place, that seems to be *the thing* that will finally get you closer to what you desire. "The affective structure of an optimistic attachment," Berlant writes, "involves a sustaining inclination to return to the scene of fantasy that enables you to expect that *this* time, nearness to *this* thing will help you or a world to become different in just the right way."[51]

. . .

Just one more time, *this time* is going to be different, I promise. *This* time, *this* therapy session, *this* method, *this* therapist will work. I promise, just one more time.

. . .

I have this draft email I wrote to Lauren Berlant in my mailbox. I wanted to ask them about cruel optimism and melancholia, and to what extent cruel optimism could be described as an externalized melancholic attachment to an always already lost future. I wanted the email to be catchy, smart, and well written. A few weeks after I had started it, it was still in my draft box. Then I received the sudden news of their passing. And now I see that email every day—one of only two drafts I keep in my mailbox. And I can't delete it. I can't let it go.

Trying to write my masterpiece email to one of my academic crushes, I lost the chance to ask them a question, to communicate. Not that they would necessarily have answered, but still. The cruel optimism of a perfect email that never materializes, like the perfect book, the perfect thought, and the perfect sentence that never comes. An email I could not send, and now cannot delete. *Dear Professor Lauren Berlant, is cruel optimism a melancholic attachment to an always already lost future?*

Just send the fucking email.[52]

. . .

The concept of cruel optimism can describe all kinds of toxic attachments: to the American Dream, gambling, unsent emails, diets, social media notifications, cigarettes, writerly perfection. But it has a particularly cutting way of describing the dynamics of a romantic relationship deteriorating in slow motion. Simona and Enrique's everydayness gathers relational frustration, boredom, built resentment, and misaligned desires, all of which bear the trace of past events but also of imagined futures. The future of a loving caress that never comes, the future of newly painted walls, the future of a family vacation, the future of a different togetherness.

The affective pull of cruel optimism keeps them stuck to their chairs.

. . .

Simona keeps coming back to the promise of having a life—or something—with Enrique, but the present tense of their couple form doesn't deliver the promises it holds captive. Now Micol, too, has become part of a loop that sustains Simona and Enrique's never-fully-collapsing couple form. In the name of the romantic promise, Micol is trying to foster a therapeutic process that could keep them together, an attempted solution that might be sustaining the reproduction of a cruelly optimistic loop.[53]

. . .

In the therapy room, Enrique is looking down, talking loudly while shaking his head. After many years spent trying to find a stable position, he is still between jobs. Simona interrupts her husband, saying that she loves her work and that she loves growing professionally day after day. Enrique's voice overlaps with Simona's as he complains about his current job as an electrician and talks about the daily difficulties that he faces with the clients of the company he works for. Simona and Enrique's voices are indistinguishable for a few seconds. Like many sessions I observed, the couple overlays and intertwines narratives about quotidian problems and relational issues. The narratives rarely follow a linear structure. Enrique explains that he is building the outdoor stairs on the patio of the house only because *she* asked for it. "But . . . we were talking about how you didn't show up at your nephew's birthday! This has nothing to do with anything!" Simona interjects, seeking Micol's support.

. . .

Sitting on my chair, my neck stretched toward the screen, I feel like Simona and Enrique's atmospheric malaise is descending into the observing room and filling up the space in between us. The camera, the screens, our bodies, the walls.[54] An invisible force takes hold. It's like Almibar, Clara, and I are waiting for something to happen, but we don't know what it is.

. . .

Atmospheres envelop us just as they can radiate from specific spaces and relational configurations.[55] To be able to radiate from something, affective atmospheres need an enclosure that delimits them, a space that gives form to the way affective forces circulate, so that an atmospheric intensity can take shape.[56] This is to say that however rarified an atmosphere can be, to become anything at all, it needs to be structured in some way, or enclosed within a form; or else there would be no affective buildup, just an infinite expansion of no-thing at all.[57]

The couple form is one of such forms of enclosure, where the affective patterns solidify and build up so much across time that they start to radiate from the couple itself.[58] So, just as rooms have their atmospheres, couples themselves have their atmospheres, ones that are composed through particular affective loops that characterize the couple's way of being together.[59] Enrique and Simona's cruel optimism, which is an affective structure of attachment, is thus an affective atmosphere too, one that radiates from them and cuts through the walls. An irradiating atmospheric impasse that *has* and *exceeds* them.

. . .

How would you describe your couple's atmosphere?

. . .

In the therapy room, Micol interrupts Enrique's account of his latest problems with the building of one house's electric system—her voice breaks through the screen. "During the last session," Micol says, "you both mentioned that your relational problems were accentuated after some economic issues in the past. . . . What happened?"

Micol's voice is shaking. She clears her throat as if to scratch away a *something* stuck in her chest, then resumes speaking: "I remember you mentioned during our last session that you had some economic difficulties in the past. . . ."

Micol's voice struggles to hold within itself a quivering elsewhere.

. . .

After a moment of silent suspense, Enrique looks up at Simona, then back down at his shoes. He starts murmuring, "The crisis . . . it is all my fault. I had a family business, a restaurant, and . . . don't get me wrong, I knew I had to sell it, but I did it all wrong." Enrique hints at a difficult relationship with his father who left him a small restaurant in downtown Buenos Aires, concluding he should have made a clothing store out of that damned restaurant. The restaurant failed during the economic crisis of 2001, bringing Enrique and Simona, along with their three kids, to the brink of economic collapse.

"A fatal crisis, *fatal*. . . ." Simona continues, "I was at home with the kids and didn't even have the money to buy some milk." She starts crying. "Not even to buy some milk. . . ." With their three young daughters, Simona and Enrique had to move out of their house and live with Enrique's parents—with no money and an unquantifiable amount of debt.

Simona suspends her narrative. She breathes and welcomes a tissue Micol hands her. Simona takes her time. She takes her time to cry in silence while shaking her head and gently covering her mouth with the wet Kleenex. Enrique keeps staring at his shoes; he draws an imaginary figure eight with his right foot. Simona cries. Enrique looks down. Time hangs somewhere suspended.

. . .

(*Uff...*)

. . .

Our attention is captured by a force that draws us toward the screen in the observing room. We perform a sort of scopic tiptoeing around Simona's outline appearing on the screen. Two doors and less than thirteen feet are separating Simona, Enrique, and Micol from us. I glance at the therapists close to me and notice that Clara's eyes are filled with unshed tears. Wanda is pensively looking at the screen, while Almibar seems to be blushing, ever so slightly.

Thirty years together, twenty years of doubts, ten years of unending impasses —the *longue durée* of Simona and Enrique's coupled malaise takes hold of us.

. . .

Silence lingers for a moment. Then Simona continues recounting her experience of the economic collapse. After being deprived of the middle-class fantasy of upward mobility and stability, she began selling used clothes in the streets while Enrique was unemployed.[60] She then slowly "made her way up," gaining more credit and credibility with wholesalers until she started selling clothes to shops around the city.

"I was working all the time," she says with a broken voice, "and he would rarely help me. He was at home, depressed, sad. He couldn't find a job. He tried, he tried, but nothing came up. He was mostly sitting on the couch, watching TV." Trying to navigate through the storm, Simona kept the family together, taking care of the children while progressively professionalizing herself, thus carrying the burden of both emotional and economic labor. Meanwhile, the event of the economic crisis left Enrique stupefied as he experienced the floundering of his own gendered expectations about household economics.

Micol passes Simona another tissue, and Simona dries her tears, only to welcome new ones. "Slowly...slowly," Simona whispers, "we managed to rise up."

Micol listens attentively and then, with a firm tone, she says, "It's thirteen years that you, Simona, are doing it [*venís remándola*] all by yourself! And you, Enrique, how do you feel about this?"

Enrique looks down, mumbling something about how he should have sold the restaurant.

"I didn't know what to do, I didn't. I didn't want to see her working, and I had nothing. Look at her now, she works too much. . . . I don't know what to do." Enrique seems to be getting lost in a detail as Simona keeps crying, enveloped in the memories of these economic difficulties.

"Enrique, how do you take the fact that today Simona is still sustaining something like 80 percent of the household?" Micol is speaking with an almost provocative tone. She sounds tired, her voice producing waves across rooms.

. . .

In the observing room, Micol's trembling voice unleashes something, as if a different atmospheric force field suddenly finds its composition. The aural texture of her voice channels an overflow of air that cannot be fully contained by her vocal cords. An affective force is *forcing* itself through—like when you are talking about your day to a friend and suddenly you choke on a word, your chest compresses, and that word reverberates across the space between you and your friend.

Something you didn't foresee knocks at the doors of your voice.

. . .

Enrique and Simona's economic past emerges from a collective experience of the Argentinean economic crisis in 2001–2, when the whole country collapsed under the largest sovereign debt in history, disrupting a decade of neoliberal policies and uneven economic growth. From one day to the next, the 2001–2 crisis vaporized the savings of a wide sector of the population. During a national state of emergency declared in December 2001, people like Simona and Enrique couldn't withdraw their money from the bank—their savings, often converted into US dollars, would be forcibly reconverted to pesos and lose about 75 percent of their value.[61]

While the 2001–2 crisis was particularly dramatic, by that time Argentina had already undergone about forty years of economic crises and currency devaluations.[62] In my experience living in Buenos Aires, the cyclicity of these crises gives people the recurrent feeling that at any moment things could collapse again, that they are walking on thin ice, and that whatever money they have would be better converted into US dollars and kept hidden in a cookie jar. This is what makes the crisis atmospheric—it permeates everyday life and transforms the economic crisis from an extraordinary sociopolitical event to a permanent state of precarious malaise.[63]

Affects of precarity choreographing a collective crisis force field.

. . .

The psychoanalytic idiom has been widely mobilized in the Argentinean public sphere to analyze the relationship between Argentina's socioeconomic situation and the national psyche. The psychoanalyst Silvia Bleichmar, among others, writes about the psychic impact of the 2001 crisis in terms of a psychic exhaustion and suffering provoked by infrastructural forms of violence and economic exploitation.[64] The psychic impact of the crisis is not only about the individual psyche but about a collective psychic life that exceeds single bodies and permeates across the local environment.

An exhaustion emerging from a recursive return to an always already collapsing economy that never fully collapses. An economic crisis that is refracted in Simona and Enrique's coupled exhaustion.

But one thing doesn't fully explain the other—it is about loops, resonances, and refractions, not linear causation.[65]

. . .

"I don't know, I don't know what to do," Enrique says.

Taking a deep breath, Simona stares into the void of her own exhaustion—the drained vitality of a broken system that keeps moving toward nowhere.

. . .

Teresa Brennan writes that affective exhaustion can result from an asymmetrical transmission of affect, an unbalanced exchange of psychic forces along a gendered axis. Brennan draws on child development studies which suggest that even if a child's basic physical needs are met, the affective care and attention of the mother or the caregiver has a radical impact on the biological development of the child.[66] Brennan writes that bodies occupying the feminine position tend to offer an absorbed attention that transmits a life force to bodies occupying a masculine position. She calls this "living attention," an affective transfer of energies that allows bodies who receive it to flourish. Living attention is a vital transfer of affects that can drain the ones who give it, especially when there is no reciprocal exchange.[67]

A scene that exemplifies what Brennan calls living attention: Imagine a body occupying the feminine position looking at a body in the masculine position who is playing. Think about "the girlfriend position" sitting on a chair, looking at "the boyfriend position" on the couch playing video games with his friends. He has been playing for about half an hour. She is there watching him playing. "Whoa! Did you see that?!" he might ask her in the middle of a game, assuming that she is always already just there, watching every single move he makes with his little joystick, watching him with her fullest attention.[68]

Or think about a dinner table with your friends—who is talking? Who is listening? Where is the attention directed toward? The other day, by a fountain in Montreal, my partner Haley and I watched a girl sitting on a bench looking at a boy juggling a soccer ball. I think about half an hour passed. She was looking at him; he was looking at himself being watched by her.

Think about the amount of psychic energy and affect that, in these scenes, goes from one direction to the other. Juggle after juggle.[69]

. . .

I write about masculine and feminine "positions" because it is not exclusively about sex or gender.[70] Anybody can occupy any position. Of course, violently gendered, racialized, and class-based infrastructures tend to squeeze specific bodies into specific positions.

(Also, now that I think about it, if you are a body occupying the masculine position and you think that "living attention" is why you get so exhausted when you listen to your partner for literally two minutes, you need to think about this a little more. Bodies in the masculine position tend to perform exhaustion to avoid listening. This is how you get to a point where you are looking at someone in front of you who is screaming at you—*it's because you are not listening*.)

. . .

Simona and Enrique are receiving the living attention of four therapists—one with them and three behind the screen—and one anthropologist. If we start getting into the perspective of energetic transfers between bodies through focused attention, psychotherapy is a reparative form of curated living attention.

. . .

The era of attentional disorders, polarized political rage, and drained vitality could likewise be understood in relation to a widespread exhaustion of living attention, all sucked up by imagistic platforms of consumption. In order to escape exhaustion, we often end up plugging our life force reservoir into an algorithmic binge that sucks out whatever attentional force it can find at the bottom of our already-drained psyche.[71]

Where is your vital energy going? Who is getting your living attention? Who is flourishing, and who is getting drained? Why do you feel so exhausted?

. . .

Enrique doesn't talk about, nor understand, the Argentinean economic crisis as a social event, or as something that happened to him but that was completely out of his control. "The crisis, it was my fault," he will repeat six times throughout this session. Enrique's interpretation of the crisis is an individualized etiology that doesn't allow him to discharge the psychic toll of a wider socioeconomic situation. In the absence of a discharge, Enrique "keeps it all inside," which itself becomes a symptomatic request for more living attention, a request for Simona to be there and absorb his anger. The symptom—Enrique's stupefied impasse and angry silence—is an accusation of sorts.

Enrique is angry at himself for not being able to provide for his family, but he is also angry at Simona's resilient capacity to keep things afloat and progressively professionalize herself—thus gaining social and economic independence. "She shouldn't work so much," he says with a paternalistic tone that barely manages to hide his resentment. Dedicating herself to her work, over time Simona started giving less and less living attention to Enrique—and he is now full of an immobilized, objectless rage because he is not the primary recipient of Simona's life force. He works even less, speaks even less, does even less. Enrique's aimless wanderings through the streets of Buenos Aires seem to be his only possible form of movement.

. . .

Wanda looks at me and says, "In the perspective of systemic therapy, Simona and Enrique are stuck in a loop. The more Simona is trying to keep things together, the more Enrique retreats into his immobility. The more she tries to talk to him and work things through, the more he falls silent."[72]

"Now the point," Wanda continues, "is to create an interruption of this loop. But Enrique doesn't want to 'work through his sadness,' that's the thing— sometimes we need to journey through our sadness [*hay que transitar la tristeza*] to break a loop. Holding onto this sadness is what keeps the loop spinning. Anger is Enrique's way to resist sadness, no? You know, Samuele, I am saying this because you also look so angry sometimes. We talked about it the other day. . . . Anger is repressed sadness, to let go and interrupt the loop you need to face your sadness Samuele."

As we keep watching Simona and Enrique's unfolding session, I feel a pinch right under my lungs, at the entrance of my stomach. Hashtag burn. I nod to Wanda. "I know, I just don't know where to put this sadness. Who can hold it, you know? Or something like that. . . . "

Wanda pats my right shoulder. "I don't know, Samuele. . . . Ask your therapist!" We both laugh briefly and shift our focus back to the screen.

. . .

Enrique and Simona's couple form is a system in the sense that their actions and reactions always include the other person's feedback. *I do this because you did that, because I did that other thing, because you did that other-other thing*—this is what systemic therapy would call circular causality.[73] I have often heard systemic therapists ask their patients, with a slightly provocative tone, *What are you doing so well to cause your partner to act in this way?* A question that prompts patients to think systemically about their relationships.[74] This way of thinking requires you to look at what is in between you and your partner. In Gregory Bateson's terms, what exists between you and your partner is the emergent "mind" of a system, a shared space that extends outside the boundaries of your skin.[75]

What are we doing to create this emergent space in between us, a space that has its own life and that is stronger than you and me? To think systemically is humbling, because it forces you to accept being part of a loop that runs through your veins but doesn't belong only to you or your partner. It's never only your fault, it's never only your partner's fault. So simple—yet most of us have the unshakable habit of putting our partners on one side or the other of the equation.[76]

. . .

You can't really separate Simona's actions from Enrique's. But across this loop, the displacements and transmissions of affective energy follow a specific axis, from one position to the other. This takes us back to the idea that couples have their own force field, one shaped and sustained by the way affects travel across their looped and looping exchanges. Closed loops feel suffocating because they don't allow for a discharge—toxic affects pile up in one's body when they can't circulate.

The couple form is a gendered loop that enfolds nonreciprocal transfers of affective intensities.

. . .

Teresa Brennan writes about "affective dumping" as another type of affective transmission. Affective dumping involves the discharge of negative affects onto a body that becomes the holder and the container of the discharged affects.[77] Here is a domestic scene to exemplify affective dumping—so we can let Simona and Enrique catch a breath. I am writing right now in my office, where I have the privilege of having a door I can close when I don't want intrusions from the external world.[78] Imagine that I am writing in total silence, wearing some ridiculously big earmuffs, and then something happens, say that I get an email. (Yes, I forgot to activate my Freedom app, so my emails are open.)[79]

I read the email, and it makes me instantaneously upset. I am angry at myself because I was checking my emails while trying to write "the book," but I am also feeling defeated because someone just told me that I didn't get that thing that I wanted to get. Even before getting up from my chair, I start screaming, "What the fuck, Haley, I just can't do this, I can't figure out how the fuck to do this! Whatever the fuck they want. . . . Fuck this shit! It is just the fucking end of thinking anyway! Motherfuckers!" I am screaming this while still in my office, but I am addressing my partner, as if she were just there, ready to listen to me and give me living attention. Then I walk out the door and find her working at her desk—she doesn't have a literal and metaphorical door she can close. I interrupt her workflow, telling her I didn't get that thing that I wanted. She looks up and listens to me. I tell her that everything is fucked, then take a deep breath.

I go back to my office, sit down, and start feeling better. I keep writing.

In this scene, my partner becomes the container and the receptacle of an anger I dump onto her. She becomes the dumpee and I am the dumper. Even before getting out of my office, I am dumping my anger and disappointment onto her, addressing her, and forcing her to become the affective sponge that soaks up my discomfort. As Brennan writes, this type of affective discharge usually follows a gendered line wherein bodies occupying the masculine position are in the position of the dumpers, while bodies occupying the feminine position become the holders of negative affects such as anger.[80]

. . .

It is hard for me to write what I am writing about living attention and affective dumping because I am on the masculine side of the equation—and I am writing as if I could do better than Enrique's angry silences. Most of the time I don't do better. Even the concept of the masculine position might turn into the object of my own affective dumping. I fear being the Enrique of the situation, and I single him out as someone I shouldn't be like, while knowing that I am also like him—recursively trapped in my own positionality. As Wanda said, "I am saying this because you also look so angry sometimes."

Thinking about the relationship between the colonizer and the colonized, Frantz Fanon writes that the white man needs to liberate himself from his own whiteness.[81] Similarly, we might need to liberate the masculine position from its own positionality. But how? Affects can have a central role in a liberation phenomenology of sorts.[82]

. . .

Think about that draining friend of yours I was mentioning (the one you started thinking about when I suggested thinking about a friend who drains you). Maybe they are so draining because they keep dumping their negative affects on you, and you keep absorbing them—a dark cloud moving from their body and getting into yours. Or maybe they keep plundering your living attention. And maybe this is a nonreciprocal situation where your turn to share your own affects or to get living attention never comes. Imagine being in a romantic relationship that is structured in this way, a relationship where you are the go-to affective sponge of your partner's negative affects and the go-to living attention supplier. Imagine you have no place or space to discharge the affects you keep holding for your partner.

Imagine this could go on for a day, a year, a decade, a life.

. . .

Who is your go-to affective sponge?

. . .

I am talking to my partner, and I say something that hurts her. I feel bad seeing her hurting. In the space of half a second, I get upset at her and scream something about not ruining our whole day for this little thing that I said. I am unable to deal with a discomfort in my own body, unable to accept the fact that I have hurt her, so I dump this negative affect onto her by becoming upset. I then leave her with a negative affect that has entered her body.

She might end up spending her whole day holding my rage in her body. She might hold onto my anger so tight that she forgets it was my rage in the first place. She might forget it so well that she starts to identify with that anger as if it was hers. Identifying with someone else's anger, according to Brennan, facilitates gendered forms of depression.[83]

This is an example of how affective dumping could be tied back to what I wrote in chapter 1 about gazes and identification. Affects can be thrown at and discharged onto you like gazes. And anger is a particularly effective affective discharge. It can expand and fill the space like a gaze.[84]

. . .

Simona's gloomy exhaustion can't be disentangled from her absorption of Enrique's anger. An anger she holds within her body without finding a way to release it.

. . .

In the therapy room, a long and slow inhalation punctuates a temporary closure of Simona's memories about the economic crisis. Simona looks relieved, as if talking about her past to Micol allowed her to shake off an atmospheric impasse, however briefly. Micol is quietly nodding while Simona is drying her tears. Simona suddenly turns her attention toward Enrique, who is staring at the window with an absent-minded gaze. *Enrique, are you even here?*

Simona shakes her head; Enrique keeps looking away.

"Enrique is always like this at home, silent and checked out. I talk to him, I scream, I tell him I need him to listen to what I am saying, but he just looks down or out the window if there is one. Sometimes he mumbles that he doesn't know what to say or do. I am so tired of it, tired of screaming trying to be heard. So tired. It's just more of the same every day."

"Enrique, what's going on?" Micol asks. "What are you thinking about?" Her voice is shaking again, as if her chest were trying to suffocate and release something at the same time. Enrique looks at Micol, then looks straight into the camera. "I don't know," he says with a faint smile. "I am thinking that I don't know what to do. I don't know what to say." Simona shakes her head again.

Despite what seemed to be an atmospheric opening, the therapy session loops back to Enrique's *I don't know* and Simona's *more of the same*, as if to persist any longer within the new atmosphere that was taking shape would have been just too long, too much, too hard, too scary, or too something.

"I don't know," Enrique says again while looking down.

In a rapid exchange of glimpses, Simona and Micol align themselves in a gendered complicity, folded within an atmospheric exhaustion that has them both. Simona keeps shaking her head in silence.

Micol takes a slow deep breath.

. . .

"No la registra, no la contiene, no le da contención, eso es [He doesn't register her, he doesn't contain her, he doesn't provide containment, that's what it is]."
—*Micol talking about Simona and Enrique after her first session with them.*

. . .

The affective atmosphere of what has been piling up—a draining attachment to the undelivered promises of the couple form, a gendered exhaustion of living attention, a diffused sense of economic precarity, Simona's *more of the same*-ness— seems to linger on a threshold of tolerability.

Imagine a pot of boiling water about to knock the lid off.[85]

. . .

Micol suddenly decides to interrupt the session and take a break to come debrief with the team in the screening room. I hear her leave the therapy room and close the door. She abruptly opens the door of our room and then attempts to close it gently. Standing in front of us, she scans the room.

Then Micol looks at me. "When I passed through the door, I thought *this couple needs to separate*. You see," she says, "I am finally losing my optimism!" I know she is talking to me in reference to my snarky comments about her therapeutic cruel optimism—but she also seems to be addressing someone else, a wider audience, or maybe herself. An affect-full, impersonal address.[86] I don't say anything. I don't know what to say—she looks shaken. I don't know what to do.

Almibar the psychotherapist reacts more promptly than me, the slow ethnographer: "What's going on? How are you, Micol?" he asks her. Micol mumbles something, bringing her right hand over her lips. Her trembling lips announcing copious tears to come.

"I have to stop trying to save the couple," Micol says. "I have to stop trying to save their couple."

. . .

Nothing changes, it's just more of the same.

But things do pile up—and sometimes something spills over.

. . .

Cruel optimism is the persistent return to an atmosphere you got so used to that even the slightest change in the air feels like the end of the world. So as soon as there is an atmospheric opening, Simona and Enrique quickly fold back to their loops, to a more familiar atmosphere, however detrimental. But atmospheric changes herald the end of *a* world, not of *the* world. A compositional force field that might need to burst, like a foggy bubble popping in the middle of a storm.

And if you let the bubble pop and dissolve into the storm, however scary it sounds, maybe you can let go. Just like Micol when she realizes that she needs to let go of her attachment to Enrique and Simona's couple form, to the idea that they should be helped to stay together rather than separate. Something needs to burst.

. . .

Micol holds her tears for a bit longer. I feel frozen on the chair, unable to react. I have an initial desire to write something down. I stop myself. I am thrown into a temporal divergence as I relate to the unfolding event. "The therapist is falling apart," I think to myself. "This moment is just . . ." My thoughts slip away as

Micol breaks into tears. She cries. Drop after drop we are all enfolded within a relational space orchestrating different affective intensities. The trembling elsewhere that was haunting Micol's vocal cords is here now—the textural background of her voice comes to the foreground.

After a moment of silence, Almibar asks Micol if she is personally relating to Simona and Enrique's situation and whether she experienced something similar in her life. I am confused and intrigued: The therapeutic setting has moved from the room on the screen to the room behind the screen. On the other side of the wall, Simona and Enrique are waiting for Micol to come back. On the screen I can see Enrique looking out the window and Simona searching for something in her purse.

But Micol, their therapist, is here now; and she starts talking from beneath a cascade of tears.

. . .

Affects and memory are deeply entangled.[87] Something someone says, an image that pops up on the screen, the sound of a smile, the mannerisms of a person you've just met, the smell of rotting leaves. When you are affected by the world around you, it can activate memories, fantasies, or projected desires that are not directly connected to what you are hearing, smelling, or seeing. Proust has famously described the eruption of memories brought into his present by the taste of a *petite madeleine*.[88]

In psychoanalysis, the psyche is conceived of as a reservoir of images, events, relational forms, and structures that belong to your individual past but also to a social and cultural imaginary that exceeds you.[89] In this individual and collective unconscious reservoir, affects lodge themselves in, and attach themselves to, specific memories and fantasies. So when I say that the world around you can activate memories I mean, quite literally, that it can summon the affects attached to specific images residing in your unconscious reservoir. This activation brings a memory—or fantasy—into your present. What makes the memory feel real is the affect that comes with it—a psychic force erupts into your world, and your body is transformed by the arrival of a memory.

. . .

While Clara is giving her a tissue, Micol says she identifies with Simona's suffering, feeling a punch in her stomach when thinking about Simona's fears of being unable to feed her children. Micol shares her feelings with us, acknowledging she cannot look at Enrique as he triggers an uncomfortable rage in her. Enrique's passive stupor is the signifier of an unbearably gendered affective loop.

Almibar performs a therapeutic intervention, a kind of therapy within a therapy, and asks Micol a few carefully curated questions. Responding to Almibar, Micol tells us she grew up in a very similar situation, with an absent father and a struggling mother. She grew up scared that there wouldn't be enough food in the house. Micol's mother was always out working while her father was sitting on the couch watching television.

The affect attached to her past economic difficulties descends and condenses within the interstices of Micol's words. Micol interrupts her own story in the middle of a sentence to repeat that she needs to let the couple go. "They need to figure out a way to separate," she says. "I have to help them let the couple go. *I have to let the couple go.*"

. . .

The activations and resonances that emerge between patients and therapists are part of an affective dynamic called *transference*.[90] In psychoanalysis, transference refers to the capacity of your therapist to activate in you the affect of primary relationships, ones that impacted the development of your identity.[91] In a transferential relationship with the psychoanalyst, "the thing past can be experienced" because the trace of past relationships, a trace inscribed in your body, comes to the foreground.[92] Transference is a mostly unconscious affective process that animates the therapeutic relationship.

Your traumatic relationship with your father suddenly knocks at the doors of your throat during a therapy session—maybe it's because of your therapist's voice, or maybe it's the way the therapist frowns at you every time you say you are exhausted. Through therapeutic transference, deeply ingrained patterns can be worked on because even if your therapist activates the affective atmosphere you have with your father, the therapist is not, in fact, your father.

This makes the affective loops generated during therapy a bit less intense and easier to work with. To become aware of one's own transferential activations can interrupt the affective loops you tend to repeat with therapists, patients, and lovers alike.[93]

When the reverse happens—when a patient triggers a memory in the therapist—it's called *countertransference*. We can thus say that Simona and Enrique, during their session, activate a countertransferential response in Micol. Enrique summons the affect of Micol's father into the room, while Simona activates in Micol an identificatory process. The transferential relation between Micol and her patients vibrates in the atmospheric background until the affective buildup reaches a tipping point.

. . .

The notion of transference is another way to think about the impact of unconscious affective exchanges that hold together the atmospheric force fields and loops we get sucked into. But transferential relationships exceed psychoanalysis and psychotherapy itself. We are constantly activated by transferential relationships as we bump into other objects, atmospheres, and people. "The limits of my capacity for transference," the philosopher Peter Sloterdijk writes, "are the limits of my world."[94]

. . .

Micol's tears pierce through the atmospheric crisis, altering its affective qualities. The atmospheric foggy vapors of both rooms condense, pile up, and then turn into a thick rain.

I have to help them let the couple go. I have to let the couple go.

. . .

Micol's past invades her present. But her present doesn't fully coincide with her past—it is an affective composition enclosing Micol's relationship with her father, her present doubts about her work as a therapist, her affective attachments to the promises of romantic love and to this particular couple, her gendered imaginaries, her relationship with a cynical ethnographer, and her surprise about the emergence of this intensity during a therapy session she is leading.

But there is also something that exceeds Micol herself—Micol's body is an atmospheric decompression valve discharging the affective weight of multiple temporalities and relationships.[95] This means that what is running through Micol, the affects she is discharging and processing, are not only hers. They belong to a historical moment, a national atmosphere, and to her patients themselves. Micol's body is the decompression point of a system that should be understood ecologically.[96]

Following a systemic perspective, Micol is not just Micol but also the emergent property of a set of relations with her environment. Thinking about the setting of systemic therapy as, precisely, a system, we could say that Micol's breakdown is part of an ecological catharsis. She is channeling the symptom of an atmospheric system composed of the screen, the camera, the anthropologist, the walls, the therapists, and the patients. A whole system built around Simona and Enrique's cruel optimism.[97]

An affective and atmospheric impasse suddenly releasing itself in their therapist's tears.

. . .

Something pushes itself through the cracks of your voice, and you start crying, knowing you can only surrender to whatever else is taking over.[98] Even if just for a second. The reproduction of the loop bumps into a momentary interruption—something breaks the spell, the enchanted loop trembles and the fog around you dissipates. You sense the emergence of a new possibility, but you don't really know what it looks like. An affect finds its way through your body and knocks at the doors of your throat.

You can only scream, *I don't know what else, but not this.*[99]

. . .

There is a resonance between Micol's affective discharge and non-Western healing rituals as described in a wide range of anthropological research. I am not saying this literally, but, influenced as I am by anthropological theories of rituals, I see Micol as a contemporary shaman who is being temporarily possessed (or taken) by a composition of affective forces—some of them sustaining Simona and Enrique's cruel optimism.[100]

Especially in rituals of spirit dispossession, it is often the shamans, the exorcists, or the ritual leaders who take onto themselves the spirits that are disturbing or occupying the life of the possessed; it's the shamans who enter the spirit world to fight against the forces keeping their patients captive.[101]

Micol here is doing a type of affective work that also needs to be done by her patients. But she does it first, entering the spirit world where the gods of cruel optimism and romantic love are entangled in an infernal embrace. *When I say spirit here, I mean a culturally located force.*

Simona and Enrique's journey thus becomes Micol's journey into the atmospheric abyss of cruel optimism. Absorbing the sense of stuckness and more-of-the-same-ness, Micol realizes that the couple's impasse is also her impasse. "I need to let this couple go. They need to separate," she repeats in front of us while recalling her own past. Something crucial has to be let go, and Micol does it first; with her patients on the other side of the wall, she does it together with us.

The possessing spirit needs to go.

. . .

The body of the therapist has become the medium for a ritual of affect dispossession. The affects of impasse territorializing Simona and Enrique's relationship are condensed, channeled, and released in a way that makes transformation, letting go, suddenly possible.

And it happens through the body first.

. . .

Anthropological analyses of therapeutic rituals are often grounded in the idea that psychotherapy is effective because it provides patients with a language to articulate and understand their symptom, situation, or condition.[102] Lévi-Strauss's notion of "symbolic efficacy" effectively represents this perspective. The French anthropologist famously analyzed the incantation song of a Kuna shaman to suggest that shamans are similar to psychotherapists in the way they help patients to find a narrative frame.[103] Verbal communication between the patient and their therapist (or shaman) as well as their coconstruction of a narrative are indeed central aspects of what we call the talking cure.

However, it has been noted that in shamanic rituals, shamans themselves might not even speak the same language as ritual participants, and what seems to do the trick is the therapeutic atmosphere, a force field generated by a whole series of elements—from the use of ceremonial substances to the performance of ritual songs.[104] What happens between ritual participants and shamans, or patients and therapists, is not only linguistic, because all participants are folded within an atmosphere that distributes the affective forces circulating between them. This atmosphere tends to elude or exceed what is being said by either the therapist or the patient but can still offer a deeply therapeutic outlet if it manages to redistribute, refract, or diffract the affective buildups that patients bring to the session.

The embodied and affective component of healing rituals can indeed be considered as one of the main determinants of therapeutic efficacy across cultural configurations.[105] The presence of a community witnessing and participating in the ritual, in particular, has the capacity to create an affective resonating chamber that can play a central role. Émile Durkheim has vividly described the emergence of a "collective effervescence" amid bodies that gather in a ritual context— an effervescence that he describes as a "sort of electricity" generated by the closeness of the participants' bodies.[106]

. . .

With its video cameras, screens, one-way mirrors, and teams of therapists, the setting of systemic therapy seems to afford the emergence of a collectivity sui generis. While focusing on relational systems, this therapeutic model itself seems to build a system—composed of anonymous observers, video cameras, and the one-way mirror. This system surrounds and embraces the patients and the leading therapist, creating a very particular atmosphere.

We can think of this as an odd version of what you could imagine as the circle of community members standing around the possessed person who is being treated by a shaman. The witnessing role of the community is activated and actualized, as I write in chapter 1, by the capacity of visual devices to summon the presence of an imagined gaze. At the same time, the presence of a team of therapists on the other side of the wall can become a holding space, a resonating chamber allowing even the therapists, as in Micol's case, to find an affective outlet.

The systemic setting seems thus to create a holding system that allows for a series of affective discharges—discharges that belong as much to a system of relations as to the individual psyche. In the scene I am describing, the atmosphere of cruel optimism finds a decompression point through Micol's temporary exit from the therapy room and, eventually, through her tears.

. . .

What I mean is that it's about the distribution of affective charges. Like Enrique who needs to release the affective weight he holds in himself about the crisis, like Simona who needs to discharge the anger she absorbs from Enrique, like Micol who needs to discharge the pressure of a past memory entangled with her attempts to save the couple, like the therapists in the other room who need to discharge the affective force of a collective memory of the 2001 economic crisis, like the ethnographer who needs to discharge his identification with a man who doesn't know what to do. And holding spaces created by therapeutic atmospheres can allow for the discharge of affects in a more spacious way.

In the affective economy of the couple form, *who can hold what and for whom* seems crucial.[107]

. . .

The cybernetic systems that compose our environment today have become the distorted container of affective discharges we direct at the screen while hoping they will bounce back, giving us a confirmation of our identity. There is no affective holding space, only a buildup that makes us more and more angry, so we keep discharging our anger against a reflecting mirror that has no power of absorption.[108]

I wonder how we can engage in the collective curation of holding spaces that exceed individual bodies, in the creation of environments that are not composed by reflecting surfaces, that move away from ubiquitous digital mirrors that solidify the identitarian positionalities we have learned to consider our *self*—so that we can elude the spirals of foggy atmospheric force fields.

. . .

When I say I watched live sessions of couple therapy for one year, people often ask me what I have learned about love, or if I have any tips or suggestions. I never know what to say, because in some sense I know as much or as little about love as the person who asks the question. But the other day I was at a dinner with my neighbors, and I ended up saying something like, "Open the windows. That's what I would suggest." The interrogative faces around the table forced me to specify: "I mean, affective charges need to be discharged into a holding environment, not your partner's body. Open the windows. So, the affective discharges are not directed at your partner's body. Better to diffract them across the air. It's a gendered thing too." Maybe it was my slightly—ever so slightly—buzzed reluctance to say much more, but it most definitely didn't fly as a response from an academic who is supposed to know stuff. An awkward silence followed my response.

Maybe the reader knows what I mean by now. #OpenTheWindows.

. . .

After a few minutes, Micol stops crying, and the therapy inside the therapy fades away. The rain is evaporating back into the background, becoming a vague cloud again. With an almost invisible deep breath, Micol wipes away her tears and readjusts her hair. We all look at the screen: Enrique and Simona are waiting for their therapist to come back. Enrique is looking up to the ceiling. Simona is checking her phone. They both look exhausted, worn-out citizens of a collapsing coupledom.

Micol smiles at us with an apologetic expression. She is ready to go back. She opens one door, closes it, opens the other door, then closes it behind her. She is back on screen, back in the therapy room. Micol sits down and looks straight at Simona, and with a severe, yet motherly tone she asks:

"Until when . . . how many more times you will give Enrique chances? Until when?"

Simona nods at Micol without replying. Simona then looks at Enrique and shakes her head. Enrique stares at the wall in front of him without saying anything. After a few seconds of silence, Micol decides to close the session: "Okay, let's stop here. We've worked through a lot today. . . . I will leave you now with a question. I want you to think about this in the next two weeks: In the name of what will this couple continue? In the name of what?"

. . .

While Simona is getting up from the armchair, looking almost revitalized, Almibar turns off the screen. I can hear the muffled echo of Enrique and Simona leaving the therapy room.

In the observing room, it is us again: We all peer into each other's eyes. It is a subtle yet sudden passage from the dry eye of the camera to our watery eyes. Almibar comments briefly on the session, saying that Simona is progressively gaining her independence and that she is emotionally ready to leave him, *if she will be able to let go*.

Micol comes back into the room. She tries not to cry for a few seconds, then starts crying again, even more deeply. After wiping her tears, she leaves the room again. Almibar seems calm, but his cheeks are burning red. Wanda is wrapped within a smiling warmth. I rub my eyes, squeezing out a teardrop while caught within the affective fragments of multiple temporalities entangling personal and nonpersonal histories. Micol comes back into the room, having exhausted her tears.

She sits down and takes a deep breath.

COMPULSIVE REPETITIONS

Maybe I should warn you. This chapter is fastidiously obsessive. I repeat many things, over and over again. I repeat questions I cannot answer about compulsive repetition and temporality, about why it's so hard to stop fighting, why it's so hard to click "stop" when Netflix is on auto-play. I write about intoxicating repetitions, intoxicating myself with repetitions—but there are also some openings toward transformative and vital repetitions. And love, love as a habit, love as an insistent return, love as a generative force. And two armchairs, there is a lot of talk about two empty armchairs.

. . .

Romina and Julio are both in their mid-thirties, and they have been together for about six years. Romina recently confessed to Julio that she had been exchanging intimate texts with one of her colleagues in the downtown office. Romina says that nothing really happened—it was nothing, really, just a few texts.

But Julio feels deeply betrayed now, and he is growing distant and angry. In an attempt to repair their relationship, Romina proposed that they go to couple therapy, and Julio accepted. During the first few sessions, things seemed to be going better. Romina and Julio reconnected. Julio apologized for the angry outbursts he had in the past few years; Romina apologized for her emotional unavailability. Julio cried, Romina cried—they kissed, they hugged, they smiled, they began making love again (even in that room at that birthday party yesterday).

But around the third session of therapy, Julio developed an explicit antagonism with Dr. Almibar, their psychotherapist. Almibar indirectly suggested that if Julio wants to keep being with Romina, he will have to accept what she did and, in one way or another, let go of the anger and insecurity triggered by Romina's texts. Julio is furious now because he feels cornered by the therapist, who seems to take Romina's side. "*She* is the one *who cheated* on me for fuck's sake!" he screams while storming off at the end of their third session of therapy. "I didn't cheat on him," Romina says in a tired murmur while following Julio out the door.

. . .

Buenos Aires, Argentina. February 2013. About fifty minutes into the video recording of Romina and Julio's fifth session, the therapeutic process has reached a tipping point. Romina and Julio are sitting on their armchairs and looking at Almibar. They have just decided to separate. Romina is crying. She sniffs and picks up a tissue from the box on a small coffee table close to her—she sniffs again, and again. She sneezes into the tissue. The sound of Romina's sniffles offers a rhythmic cadence to a silence that expands and contracts across the room. Julio is staring at the therapist while nervously tapping his right hand on the armchair. He seems to be keeping time, following the uneven beat of a forgotten tune. Romina's sniffing and Julio's tapping orchestrate a musical echo of their offbeat relational metrics.[1]

. . .

Suddenly, Almibar's whispered sigh pierces the silent bubble with a closing question. "*¿Nos quedamos así?*" (Shall we leave it here?) Neither Julio nor Romina reply. Julio quickly stands up from the armchair with an affirmative gesture. Romina nods to Almibar but dwells longer in her chair, as if holding a sitting pose, the pose of someone contemplating for a last moment the evaporation of a world she has shared with her partner for six years. Almibar has been out of the frame of the video recording, but he appears now standing up and going toward Julio, who reaches for his wallet to pay for the session. Julio and Almibar both step out of the frame. The video camera is still running, as if recording the audience at the end of a movie in a theater: The lights are turned back on, and the spectators gather their belongings, distractedly looking for things they might have lost during the show. The spectators are still half caught in what they have seen, but already elsewhere.[2]

. . .

A door swings shut.

We hear Almibar and Julio leaving the room, their voices becoming indistinguishable. Romina is still in the frame, sitting in the armchair. Spectator of her own figuration, Romina offers herself to the eye of the camera.[3] Then she stands up and comes out of her contemplative pose. Turning her back to the eye of the camera, she reaches for the Kleenex box and picks up a few more tissues. She collects two crumpled tissues she left on the side of the chair. For a few seconds, she dwells on her own shadow reflected on the back wall. She scans the room, as if searching for a last thought, as if trying to recall what it is, exactly, that just happened—what it is, exactly, that has been lost.

She leaves.

. . .

The psychotherapist forgot to turn off the camera, which now keeps recording the still life of the therapy room. We see two armchairs, a coffee table with a table clock, a dim light, a wall, a painting on the wall. In the recording, we hear a closing door and the reverberation of Romina's footsteps walking away from the therapy room toward the entrance of the building. The steps reverberate like a drumming sound coming from another world. The two armchairs remain motionless on the screen. We can hear the white noise of the camera. Step after step, Romina walks away from the therapy room.

She walks away from a last session spent trying to save the collapsing relationship with Julio. We hear another door closing. She is out of the building. As far as we know, this is the end of Romina and Julio's relationship.

After a few minutes the screen turns blue.

. . .

Toward the end of my fieldwork in Buenos Aires, Dr. Almibar gave me three different sets of video-recorded therapy sessions he thought I would find useful to continue my research once back in Berkeley. "I think you will especially like these ones. They are fascinating," Almibar told me while holding the DVD of Romina and Julio's five therapy sessions. Romina and Julio's sessions were recorded in 2013, a few months before my arrival in Buenos Aires. I assumed that if Almibar wanted me to have them, it was probably because they documented a successful therapeutic process that brought Romina and Julio back together. However, the recordings captured a spiraling therapeutic process that would eventually lead to their separation. Session after session, the interactions between Romina, Julio, and their therapist would get more tense. It was like watching a scripted narrative, as if from the very beginning it was always going to lead to Almibar's closing comment—*Shall we leave it here?*

For a few weeks I was haunted by a question I was too shy to ask. What did Almibar want me to see in Romina and Julio's recordings?

. . .

I never asked. But while writing my PhD dissertation, Romina and Julio's recorded sessions exerted an enthralling power over me, as if holding the secret of a final lesson I had to learn about affective attachments, psychotherapy, and screens. Why did Almibar tell me I would like these sessions? With the desperate obsession of someone who is looking for something but doesn't know what that something looks like, I ended up watching these recordings over and over again.[4]

One night I was rewatching Romina and Julio's fifth and final session, and something in the last minutes of the recording acquired an uncanny vitality.[5] As I described, after Almibar's *shall we leave it here* and after Julio and Romina had left the frame, for a few minutes, the camera kept recording the empty therapeutic setting. With the mildly delirious excitement you get when you think that you have bumped into something you don't know anything about but that you suspect somehow will be *something*, I made a loop of the last minutes of the recording, about five minutes, and watched it so many times that I started dreaming about it.[6] The five-minute loop starts with Romina leaving the room, then we hear her vanishing steps, then we see the two immobile armchairs on the screen for a few minutes, and then the screen turns blue.

Maybe it wasn't about what Almibar wanted me to see. What did *the camera* want me to see?[7]

. . .

The screen turns blue. The loop starts again.

Romina has just left the room, and we can hear the echo of her heels hitting the floor. Romina's steps progressively vanish, becoming an acoustic trace in the eyes of the viewer. The camera captures a crystallized composition, everything so still that you could say it's a photograph of two armchairs.

But in the background, we can hear the white noise of the camera, which intermingles with the almost inaudible sounds coming from the streets of the city.[8] Buenos Aires is murmuring a dystonic lullaby that flows through the empty spaces of this frozen image. The white noise, the rhythmic steps—this aural texture reminds the viewer of the passing of time, a temporal movement hiding under the armchairs' legs.

. . .

My insistent return to Romina and Julio's five-minute loop animates this chapter, which addresses how rhythms, refrains, repetitions, and recursive returns define and redefine affective attachments.[9] Of course, it is the return itself that makes this five-minute loop seem important. It is the act of returning to this scene that gives it life, that injects movement into it, that transforms it into a "scene of instruction."[10] A scene of instruction about relationships and temporality, about the capacity of returns to suffocate us, liberate us, transform us, teach us, or numb us. This insistent return to a five-minute loop is, then, more widely, about insistent returns themselves.

. . .

You can transform anything into a scene of instruction if you keep returning to it.

. . .

The screen turns blue. The loop starts again.

I hear the rhythmic echo of Romina's footsteps. As I stare at the immobile armchairs, I am suddenly brought back to Romina and Julio's conversational refrains, which accompanied the slow motions of a breakup that went on for a couple of years—refrains telling a story about everyday repetitions, incremental transformations, breaking points, and vanishing steps.

What? I *never* said that!

You *always* forget to turn that damn thing off!

You never tell me you like me!

What are you talking about? I *always* ask you first!

This is it, *let's break up....*

Please love, *one more time, this time* it is going to work.

I promise I will remember next time!

I love you,

I *never* did!

Stay here, but not too close, okay?

Nothing *happened! I* never *told him that!*

That's it, I am leaving.

I can't believe this is happening *again!*

You never *listened when I tried to talk to you!*

Yes, *I did kiss him* when we were in high school! So what?!

I hate you,

I hate you too, sweet love.

What about her? She is the one who put us in this mess!

And what about him?

I *never* ...

I always ...

. . .

Relationships are made of refrains, repeated sentences that freeze your partner in a present that is never past nor future. "You always leave the lights on!" "You never ask me if I need help!" I like to think about this always-never temporality as a mythical present. The historian of religions Mircea Eliade writes about the capacity of rituals to bring into the present the generative force of a mythical time.[11] This mythical time, which varies across religious cosmologies, is an immemorial time—not past, not future. A time that can be brought into the present through ritual practices and ceremonial repetitions.[12]

Always-never refrains are like incantations that activate a similar mythical present, which freezes our partner in a temporality that is abstracted from the unfolding of time—not past, not future—an immemorial time dissociated from the infinite motions of becoming.[13]

. . .

You always.

You never.

. . .

Next time you catch yourself uttering an always-never refrain, think about it. Do they really *always* leave the door open? Do they really *never* tell you they love you? Every time you sing your always-never refrain, you spin an adverbial "web of significance" around your partner. You wrap them into a sticky temporal bundle so they cannot move, and they are forced to comply with the spell you cast on them.[14] Caught in this spell, your partner becomes the person who never ... who always ...[15]

. . .

The screen turns blue. The loop starts again.

The percussive sound of Romina's steps marks the unfolding of time and keeps the beat, a beat that repeats itself, but also keeps moving until it finds its vanishing point. The repetition of this transforming beat embraces the immobility of the two armchairs—a static structure animated by the moving sound of the steps. Like the forms and structures we return to, day after day, forms that give shape to our affects, that organize our returns. Like the couple form, a "structure of feeling" that organizes and orchestrates our attachments—a libidinal stricture of feeling.[16] And there is something impersonal about these structures—the empty armchairs are not about Romina and Julio anymore. Romina and Julio left the room, but the two armchairs remain.

. . .

Buenos Aires, Argentina. June 2013. Silvia and Nico position themselves on the two white armchairs and face their therapist, Wanda. It's their first session of therapy. "We have been married for almost thirty-two years, and we don't share anything anymore. Everything is so bad, bad, bad," Nico says, shaking his head.

Nico and Silvia have entered a well-known stage of the couple's life cycle: The kids are out of the house, and both partners are, quite literally, facing one another again. As therapy unfolds, Nico explains how things have been falling apart for the past ten years.

"It's at least ten years that we have been fighting nonstop."

Silvia looks at her fingers as she moves them through the air, drawing irregular shapes. Her gaze lands back on Nico, then Wanda, then the eye of the camera.

"At some point, will it also be my turn to say something?" Silvia interrupts Nico.

"We have problems with everything," Nico continues, "even when we have to decide about the new floor of the bathroom. We got so stuck about it, it's like two years we have to renovate the bathroom. I never have a choice. All my life I tried to do things differently, but I can't do otherwise; we don't even have a common project, something we share. All I can do is to do what she wants me to do. 'Yes, yes, of course!' That's what I can do, just to say this, 'Yes, my dear, of course my dear!' I have no space to do anything else...."

"It's true," Silvia intervenes. "We never agree, not even on basic stuff. We have a different concept of what a couple is. I say white, he says black, and now we are older and ... I am looking for ... I want a partner, but we suffer, we suffer, we always argue, and we could be better, but we never agree. Before it was about the kids, but now that they are out of the house ... now we need to find a project, we could have a new common project, but instead we suffer...."

Nico is looking out the window. "She never listens to me!" he suddenly erupts. "No one listens. She talks and talks, and people think I am exaggerating, but no one listens! She doesn't listen!"

"What's the connection with what I was saying right now?" Silvia replies.

"Well ..." interjects Wanda with a slow and peaceful tone, "now that you are here, and you have all the attention, my attention, the team's attention, the video camera's attention, Silvia's attention, what would you like us to hear, Nico?"[17]

Silence falls over the room.

"That ... that she could accompany me in some project or something! '*Not this, not this, not this!*' Nico bursts out, mimicking Silvia's disapproval. "What can we do then? Nothing! A dinner? A vacation? Renovations? Hanging out? Going to the movies? Exercising? Singing? Nothing!"

"Whatever, Nico! That's so stupid! I would like someone who calms me down. You know, I need someone more 'on point.' I need security, and you ... well you are not doing that!"

"What? What's this? Where is this coming from? I told you, Wanda, she just doesn't listen! I am talking about the fact that we don't have single project in common. We don't find a way to invest the little savings we have to do something together, and we can't figure out ways to entertain ourselves, to take a break from work—that's it, that's where we are at, no investment and no diversion [*ni inversión ni diversión*]. We are so lost."

. . .

Repeated refrains punctuate your relationships—and sometimes you can't find a common beat to riff on. Sometimes the overall rhythm is more like a random beat without tempo.[18]

. . .

Nico repeats the phrase *"ni inversión ni diversión"* nine times during the first session, often followed or anticipated by a comment about how he doesn't share any projects with Silvia. A repetition that becomes a refrain, a refrain which captures two hollowed-out temporalities—we have no economic investments that would allow us to share an imagined future, and we don't find ways to divert from our present, to drift aside from everyday repetitions.[19] We are trapped in a present that holds a future we can't imagine; we suffocate in a present we can't animate with a diversion—but we keep coming back to it. We keep sitting on those chairs, unable to separate. *Ni inversión, ni diversión*, a catchy refrain that indexes the temporal aridity of Nico and Silvia's circular present.

. . .

Tied to a quintessentially modern temporality that draws its ticking force from an imagined future that we move toward, the couple form is often projected into a future to come. The couple form holds within itself the promise of a future good life, and it's amazing how fast the future can territorialize the present tense of the couple form.[20]

Think about a classic initial conversation you might have when you meet someone that you are really into. It usually starts with something like *Do you know what we should do?* An imagined future irrupts into your shared present in the name of a potential relationship. "We should totally drive to Utah next week! Have you ever tried that post-neo-vegan place down the street where they only serve lukewarm water? I think you will love it! Oh, and there is this friend of mine—I want you to meet them!"

As I often say to my students, when you hear any variation of the question "Do you know what we should do?" that's a good moment to make some distinctions and decide whether you're interested in what you're getting into. It's a good moment, for example, to push an imaginary eject button, to fly up in the sky and dissolve the futurity cloud. Or maybe drive to Utah.

. . .

What's left when there is no temporal movement or direction, no imagined tension toward, just the exhausted repetition of refrains that make everything frozen in time? Two armchairs.

. . .

Refrains are comforting. They delimit a habitable territory, a relatively predictable and secure space. It's warm and cozy to be at home, to inhabit the predictable territory you keep re-creating with your repeated refrains.[21] In *A Thousand Plateaus*, Deleuze and Guattari open their chapter on the refrain with a beautifully haunting image: "A child in the dark, gripped with fear, comforts himself by singing under his breath. He walks and halts to his song. Lost, he takes shelter and orients himself with his little song as best as he can. The song is like a rough sketch of a calming and stabilizing, calm and stable, center in the heart of chaos."[22]

. . .

Refrains provide a center in the heart of chaos. We cast our refrains over the infinite motions of becoming to protect ourselves, to find shelter in a fundamentally arbitrary world. And we cast the always-never spell on our partners to diminish the likelihood of an extremely chaotic possibility: They can change. They are not frozen in time.

. . .

But this is most definitely not something that happens only in the couple form, and refrains are only one of the things we mobilize to restrain entropic chaos. Humans have the biocultural tendency and evolutionary necessity to predict, anticipate, and delimit the realm of possibilities around them. There are many (many) ways to think about this across different disciplines. The so-called Bayesian brain hypothesis, which seems to prevail in contemporary neurosciences, suggests that a central characteristic of our brain is to make predictions about the world around us to minimize surprise and to reduce entropy.[23]

These predictions allow us to move through the world as if the world was a stable system. In cybernetic terms, predictions help us maintain homeostatic balance. One of the main goals of our brain, from an evolutionary perspective, is to save energy, and that's what predictions allow us to do. *If you are in the middle of a city and don't spend all your brain juice to figure out if what you see is a jaguar coming to hunt you down or a friendly urban dog, you can save some brain juice for other, potentially more important, tasks.* To preserve energy, we see in the world around us what we expect to see. We perceive what we expect to perceive.

It's like being run by a hermeneutic autopilot that eliminates all the noise, all the inputs that might point our attention to something unexpected, like when you open your fridge already thinking that there is no maple syrup left, and you don't see the can right in front of your nose.[24]

. . .

I think about this every time I end up watching a TV show instead of a movie. I want the stability of repetition. I crave the comfort of something predictable, something that I can binge for extended stretches of time, something that could potentially never stop. Something I already know, or even better, something that already knows me. Like when Netflix or Spotify suggests you watch or listen to something that is so perfect for you that you start having an uncanny sentiment toward an imagined algorithm that might "know you better than your mother."[25]

Your digital m/other is on auto-play.[26]

. . .

When you binge-watch whatever content you like to binge, you can always tell yourself that you are just doing what your brain is supposed to do: saving hermeneutic energy because you never know what's going to come and hunt you down in the desert of your existence. And the sagging couch is a shelter that protects your neural apparatus from the chaos that impinges on the fringes of perception.[27]

. . .

Different temporalities haunt, animate, and sustain the beating sound of our returns—the mythical present, the future perfect, the expected future that never comes, the present that should be almost exactly the way it is but different, the past that never goes away.

I dream of a present that unwraps like a gift.

. . .

The screen turns blue. The loop starts again.

Romina's vanishing steps are the soundtrack of a primal scene of departure— and I am left here, alone, in front of the screen, looking at two armchairs and thinking about affective attachments. Will Romina ever come back? I can start the loop yet another time to feel closer to her for a moment, but I will only hear her leave again. *Click*—Romina is back/now she is gone. Repeat. *Click*—Romina is back/now she is gone. Playing on repeat this painful game of arrivals and departures, I slowly master my solitude, a mastery obtained through a repeated encounter with Romina's departures.

. . .

In *Beyond the Pleasure Principle*, Freud offers a speculative exploration of the psychic forces that underlie and sustain compulsive repetition. One of Freud's most provocative ideas is that at the core of the human being there are forces that can override what he calls the "pleasure principle"—the regulatory mechanism of mental life that aims to lower or discharge "unpleasurable tension."[28] While this tendency to decrease unpleasure seems to characterize our psychic life, humans, according to Freud, also compulsively return to experiences that are fundamentally distressful. Thinking through a wide range of material, from biology to children's games to the posttraumatic dreams of soldiers after World War I, Freud posits the existence of the *death drives*, which he imagines as *unconscious psychic forces* that propel our unconscious repetitions.[29] These repetitions, among other things, hold within themselves an attempt to master, or at least come to terms with, painful experiences that can't be processed consciously.

To make this point, Freud famously describes a game that his grandson plays when he is about eighteen months old. The "good little boy" has a "wooden reel with a piece of string tied round it."[30] When his mother is gone, the child holds the reel by the string and throws it far away from himself to make the reel disappear. The little boy then celebrates the disappearance of the toy with an expressive "o-o-o-o," and Freud interprets this sound as the German word *fort*, which means "gone." The boy then pulls the string and "hails" the reappearance of the wooden reel with a joyful *da*, which in German means "there."

This *fort/da* game of "disappearance and return," Freud writes, is a game wherein the child develops a mastery over the mother's departures and returns through the repetition of a distressing experience.[31] A compulsive repetition of an essentially painful experience in order to gain a pleasurable mastery over the departure (and return) of a primary object of attachment.

. . .

Go away and come closer, always and never. Dance over the beats of this mythical present.

. . .

Clara, Almibar, Micol, and I are watching the blue screen that will soon project Silvia and Nico's second session. While we are waiting, I tell Clara how often I notice that there seems to be no continuity between different sessions of the same couple in therapy.

"Every session of therapy is different from the previous one. We take what [the patients] give us," Clara responds. "Sometimes there is no continuity between sessions. They develop around a different theme. Other times the session produces constant variations on the main, recurring theme. It's like in classical music . . . but I don't know who wrote the score and who the director is. But you have to follow the recurring theme. You have to get in there because that's where change can happen. That's where you find the most resistance to transformation. Couples build their relationships around common themes. They keep repeating them, and they tend to emerge during the sessions. And you have to dance with the theme, return to it, slowly, patiently."

. . .

One of my favorite neoliberal gurus has this refrain that he repeats almost every time he speaks. *Repetition is the mother of skill.*[32]

. . .

The screen turns blue. The loop starts again.

The two white leather armchairs are at the center of the frame. The leather still shows the traces left by Romina and Julio's bodies. The spectrality of the empty armchairs now seems animated by two gazes that radiate from them.[33] What are they looking at? The armchairs are slightly oriented toward each other, but their gazes converge on a third focal point that is outside of the frame—if you follow the chairs' orientation, you can suddenly feel the absent presence of the psychotherapist's chair.[34]

. . .

The screen turns blue. The loop starts again.

"Is it true that we can learn only when we are aware that we are being taught?"[35]

. . .

However you want to sit on them, chairs orient your posture. Even if you think you are stronger than the chair and that you are the one deciding how to sit, after some time sitting on a chair it's easy to forget about it—and then the chair silently takes over your body. It wraps around your muscles, it takes in your weight from whichever pressure point it pleases. The infrastructural sovereignty of the chair orients your body, which is the ground of your experience of the world.[36] That's why some chairs are so bad for your posture—and there is a whole debate about what a good chair is supposed to do to your body. Hold you? Make your core work? Help you relax? Boost your productivity? Or like some posture gurus would have it, is the best chair basically not a chair?[37]

. . .

Even if it appears to be the most natural thing in the world to you—what you face, what you are attracted to, what you tend toward, what you return to, what you are affected by—is always already mediated by "orienting devices" that configure your affective life and define what you are turned toward. In *Queer Phenomenology*, Sara Ahmed writes that to be oriented is to be "turned towards certain objects," which, in turn, orient us and turn us around.[38] And chairs are a good example to think about the infrastructures that orient us in the world and shape what I would call our *regimes of availability*.[39] Orienting you, a chair makes you available to one order of reality over another.

Romina and Julio—or whoever sits down—are oriented by the chairs in the very moment they sit on them. When Romina is about to leave the room, she looks at the chairs, almost taking leave from them—as if the chairs held the couple form together, as if the chairs were the couple form itself.

. . .

The chair is a good way to picture what the philosopher Giorgio Agamben calls a *dispositif*, a word that in English has been translated as "apparatus."[40] A *dispositif*, Agamben writes, is "literally anything that has in some way the capacity to capture, orient, determine, intercept, model, control, or secure the gestures, behaviors, opinions, or discourses of living beings."[41] What *dispositifs* do, according to Agamben, is to produce subjects. "I call a subject," Agamben writes, "that which results from the relation and, so to speak, from the relentless fight between living beings and apparatuses [*dispositifs*]."[42]

The living being you were before being captured by the *dispositifs* that shape you is most definitely not what you are now, which is a being who is subjected to, and shaped by, multiple *dispositifs*. According to Agamben, *dispositifs* are indeed what make a subject into a subject.[43] To say it more bluntly, there is no subject without a *dispositif*. This is not good nor bad, it just means that there is always a process, a device, an infrastructure, a situation that makes you into you, that makes the you that you are possible, and, in what concerns me here, oriented-toward.

So *dispositifs* dispose you. They, for example, arrange your posture, orient you toward, and make you available to specific orders of reality instead of others. Romina and Julio are sitting on the *dispositif* of the two armchairs, which indexes another *dispositif*, the one of the couple form. The couple form, as a *dispositif*, determines what we are relationally available to, what we can or can't experience as love. As Ahmed writes, the romantic couple form orients us toward normative ideals of love and intimacy. It determines what is available *for* and *to* love.[44]

. . .

When Agamben writes that literally anything can be a *dispositif*, it means that what shapes your subjectivity can be anything you submit to, and are oriented by, however intentionally or unintentionally.[45] Just to name a few, you are subjected to the *dispositifs* of language, culture, biopower, the family form, the couple form, the schooling system, and so on.[46] If we think about language, as an example, anthropologists and linguists have shown us how different words in different languages make you available to completely different experiences of the world.[47]

. . .

To be a subject, to be "you," thus means to be subjected to the affordances of a *dispositif*.[48]

. . .

If you write your book on a "chaise longue all day long," it is not the same thing as writing it while standing, or jumping up and down—embodying different postural forms, you become available to different thoughts, different ideas, a different voice.[49] Or think about writing your book while sitting on one of those chairs that make you sink into their tender and soft existential melt—those armchairs that make it hard to even ever so slightly engage your core and bend toward the mousepad to pause the TV show you have been bingeing for the past three hours.[50] That's why after a few hours on the binge train, I force myself to stand up—bingeing a show while standing gets trickier.

Now, for example, the *dispositif* of reading is subjectifying you as a "reader," and this makes you available to a very specific reading bubble, an imaginary space between you and me.[51] And the tone and temporality of this chapter is making you feel differently than the other chapters.

Different *dispositifs*, different affective experiences.

. . .

The screen turns blue. The loop starts again.

The percussive sound of Romina's steps embraces the immobility of the two armchairs—a static structure animated by the repetition of a heel-to-floor impact. Romina and Julio left, but the two armchairs remain. Like the forms we return to, the forms that shape our affects and organize our returns.

. . .

It's not just me, you know. I am writing this chapter in conversation with the work of Eric Taggart, a psychotherapist and critical media theorist who writes about the Strange Situation Procedure, the founding experiment of attachment theory.[52] In this experiment, which is held in the same type of setting as systemic psychotherapy (closed-circuit television, one-way mirrors, screens), a child—between twelve and eighteen months old—is subjected to different separations from, and reunions with, the mother, as well as encounters with a stranger. Psychological researchers study and code in detail the different reactions of the child—what happens when the mother leaves, when the child encounters a stranger, and when the mother returns—to determine the child's "attachment style."[53]

In his work, Taggart is also mildly obsessed with the different objects present in the Strange Situation Procedure experiment room—like the two chairs where the mother and the stranger sit or the toys that are there for the child to play with. Yes, the two chairs—*I told you it's not just me!* Taggart writes about how the arrangement of the room where the experiment is held offers a "techno-primal" mise-en-scène of the ways in which objects organize and mediate the child's psychic life. That is to say, the experiment room itself *theatralizes* the ways in which the child's psyche develops, through a play of separations from, returns to, and reunions with external objects that capture the child's affective investments—from the mother to the stranger, from the toys to the chairs.

Objects, Taggart writes, compose "affective infrastructures" around us, ones that capture, dispose, and distribute our psychic attachments.[54] Objects of attachment are *dispositifs* that structure (and stricture) our affective life. These objects can be as concrete as a piece of wood and as abstract as the idea of the idea of a concept about something. Throughout our psychic development, we experience and build different relationships with different objects that organize our affective attachments—from the feeding breast to the algorithmic feed. The couple form is one of these objects (or one such form).

We keep returning to some of these objects throughout our life, just like children who keep playing the *fort/da* game, never getting tired of seeing something disappear and then reappear again.[55] We keep returning because our attachment to these objects literally holds us together.

And so we return. Again, and more, and over again.

. . .

In psychoanalysis, some objects matter more than others, particularly in specific developmental stages—think about Lacan's mirror in chapter 1. The psychoanalyst Winnicott writes about "transitional objects," which he describes as the first "not-me" possessions of the child. The transitional object facilitates the passage from the internal to the external world of the child; it is an object that is "not part of the infant's body yet [is] not fully recognized as belonging to external reality."[56] Think about a soft piece of blanket you used to suck on, or your favorite stuffed animal that you progressively destroyed because you loved it so much, or a little sound you used to make to soothe your distress. Transitional objects allow the child to enter an "intermediate area of experience"—the object is not the result of the infant's imagination, but it is not completely detached from the child's inner life either.[57] Softy Bunny does, in fact, exist in the objective world but still functions as a prosthetic extension of the infant's inner life.[58] In their being in between inner and outer reality, transitional objects allow the child to practice, over and over again, a relationship with an object that is almost distinct from the child herself. This, progressively, allows the child to develop a mastery over her own boundaries, to distinguish what she wants the object to be and what the object is. This mastery is obtained through repeated returns to the transitional object, a repetition that often leaves its mark on disintegrated objects that have weathered our insistent returns and departures.

When a transitional object has done its job, Winnicott writes, it gets left behind, forgotten, without being repressed, mourned, or internalized. The object "loses meaning, and this is because the transitional phenomena have become diffused, have become spread out over the whole intermediate territory between 'inner psychic reality' and 'the external world as perceived by two persons in common,' that is to say over the whole cultural field."[59] The idea here is that if we have abandoned our early childhood transitional objects, it's because the "whole cultural field" is now covering us up like a warm blanket we can't let go of. A blanket that blurs the borders between inner and outer worlds.

. . .

I know, I know. I am zipping through different approaches and vocabularies— from psychoanalytic object relations to attachment theory. Let me offer you a repetition with difference, so we can return to the theme, dance with it, slowly, and let it breathe between us.

You are a subject. And this means that you have been subjected to a series of *dispositifs* that orient your perception, behaviors, beliefs, and so on. *Dispositifs* orient you toward and determine what is available to you, what you can perceive, what you can or can't love. *Dispositifs* can be as concrete as a chair and as abstract as the idea of love. Some *dispositifs* have a great impact on your psychic development, like transitional objects. Whatever *dispositifs* you are subjected to, whatever the degree of conscious awareness you have about them, they produce what you end up experiencing as your own self. More often than you think, you are submitted to hegemonic *dispositifs* that didn't ask your permission to make you into their malleable subject.[60]

The *dispositifs* I describe in this book tend to orient your psycho-affective life—like the gaze in chapter 1, which we can now understand as a *dispositif* because it shapes your subjectivity. Or the couple form, a *dispositif* that structures dominant affective attachments. Being a form, the couple gives shape to your affective life—like an empty cylinder lends its form to whatever gas fills it up. I wrote in chapter 2 about affective forces and enclosure, and about how affective atmospheres need to be enclosed within something to be atmospheres at all. Remember the atmosphere of cruel optimism encapsulated within the *dispositif* of the couple form?

Atmospheres, we can say now, need a *dispositif* to become anything at all. Affective infrastructures, or psychic *dispositifs*, orient and organize our attachments. And we keep going back to them, like to the toys in a room, like to a mother that comes close and goes away, like to a smartphone.

. . .

In this chapter, I am trying to tie all of this to a haunting question, which is about what fuels what Berlant calls *cruel optimism*. Why do we keep returning to affective *dispositifs* even when they are destroying us? Why do we keep playing with a toy that cuts our fingers every time we pick it up? This question can't have a single answer, like all good questions. So to engage with it, as I keep doing in this book, I drift aside from the possibility of faking an answer I don't have, and instead I dance around the question. I dance around repetition itself, repeating the steps, dancing over repetitions, repeating the question. *What does repetition do?* Why do we keep repeating, returning, and, basically, looping?

One way to think about it, as I began suggesting, is that humans are animated by a compulsion to repeat, which Freud understood as tethered to the death drives, forces that fuel our insistent returns to pleasurable as well as unpleasurable experiences. A repetition of unpleasant experiences, but also a repetition that fosters mastery, a repetition that holds us together as we return over and again to objects that regulate our attachments. This death instinct can be, as Herbert Marcuse vividly described, both deadly and vital, or as reactionary as revolutionary.[61] So what I am running after, really, is to let this double movement, these two sides of repetition flicker through the chapter—repetition as trapping suffocation, repetition as a doorway to transformative mastery. Both repetitions need a subject, which means someone who is, consciously or unconsciously, willingly or unwillingly, subjected to a *dispositif* they return to.

. . .

You can transform anything into a scene of instruction if you make it your *dispositif*.

. . .

Another important take on this repetition bonanza: Repetition generates and sustains affective states.[62] We compulsively return to our go-to objects of attachment—subjectifying *dispositifs*—to regulate our affective life. We return to the couple form seeking an affective state, one that might or might not be delivered. The state triggered by repetition is key here, and I will explore the more psychedelic side of it in chapter 4. For now, consider the affective states you get into when you return to the objects that dispose you, that organize your relationship with the world—you can even just start with the chair you keep sitting on when you read, or write, or binge, or . . .

But maybe armchairs are too low-tech to make this point about affective states.

Think about digital devices then, the ultimate *dispositif* of the contemporary condition.[63] The smartphone is today's *fort/da dispositif*, a toy the user wants to throw away only to see it bounce back again.[64] But there is more. Today the smartphone is literally a prosthesis of your identity, the transitional object that screens your relationship between the internal and external world. As a transitional object, the phone is both not-you and also still kind of you, and it gets harder to make the distinction the longer you scroll. Where do you end and where does the feed begin?

. . .

I return to digital *dispositifs* longing for notifications that both haunt and animate me. And the red notification is just the shiniest part of a dopamine bait that is as big as my soul. On the other side of that blinking redness, my whole existence might be on the line. *Did I get that grant? Did my friends like the song I have recorded for them? Wasn't yesterday's dinner so awkward—why aren't they writing back now? Oh, my god, I shouldn't have posted that picture! Wait, one second, this could be important. I can't turn it off now.* It's all about me, of course. The notifying bait is the dinging and buzzing sound of my submission to digital *dispositifs* that hold my soul, shape my days, channel my attachments.[65] "When I undergo my existential breakdowns—they are usually on a Monday-Wednesday-Friday schedule—the buzzing sound of a notification keeps me alive, I feel like it can snap me out of my depressive state."[66]

Hit me, hit me constantly with something that pokes me, something that brings me back into the loop, something that asks for my attention, something that gives me attention.[67] Something. Buzz me into the digital cathedral of the self.[68] Han describes smartphones as a devotional *dispositif* used to stabilize dominion. "Smartphones," he writes, "represent digital devotion—indeed, they are the devotional objects of the Digital, period. As a subjectivation-apparatus, the smartphone works like a rosary—which, because of its ready availability, represents a handheld device too."[69]

Buzzed into the digital cathedral, I bend my head each time I scroll through the rosary of my soul. In the silent interstices of the scrolling cathedral, I can hear my heart buzzing like a phone on silent mode. Our heartbeat or, better, our breathing patterns should be measured in phone buzzes.

Buzz-in, buzz-out, buzz-in, buzz-out, buzz.[70]

. . .

Last week I turned off all notifications, deleted all the distracting apps, made my smartphone a dumb black-and-white screen with nothing on it. And yet, I would catch myself looking at the screen, waiting for something, staring at the reflection of my face on the black mirror of my buzz-less soul—waiting for a buzzing notification that would keep me afloat. On the other side of the notification, an expanding network of self-adapting platforms is waiting for me, waiting to feed me a part of myself, a digital load of me-ness.[71] But waiting, actually, is not really what we do. Compulsive clicking is the erasure of the very possibility of waiting.

And *they* know it. *They* know how much I hate to wait.

. . .

So . . . the Freudian "good little boy" repeats to gain mastery, the algorithmic good little user repeats to get in a numbing trance state, and the not-so-good little anthropologist repeats compulsively to see if something new pops up through the cracks of his sentences.[72]

Repetition gets you into a state—good or bad, that's not really a question repetition asks itself.

. . .

And the more you return to the *dispositifs* that shape your sense of self, the harder it is to let them go—the pulsing beat of a cruelly optimistic type of return. To let go of a *dispositif* that shapes your subjectivity and organizes your affective attachments might mean to let go of a big chunk of your identity. It implies a potential experience of ego dissolution—even if just for a second. Because you don't want to die, right?[73] You want to keep being exactly who you are, to maintain as much homeostatic balance as possible, to reject entropic intrusions. And we are back to (the protective power of) refrains, which we can now understand as incantations that keep you glued to the *dispositifs* which make you into you. As ritual incantation, a refrain encapsulates the very logic of repetition—it *is* repetition—and some refrains offer us the narrative structure to make sense of our insistent returns to the practices that shape us.[74]

I am thinking right now about one of my classic refrains in the "Work" category: *I am so exhausted!* I have this refrain on auto-play ten months per year. This refrain delimits my experiential range of possibilities while also justifying my attachments to a whole set of *dispositifs* that make me into me—from caffeine to screens. If I stop singing to myself the exhaustion lullaby, I might have to stop bingeing on TV shows or drinking so many espressos—and I am so attached to both that I wouldn't know what to do with myself if I embrace the possibility of not being *that* exhausted.

. . .

Some repetitions keep you exactly where you are; others could untether you from your own self. Compare binge-scrolling on TikTok for one hour to doing deep, intense, circular breathing for one hour. Both repetitions can get you high, but the kite will fly across different skies.[75]

. . .

"We have finally decided where to go for a fifteen-day vacation! It's a victory! But I already know, she will be walking around with three cell phones obsessing about our kids in the city or talking with her father! It's always like this when we are alone," Nico complains during the fifth session with Silvia. "What about taking some time together during this vacation to talk about possible projects, something you might want to try to do together?" replies Wanda. "Of course, you are so well rehearsed in fighting and arguing, so don't ask too much of yourself. Follow your rhythms, but you could take some time every day to talk for a little bit about something you would want to do together, something small, a little project.... What do you think? Just to start practicing a new rhythm, to rehearse a new pattern, a pattern where you can get together without fighting and talk about new projects, future projects...."

"What do you mean?" Silvia asks.

"I don't understand. What do we have to do?" echoes Nico.

. . .

What's your go-to refrain?

. . .

Nico and Silvia have returned from their vacation. It's their sixth session of therapy. Silvia says that the vacation was good—they didn't fight as much. "But then of course, yesterday he comes home late for dinner—he has no notion of time!" Silvia abruptly changes the subject. "You always tell me, 'I'm coming, I'm coming,' but you never arrive!"

"What else should I tell you? I can't tell you anything else! If I'd tell you, 'I'll be there in twenty minutes,' you'd be like, 'Why? What do you have to do? Read your stupid blogs?'"

Wanda tries to slow things down. "Okay, so ... Silvia ..."

"Words have meaning!" Silvia interrupts.

"I told you I'm busy at work!" Nico screams back.

"How do you even know what I'm going to tell you? What are you, God?"

"It's control! You need to control me, like a little dumb puppet!"

"Okay, Nico and Silvia, here we need to slow down a little, so we can ..." Wanda tries to say gently.

"Say it! Just say it's control! Say you just want to control me and put me in a little corner!"

"I'm not controlling you! If you never show up, how the hell would I be controlling you?"

Their faces flushed with choleric redness, Nico and Silvia's fighting systematically cuts Wanda out. On the other side of the wall, we all look at each other, a little dazed from the intensity of Nico and Silvia's constant arguing. The tension in the therapy room spills over into our room for a second. Almibar gets up and goes toward the TV to lower the volume. "Where is the remote? Always hiding somewhere when you need it."[76]

"It *is* control, and you know it!" Nico's voice is shaking.

"How can I control someone who is out at 7 a.m. and comes back at 10 p.m.?! Huh?!"

This time Silvia's question is addressed to Wanda, who finds a small interstice to say something.

"When do you feel the most controlled, Nico?"

"When we have to meet," Nico whispers defeatedly.

After a moment of silence, Silvia says, "It's about connection. For him every weekend with us is a lost working day." For a second, things seem to slow down. Nico shakes his head—he seems to be getting a running start to rekindle the fight: "If I have to work, I have to work! If . . ."

"That's not at all what I'm talking about!" Silvia interrupts him. Nico and Silvia's rhythm accelerates again. They repeat their sentences, they anticipate what the other person is going to say, their voices overlap, they repeat their sentences.

"I'm a little puppy, that's what I am for you! It's control!"

"Cut it with this show! I'm not controlling you! I'm talking about . . ."

"Okay, okay, guys," Wanda steps in. "I'm going to take a little break now to go debrief with the team. . . . In the meantime, you can think about what you want to do here, today, in this space, during your therapy session. . . ." Wanda gets up and leaves the room.

. . .

In the observing room, we all feel relieved—a momentary silence between Nico and Silvia feels like something has been unplugged from our brains. Wanda comes through the door to talk to us. As soon as the door is closed, she bursts out in a short, composed, yet liberatory laughter. "I wish I could smoke a cigarette now!" she says. "It requires a lot of practice to be able to fight this well. These guys are amazing. It's like they are on autopilot," she continues, "a software running through them, or a script.⁷⁷ And now they are so worked up that they can't even wait for the other person to say their line. They are so well rehearsed that they already know what the other person is going to say. It's a tight and closed loop. They can't stop repeating the script. And now I'm captured in their loop, you know? They are showing their fights to me. . . . We need to slow this down, to create some space for them to see it."

We all nod pensively. As we look at the screen, we notice that Silvia and Nico are completely silent now. Nico is holding his head with his right hand while checking his phone with his left. Silvia has slightly reoriented her armchair and is looking out the window. We contemplate the screen, our heads filled with the echoes of Silvia and Nico's voices.

"Look at this!" Wanda says with wry amusement. "I am out of the room, and of course they stop fighting!"[78]

While we are watching Nico and Silvia's silence, the screen suddenly turns black.

. . .

How do you interrupt repetition?

. . .

In the video recording of this session, after this period of silence between Nico and Silvia—while Wanda was talking to the team in the observing room—the screen turns black for about three and a half minutes. The recording is still playing, but the screen is black. It's not certain why, but maybe the camera was also too tired of hearing the patients scream and went into sleep mode. A three-minute-long black screen evoking the texture of a pause between fights. A three-minute-long silence that maybe speaks of Nico and Silvia's paradoxical inability to act out their arguments without the presence of Wanda—the intimate spectator kept at the threshold of their loops. A black screen that creates a hiatus, an interruption, a period between sentences.

But only for the viewer of the recording, because in that moment, when the screen went black, we didn't pay much attention to it. "Remember to turn the camera back on," Almibar said to Wanda as we all promptly turned away from the black screen and kept talking about the session.

. . .

Wanda is back with Nico and Silvia and turns the camera back on.

"It seems to me," Wanda says with ethereal calm, "that you both agree on the fact that you need to connect. You said you want things to work out, that you don't want to separate, but you can't find a way. Nico, you feel pressured and controlled; Silvia, you need to know when he is coming back home. You want to feel heard. The atmosphere between you two is . . . hard. It's hard to sit here and watch you fight all the time, if you allow me to say it, and I'm sorry it's a bit strong, but it feels a little toxic to witness your fights. It makes it hard for me to help you if you keep fighting like this during a session. . . ."[79]

"Yeah, that's what it is—this is *toxic!* You see, the problem is that she calls me only because she is bored! That's all!" Silvia seems surprised for a second. Nico is calling Silvia back to the fighting ring.

"When I call you, it's because I am waiting for you at home, with dinner on the table . . . that's because I am bored!? What are you talking about! That's what happened yesterday?"

"Yeah, what? What happened yesterday?"

"What happened? What happened?!" Silvia is furious. "This guy never notices anything!"

"Tell me, then, tell me what happened yesterday. What happened yesterday?"

. . .

The two armchairs, the two armchairs remain.

And you have to dance with the theme, return to it, slowly, patiently.

. . .

What Freud writes about the death drive in *Beyond the Pleasure Principle* is quite speculative, and this notion has been interpreted in very different ways.[80] As I mentioned above, Freud describes the death drive as a psychic force sustaining an unconscious compulsion to repeat and return to unpleasant experiences. This compulsion allows humans to gain mastery over such experiences. But there is also something else he was running after, especially in his attempt to understand the death drive from a biological perspective.

Freud described the death drive as belonging to the "conservative nature of living substances," a nature that drives organisms like us to compulsively try to restore "earlier states of things" and to resist the inevitability of decay, change, transformation, and decomposition.[81] And while "decompositional" change might sound like death, it is, in fact, an essential component of organic life itself, of vitality. The infinite motions of becoming move at the beat of decompositional change.[82]

The death drive is thus for Freud also a regressive force that tries to take us back to what we were before—what we were two seconds or a few years ago, but also what we were before we were born, before there was a human species, before there was biological life. We are talking about a force that wants to take us back to the mineral state, just to be clear. And, speculating a bit over Freud's speculations, my sense is that if we think about the death drive simply as a compulsion to hurt ourselves or smoke cigarettes, we might be missing a big point.

The death drive is a psychic force that keeps hitting the brakes on whatever we might be becoming. It's a force that rows against the torrential current of entropic disaggregation; a force that resists excessive stimulations and restlessly attempts to reduce chaos; a striving toward death that tries to keep us alive exactly the way we are *right here right now*, and as long as possible.[83]

Until we dissolve into the ether.[84]

. . .

Once you are folded within the subjectifying force of a *dispositif*, you might not see anything beyond what it shows you—and whatever form of life is happening away from the two armchairs feels like an unreachable beyond.

. . .

We can also think also about compulsive returns to digital devices as an attempt to find a sheltered and predictable environment, seeking desperately for refrains that can protect us from receiving actual new input. When I am compulsively scrolling on TikTok, I am anticipated by algorithmic apparatuses that feed me what I "will have wanted" according to the time of the day, the seasons of the year or my life, and, overall, my "data-logical" patterns—I do get a lot of motivational videos around noon all year round. It's like having the present tense being swallowed by the future perfect, a tense that describes not what I am but what I will have been.[85]

And this predictive temporality is comforting because the app progressively eliminates what I don't like, so I will be fed only food that was prechewed for me, in the name of the Samuele I will have been, the Samuele that will always already have been. The future perfect haunting my compulsion constrains entropy, providing me with endless refrains to binge on.[86]

"You always," says the Algorithm.

"I always." Samuele nods.[87]

. . .

High-tech devices or low-tech chairs or mixed-tech couple forms. Pick your favorite compulsive loop to anticipate and predict what comes your way. Pick your go-to *dispositif* to return to. Pick anything, anything you want.

Anything but transformation.

. . .

So it's not just our partners who trap us with their *always-never* incantation. We trap ourselves voluntarily in a similarly frozen temporality, one scroll after another. The algorithmic m/other of the sky feeds us with a mythical present that protects us from encountering anything different, from becoming anything different.

. . .

The mythical present or the future perfect makes you feel at home, cozy and sheltered. When you are at home, the world around you can't be otherwise, which means that you are unable to see anything you haven't already anticipated.[88] This anticipation runs deep through your veins, and it feels like the most natural thing in the world. But this homey feel is the result of social and historical *dispositifs* that shape your predictive perception.[89] That's the homey feeling that the "smart world" we live in is constantly trying to create.

A seamless flow of interactions that make you forget the possibility that you could discover something actually new—like when you open Spotify and your "Discover Weekly" plays what you already like. And in the predictive world we live in, it's hard to be able to encounter a present that has never been, to sit down and unwrap the present as if it was a gift given to you by someone who has no idea what you like.[90]

Will we ever be able to bump into an unwritten future?[91]

. . .

There are days you feel so stuck and drained, and maybe you just need to change the chair, but you always forget to think about this after you sit down. Because the chair folds you in. Whoever you are. And you keep returning to it. Of course, that is until the moment when you are in so much pain, or in so much distress that you start focusing on your posture, and then you obsessively think about chairs, and especially about the amount of pain the chair you are using is inflicting on your musculoskeletal system.

Sometimes you are in so much pain that a few seconds after you sit down, you are already anxiously moving on the chair and ready to get up, but you need to write that email, and you stay there a little longer, just to write that email, until you forget about the chair again, until you pop down a painkiller and write your worst lines.

. . .

What happened, what happened yesterday? A recursive refrain that brings us back to a fight frozen in time, a resentful loop that never ends, a predictive and static bubble we are tragically tethered to—*ni inversión, ni diversion*. What happened yesterday, what happened?

. . .

Dance with the theme, return to it, slowly, patiently.

. . .

"Yeah, that's it! You don't even know what happened yesterday!" Silvia is yelling at Nico, who is yelling back at Silvia. The fight is escalating again, and Wanda can't find an entry point to say something, anything. Suddenly, the intercom in the therapy room buzzes. The buzzing sound resonates across the wall, the eye of the camera, and our screen. Nico and Silvia's argument finds an abrupt interruption—the buzzing sound catches both of them by surprise. On the other side of the wall, Almibar is pushing on the intercom's button while attentively looking at the screen. *Bzzzzzzzzzz.*

"Sorry, one second. Yes?" Wanda picks up the receiver.

"Is everything okay? What can we do from here?" Almibar, who is talking to Wanda through the intercom, knows that it is not about saying anything in particular to Wanda. The most important action was to buzz into the session to create an interruption.

"Yes, yes, of course," Wanda replies.

Nico and Silvia seem a little confused; after glancing at the intercom and the video camera, their gazes intersect. Nico smiles, shaking his head. Silvia smiles back and nods. Nico and Silvia suddenly notice the presence of an audience on the other side of the wall, as if the buzzing interruption allowed them to wake up from a hypnotic state. Wanda puts down the receiver. There are maybe fifteen seconds of silence—the room feels suddenly bigger.

. . .

So, there are also buzzes that could snap us out of the loop, like a cold slap in the face. Maybe that's where we are headed. We will have three-dimensional cold mechanical hands that emerge out of our screens and slap us out of our trance state.[92] "SLAP. You have bumped into your binge-wall MOFO!" But it's an add-on to your monthly plan, and it's so expensive that only privileged users will be able to afford the slap.[93]

. . .

I spend a lot of time designing classroom "experiments of experience" to stimulate students' engagement with all sorts of concepts.[94] But my favorite pedagogical moment is very simple and based on the creation of an interruption, any interruption.

In the middle of your lecture, you stop lecturing and fall silent for thirty seconds without saying anything. Or you ask students to stand up and make a sound. Or you turn off the lights for less than a minute. A simple interruption that creates a displacement, a discomfort, a hesitation, something. I promise that you can then spend the entire class discussing the effect of that interruption on students and what it reveals about our *dispositifs*, habits, attention, positionality, affects, expectations, dominant temporalities, repetitions. I guess that was the spirit of the situationist interruption. A thirty-second interruption that can open the door to collective transformation.[95]

. . .

"Nico and Silvia need new rituals, new practices, new repetitions." Wanda is talking to the team during Nico and Silvia's third session of therapy; the second and third sessions have gone much like the first. "What about preparing a small ritual they have to do every day, to exercise new forms of being together? We can ask them to take a few minutes before they go to bed every day, and read out loud something we write for them, like a mantra they have to repeat, a few sentences that are already scripted so they don't get stuck in a fight?"

"So, to stop repetition we need more repetition?" I ask Wanda with an ironic smile.

. . .

Repetition itself is a *dispositif*, one that orients and channels the affective forces tethering you to your objects of attachment. Repetition holds you together just like it holds the affective infrastructures holding you. Different repetitions tap into, and activate, different forces. It's interesting how, in our exchange above, Wanda doesn't really distinguish repetition from ritual. And indeed, one of the main characteristics of rituals is repetition—repetition through time but also the repetition of gestures, sounds, or sentences that make a ritual ritualistic. Think about a dance pattern, a mantra, or the repeated sound of twenty people in a circle stomping their feet on the ground; or think about binge scrolling.

Saying *ritual repetition* might actually be a tautological repetition, one that foregrounds the idea that every repetition is ritual, a ritual repetition that can become its own scene of instruction. *You can transform anything into a scene of instruction if you keep returning to it.* Even this sentence, even just repeating to yourself ritual repetition, ritual repetition, ritual repetition, ritual . . .

Anthropologists of rituals have widely explored how ritual repetitions (ritual repetition, ritual repetition . . .) make ritual participants available to experience all sort of "electric" forces.[96] Try breathing super-deep and super-fast for two hours if you think what I am saying makes no sense and come back to this page after. Émile Durkheim famously referred to a "certain rush of energy" that bursts through our bodies when engaging in ritualistic and repeated actions.[97] More recently, William Mazzarella describes the social itself as a *dispositif* that rearranges vital forces through rituals that activate the subject's affective response.[98] These forces circulate across the social cosmology that holds the ritual in place. So every repetition is an incantation, a spirited summoning of the forces belonging to a specific cosmology.

This happens sometimes on purpose, sometimes despite us—and all the pleasurable in-betweens.

. . .

The ritualistic return to a couple's *always-never*, for example, summons the forces of a mythical present holding that situation in place, freezing partners into an impossible transformation. As I explored in chapter 2, ritual repetitions can summon barely perceivable forces that come in the form of an atmospheric crisis. The mythical present is a temporal umbrella protecting cruel optimism.

But rituals can also summon the force of a liberatory *not-this*.[99]

. . .

Wanda, together with the team, did end up preparing a short ritual for Nico and Silvia, who had to find a moment every day to read to each other a short sentence that we wrote for them. The sentence contained a reciprocal commitment to find something to do together, to be open to listening to the other person's desires, and to basically let the other person *be their own thing*. Within the fractures of their compulsive repetitions, the team prescribed the ritualized cure of a new daily ritual.

After ten sessions of therapy, Silvia and Nico confessed that they had forgotten to read their ritual sentences to each other after a couple of weeks—but things, somehow, seemed to be much better.

. . .

There are ritual returns that make you available to an affective state of openness, a state where a generative force runs through your body, and the only thing you can do is to hold still while embracing a vital motion that runs through you, exceeding you—so vital a force that it might *de-compose* you.

Sometimes, that's how I imagine the love I run after. A love that looks like holding a perfectly still pose, a pose that doesn't impose itself on the loved object, a nonimposing loving pose that lets the object of attachment move at the beat of their own becoming. Following what I write in chapter 1, maybe this is a type of love that loosens the grip on dyadic projective identifications.[100] Or maybe a type of love that refuses to force one's partner into playing the part of a transitional object, an object midway between internal and external reality, an object that might still be the continuation of . . . *me*.

Aspirationally, I'm thinking here about love as a ritual return to a scene where you just let go, loosen the grip, and find a postural stillness that lets the other be their own difference.

. . .

Some repetitions keep you exactly where you are; others can untether you from your own self.

. . .

But before you can start practicing new returns and become a subject to/of different *dispositifs*, you need an interruption, something that makes the *dispositif* tremble, something that allows you to see the sequences, the practices, the gestures, that keep bringing you back to it.[101]

. . .

Bzzzzzzzzzzzzz. Click "pause" and get off the chair, champ.

The screen turns blue. The loop . . .

4

OSCILLATIONS

Buenos Aires, Argentina. November 2013. It's my second session of hypnotherapy. My eyes are closed, and Sofía is speaking to me with a slow and warm voice. A video camera is filming the session. I take a deep breath and let myself sink into the armchair. I feel heavy and relaxed, caught between wakefulness and sleep, my mouth half open. Everything is dark for a moment, until I see myself immersed in deep waters—an oceanic blue surrounds me.

As I swim underwater, I notice that my body is all flattened out. It looks like a rectangular surface. Its transparent color reminds me of the outer edges of a jellyfish, a thin membrane dancing with the waves. I swim through this oceanic blueness for a bit, until I notice different objects floating nearby. A black chair, a bundle of blue pens, and something that looks like Sofía's face all cluster around me. Some of the pens stick to my body surface, clinging like barnacles. The chair passes through me and disappears. My body is a filtering sieve.

I am silently absorbed but grow progressively restless.

Sofía notices it. "What's happening to you now?"

As I reposition myself on the chair, I feel an anxious pinch right in the middle of my chest.

"It's . . . it's a place with no space and no time," Sofía says softly, "a space of contact and receptivity . . . a space of transformation. . . . What's happening, Samuele?"

My anxiety loops in on itself, creating an intensity. I touch my stomach. Something hits me. The pinch turns into a punch.

I open my eyes.

. . .

During my research in Buenos Aires, which I mostly spent observing and absorbing the struggles of couples in therapy, I wasn't doing too well. I was drinking and smoking like a champion, my mother's death was haunting me, I had frequent panic and anxiety attacks, and my marriage was looping between reciprocal accusations and loving attempts to repair open wounds. In that same period, my partner and I were sharing all sorts of ideas and readings about hypnotic experience across different traditions—from Christian mysticism to psychoanalysis.[1] What if hypnosis could help me get out of this funk? A few months into my fieldwork, I embarked on a therapeutic journey with Sofía, an Ericksonian hypnotherapist.[2] As I was running in researcher mode, I thought it would be a good idea to film my weekly sessions of hypnosis and create a personal "hypno-archive" for a potential side project.[3] Of course, this was also a way to avoid facing the possibility that I *just* and *really* needed some therapy.

Session after session, this therapeutic experiment with hypnosis offered me a space to process personal losses and an overall sense of anxious stuckness. Today, as I rewatch the sessions, new losses and anxieties are layered over the recorded words of my past self. And it's both perturbing and liberating to watch my ten-years-ago self in therapy. It's hard to see, now with more clarity, how during that period I fueled the reproduction of detrimental and hurtful relational loops. It's liberating to discover how some of the psychic shifts that began during my hypnosis sessions are still part of my mode of existence—psychic shifts sustained through slow work that unfolded across a decade of breakdowns, nano-breakthroughs, and daily adjustments.

. . .

In the pages that follow, psychic transformation doesn't happen in a straight line, but rather in an oscillatory movement, a wavelike rhythm between different ways of paying attention to what unfolds around and within us.[4] Like when you have a symptom that disappears because something else calls your attention. But it's not about symptoms, really, as much as it's about seeing our lives as an oscillatory dance between things we are attached to and things we let go. I keep trying—and failing—to step into a playful acceptance of this oscillatory movement. Sometimes it feels like nothing is moving, like I am stuck in an endless circular movement. But things keep changing.

. . .

Buenos Aires, Argentina. July 2014. As I walk up the stairs before our last meeting, I catch a glimpse of Sofía's outline. She is waiting for me by the door, accompanying my arrival with the warm gaze of an almost-already lost friend. A therapist in her early sixties, Sofía has been practicing hypnosis for about thirty years in the capital.

Sofía lets me into her office. We both smile gloomily at the mention of my upcoming departure. I feel drained and ready to leave Argentina. As we sit down facing each other, Sofía turns on the video camera. I mumble something about how anxious and depressed I became during my fieldwork and how seeing so many psychotherapy sessions behind the one-way mirror threw me into a constant state of exhaustion. But Sofía replies that it's not only about my research, and she suggests that I unconsciously decided to come to Argentina to give a sense of closure to a period of mourning that began in Argentina six years before.

"This is where you were when they told you your mother was dying," she says. "These things leave a trace. This place is connected to a loss—we don't know how deep this connection between Argentina and your loss could be." Sofía scrolls through her notes of our past sessions.

"I have been reading my notes," she continues, "and I see so many emotions, a lot of fear, depressive and euphoric moments, anger, something about your research, something from your relationship, something from a deeper space, something that isn't even yours and maybe belongs to Argentina as a place. . . ."

She puts down the notebook and looks at the clock on the wall; she says we have time for one last hypnotic induction. I notice how slow and soft her voice has been for the past few minutes. I reposition myself on the couch, sinking into my breathing pattern.

. . .

The philosopher and hypnotherapist François Roustang writes that to enter a hypnotic state you simply need to sit down comfortably, find your breath, let yourself sink, and do nothing. If you really want or need to do something, you can keep your eyes open when you breathe in and close them when you breathe out. Or just sit down, comfortably, find your place, find your pace. The place where you are right here, right now is perfectly fine. Do what you are already doing, keep being where you are, breathe the way you are breathing, be comfortable in your own skin.[5]

Hypnosis is a disposition, a way to become available to what comes into presence.[6]

. . .

"What we call 'inspiration' should be taken literally," writes Merleau-Ponty (maybe playing on the double meaning of the French word *inspiration*, which can mean inspiration but also inhalation). "There really is *inspiration* and *expiration* of Being, respiration in Being, action and passion so slightly discernible that we no longer know who sees and who is seen, who paints and what is painted."[7]

. . .

"Okay, very good, let's see," Sofía says softly. "Very good, exactly, Samuele, close your eyes, this, exactly like this, feeling comfortable, really comfortable. You already know how to enter into a different state of consciousness, and we can use many techniques you know already, or none in particular. You just have to remember, Samuele, remember and recall your past trances, different states of consciousness, remember how it feels to sit comfortably in your chair. It's raining outside. The rain is falling down, and we can hear the raindrops, drop after drop after drop after drop. Do you hear the rain? Outside is Buenos Aires, the street where you live, the sounds of cars, the city. Outside is the rain, drop after drop after drop—can you hear it? Yes, like this, maybe you can close your eyes. As you know, the visual world drives us outside, outside. But you are here, inside. You are inside, sitting on your chair, trying to find a comfortable position, in this room, yes, like this, trying to find, to find a meaning to all this, to all the things you lived this year. Yes, like this, put your hands over your lap, sit comfortably."

Sofía's voice slows down. She asks me to start noticing the difference in temperature between my left hand and my right hand, between my right leg and my left leg.

"I am asking," she continues, "I am going to ask your unconscious mind to produce a very quick overview of all the things that happened to you since you came to Argentina. Only relax and be comfortable where you are. Let the images come to you. When you came here one year ago, where you went, who you saw, who you talked to, the places you went, your projects, people you met, moments you shared, things you have thought, friends you made, and your observations, what you saw, what you lived,[8] what you ate, what you drank—everything is now passing through you like a series of little images. Often, we don't realize it, but a long time passes before we can understand with clarity what we went to do in another place, to understand what the use of our experiences was. We always worry about knowing the meaning of things right away, but we need time. We need time. What happened? What happened to you this year? Even though it was a conscious choice to come here, your unconscious mind also knows what *else* happened—the consciousness of unconsciousness, the conscious ways of the unconscious."

. . .

In the early days of systemic therapy, pioneering figures like Gregory Bateson and Jay Haley incorporated the work and techniques of Milton Erickson (1901–80), an American psychiatrist who revolutionized the field of modern hypnosis.[9] It's quite common still today to find systemic therapy institutions that have an Ericksonian hypnotherapist working with them. As a hypnotherapist, Erickson developed an exemplary archive of induction techniques that aimed at "short-circuiting" the patient's conscious awareness to facilitate their therapeutic transformation.[10] Erickson's practice was grounded in the principle that when patients tried to change intentionally, they often ended up hindering their own transformative processes.[11]

Consider how easy it is to end up doing something after you decide not to do it. The innumerable times I end up drinking way more than I should, precisely when I tell myself that I won't drink at the party! The Ericksonian approach tends to tackle our issues laterally, which means to bypass conscious awareness and get some help from our unconscious resources.[12] Systemic therapists and Ericksonian hypnotherapists converge on one idea: Change often happens despite and besides our intentional attempts to provoke it.[13]

. . .

Into the Loop has focused mostly on systemic couple therapy. In "Seeing Yourself Being Seen" (chapter 1), I described how processes of identification with the gaze of others impact relational loops; in "Atmospheric Crisis" (chapter 2), I explored the transmission, accumulation, and discharge of affective forces between partners, therapists, and their environments; finally, in "Compulsive Repetition" (chapter 3), I engaged with the subjectifying force of refrains, returns, and repetitions.

This chapter brings some of these themes and questions together, but it does so laterally. We are taking a detour so we can look back at the question animating the book but from a different viewpoint—how and under which conditions can we interrupt the loops that define us? I consider here the possibilities afforded by hypnotic experience as one way to understand how we end up glued to a loop as well as how we can loosen our grip on it. But there won't be a straight answer.

I develop a lateral and refracted approach to describe hypnotic scenes that are never fully transparent; I offer images and thoughts that bear within themselves an opacity that calls for unconscious insights rather than argumentative knowledge.[14]

. . .

"Let the unconscious be unconscious," Sofía whispers, "and let your consciousness fall into an absorbed state. The unconscious knows what for and why you came here. You lived what you lived, you felt what you felt, you lost what you have lost, you are where you are now, and it's okay to be where you are. Let the images about your past year in Argentina pass in front of you in rapid succession. Different images of all the things that happened here. What is an image? An image, a sound. What is a sound? Do you hear the sound of my voice? Soon a new stage will come, a different one."

"This period in Buenos Aires," Sofía continues, "was a phase of incorporation, of embodying information, situations, smells, colors, new information—and it will be ordered and codified later. But now everything is passing through you, and it's forming the raw material with which you will build something else. What has been lived, listened, heard, forgotten, all this, this is the material you are bringing with you, and with which you will build something new, something else. You have the capacity to transform this into something different. And you will realize it when you do this different work, when you will articulate and put together your work, and realize what was the use of all this. . . ."

. . .

Hypnotic inductions are forms of communication anchored in the rapport established between hypnotizer and hypnotized, and they can take many forms—structured muscle relaxation exercises, eye fixation technique, improvised conversational detours, repeated sentences, or guided visualizations.[15] Hypnotherapists like Sofía, influenced by Milton Erickson's approach, tend to mirror the patient's language and mobilize what happens during the session to structure their inductions and suggestions.

In my case, Sofía knows how anxious I am about doing something with the data I have collected in Argentina; she also knows that I am in a difficult relationship, and she knows that I am confused about so many things. Sofía thus structures a long and drifting induction that, among other things, suggests I start embracing a psychic transformation, one that implies a patient movement between what I experienced in my past and the creation of new mediatic traces—like a piece of writing that refracts a loss that can't really be faced directly but can still be worked through when it morphs into words.

Sofía's induction is about a rearticulatory movement between unprocessed affective knots and things we build to process them; but it's also about voicing things that we don't even.

. . .

The Society of Psychological Hypnosis has agreed on a simple definition of hypnosis: "a state of consciousness involving focused attention and reduced peripheral awareness characterized by an enhanced capacity for response to suggestion."[16] Reworking this definition, we can say that the hypnotic state can be reached through inductions that involve focused attention and reduced peripheral awareness. In general terms, peripheral awareness is the capacity to perceive whatever is going on at the edges of perception: Whatever you are not looking at intentionally could fall under your peripheral awareness.[17] In reducing peripheral awareness by training your focus on a limited set of stimuli, hypnotic inductions thus constitute a reorientation of attention.

This is a somewhat limited and limiting definition of hypnosis, but to start thinking about hypnosis in this way foregrounds the fact that hypnotic inductions, to begin with, prompt the patient to cut out more and more stimuli.[18] The reduction of peripheral awareness then facilitates the patient's entrance into a hypnotic state, a space of deep affectability that heightens the sensory impact of what the patient is seeing, imagining, or perceiving: Smells can get more intense, memories can be perceived more vividly, visualizations feel more real, or a social media post can flawlessly hit the vibrating center of your soul.[19]

. . .

The progressive elimination of stimuli can also be obtained through a binary oscillation between two poles. The patient is asked to focus on the inside and then the outside, the left and the right, the cold and the warm, the conscious and the unconscious—as when Sofía suggests I think about the rain outside, then about me sitting indoors, then about the city's noises, then my inner sensations. This oscillation between poles has the soothing effect of being rocked back and forth by a slow, repetitive, and embracing rhythm. A whispered lullaby singing, *where does one thing start, where does it end?*

. . .

The idea is to bring the patient into a space, as Sofía says in the opening image of this chapter, of transformation, contact, and receptivity. A space of suggestibility. When we are in that space, we become more available to be affected by whatever comes our way—in my case here, more affectable by the hypnotherapist's words. There are many ways to understand and define this space.

We can consider this space as a state, a liminal state where our usual way of being in the world is somewhat suspended, disturbed, and dis-organized—think about people entering a trance while following the repetitive rhythm of drums during a dispossession ritual.[20]

The anthropologist Tanya Luhrmann writes about spiritual experiences in terms of "absorption," which she considers a "mental capacity common to trance, hypnosis, dissociation, and perhaps imagination itself."[21] In a state of absorption, whatever you are imagining and focusing on seems "more real to you," and the world around you can "seem different than before."[22]

There is also a wide range of theories in psychology that describe hypnotic absorption as a creative flow state, one that allows you to tackle problems and hyperfocus in a completely different way—because your unconscious is at work.[23]

I am mentioning different names and theories about this space so you can relate to it in case you have never had an experience with hypnosis. Different theories, of course, might point at radically different phenomena. And the more I read and think about it, the less I know what it is, exactly, that I am talking about when I am talking about hypnosis.

. . .

Freud writes about the relationship between the patient and the hypnotist to explain the experience of being in love, which involves the blurring of the boundaries between the loving subject and the loved object. When you fall in love, your boundaries tremble and shake, and you are projected into this bubbly space in between you and your loved one, a space that exceeds you both. This bubble-like "interpersonal space," Peter Sloterdijk writes, is "overcrowded with symbiotic, erotic and mimetic-competitive energies that fundamentally deny the illusion of subject autonomy."[24]

This hypnotic space amplifies, or makes possible, processes like projective identification and affective transmission.[25] In the hypnotic love bubble, lovers can leave a trace, or make a dent, in each other's psychic life. Freud suggests that in this shared hypnotic space, the loved object can even take over, and hold captive, the lover's ego.[26]

In the hypno-bubble, to borrow from William Mazzarella, "I become myself through you, but I also lose myself in you."[27] Echoing Sloterdijk, Mazzarella describes this bubble-like space in terms of *constitutive resonance*, which is "a relation of mutual becoming rather than causal determination."[28]

Hypnotic attachments transform the lover's sense of self.[29]

In Freud's perspective, the relationship between the hypnotizer and the hypnotized offers deep insights into the dynamic of the romantic couple form, where partners in love tend to loosen the grip from their own ego, their individual boundaries interweaving to form a love bubble. The bubble can be activated and brought into existence with a focused attention given to one person, the one who makes everybody else disappear—think about the classic movie scene where the camera zooms in on the face of the beloved and leaves everything else in a blurry background.[30]

. . .

"What's happening to you, Samuele, right now? What do you see?" Sofía asks me.

I have heard Sofía's question, but I can't speak. My eyes are closed. A shape suddenly emerges from the darkness of my vision. I see a spherical grayish bubble coming out of my chest. The bubble slowly floats outside of me but is still tethered to my body. The bubble glimmers, it looks soft, and it's filled with small images; the images inside the bubble are inside tiny rectangular screens that move across, and are folded within, the bubble's bubbliness. A sphere holding a bunch of rectangles.

On each little rectangle, I see different images flickering through; some images emit a crisp luminosity, some are all fuzzy. I see a sidewalk in Buenos Aires, a screaming couple, a crying patient in therapy, Brenda's face looking at me through the one-way mirror, flashing screens that turn into dark mirrors, a shattered wineglass, two white armchairs, a broken mirror, something that breathes through the fragments, something that breaks. The gray bubble pulses in front of my chest as if it had its own breathing pattern—a glimmering bubble breathing through the images it holds captive.

. . .

"It's like"—I start talking slowly—"I feel . . . I am seeing a sphere. It's a bubble. A soap bubble coming out from my chest, but it's still attached, I can see it being outside of me, but it's as if I also want to bring it back inside." I move my hands, pushing the sphere back into my chest. "It's circular, it's a circular movement. It comes out, it goes back inside."

"Yes, like this, very good." Sofía encourages me. "Yes, it's circular, circular, it's outside and goes back inside, in a circular way, exactly."

I describe to Sofía some of the images I am seeing inside the bubble. My hands are forming a sphere to hold the bubble in front of my chest, then I push it back into my chest—and it comes out again.

"Yes, like this, very good." Sofía encourages me. "Yes, it's a circular bubble, it's outside and goes back inside, in a circular way, exactly. It will be introjected again, and it will come out again. It will come out again . . . but with a different form. It's the sphere's process of coming and going. You incorporate it, and when it comes out again, it will be different. . . . After you take the sphere back inside, you let it out again. It's a work of transformation, a circular movement between different moments, different movements, different forms."

. . .

The oscillatory proposition of this chapter rests upon the tension between hypnotic inductions and the hypnotic states these inductions carry us toward. There is a strange shape to this oscillation. Hypnotic inductions work like some kind of funnel, progressively filtering out all but a few stimuli. But then, no matter the technique, if the induction is sustained or repeated long enough, and if the situation allows it, the hypnotic experience suddenly opens out into a space of receptivity, affectability, and potential transformation.

It's as though the hypnotic induction has brought the patient through the narrow end of the funnel, some sort of psychic threshold between the hypnotic induction proper and the hypnotic state—the narrowest tip of the funnel turns into the edge of a wide-open mouth of another funnel.[31]

You can think of this as a double-funnel model to imagine the relation between hypnotic inductions and hypnotic states—or an hourglass-shaped model. Attention and affectability contracting and expanding in an oscillating rhythm.

. . .

When asked about hypnosis, most of my students talk about spectacularized forms of stage hypnosis where a patient, spectator, or victim falls under the influence of the hypnotist—they describe the hypnotist as a charlatan tricking people into believing something that isn't real (or is it?).[32] A common image my students use to represent hypnosis in their end-of-semester video projects is the hypnotic black-and-white spinning spiral—and I never thought a spiral could look so evil.

There is indeed something unsettling about hypnotic phenomena, which have been studied and mobilized in a wide range of practices and disciplines, from Mesmer's "animal magnetism" to psychoanalysis and neuroscience.[33] What's particularly unsettling is that hypnosis invites us to revisit our understanding of what it means to be conscious and to have control over our own self.

The loops and affects I describe in this book prompt us to pay attention to processes and forces that exceed yet shape our individuality. Hypnosis foregrounds similar questions: To what extent are you actually autonomous, actually in control, actually . . . *you*?

· · ·

My hands keep holding the sphere in front of my chest. The bubble shrinks and expands at the movement of its own breath. Sinking into the armchair, I try to focus on all the images the bubble holds.

"Everything transforms you," Sofía says. "Everything touches and affects us when we are in this [hypnotic] space, but after this session, our last session, you have to go your own way, knowing that you added a step more in a journey you chose without much consciousness but with deep reasons."

"Now, Samuele," Sofía continues after a slow and deep inhalation, "I ask your unconscious mind to hold onto the images you are seeing inside this bubble, so that it can process them, so that it can process them in the way that the unconscious knows how to process them; in the upcoming days and more than anything during your nights, when your mind is most at work. Good . . . very, very good."

I breathe in my drowsiness and breathe it out, sinking even deeper into the armchair.

· · ·

I wrote these sections breathing in with closed eyes and breathing out with my eyes open.

· · ·

I am now bringing your attention to a specific and very partial aspect of hypnosis. But if you have read the previous chapters, you probably already know that I am fond of big, wide, and all-encompassing definitions. In these pages, I consider hypnosis as a particular register of attention (the induction part) and affectability (the state part). Hypnosis requires a reorientation of what we are paying attention to, which can then enhance our affectability.[34] This happens in a social relationship between the hypnotizer and the hypnotized, but it can also happen outside the therapist's office.

Indeed, any socially inflected punctuation of our cognitive skills can be understood as a hypnotic induction. This view offers a frame of reference to consider how cultural contexts shape our collective regimes of attention—through a hypnotic reorientation of what we pay attention to. This relatively wide (and super-narrow) view of hypnosis can help us rethink the relationship between hypnosis and screens, hypnosis and culture, hypnosis and love, hypnosis and writing.

. . .

But then I hit a thinking wall when I ask myself, when are we *not* under some form of hypnotic induction that makes us privilege some stimuli over others? When are we *not* in a state of suggestibility?

. . .

You go in and out of mild trance states multiple times during your day.[35] Like when you read these lines and feel absorbed by them, maybe so absorbed that your surroundings start fading out.[36] Or when you didn't realize how quickly you got home because you were so absorbed in that Marie Kondo podcast but couldn't help also starting to scroll on your phone, and you almost got hit by that person who was also on their phone while biking, and you both almost didn't see each other. Almost.

. . .

Today's algorithmic forms of governance work so well because they generate perfectly personalized hypnotic inductions.[37] Think about scrolling on Tik-Tok, for example, how the app feeds you only what you always already want and quickly eliminates undesired content that could potentially snap you out of your binge.[38] As you scroll, your peripheral awareness is reduced by content funnels, but it's also reduced through the repetitive (and ritual) movements of the scrolling action itself—your hand holding the phone, your thumb going up and down, up and down, up and down, up and down, up and . . .

This gets your body ready to hop on the trance-train.

And once you hop on the T-train, you morph into the one and only addressee of digital influencers who are talking to *you* as-*you* inside a hypno-bubble that allows for all sorts of affective exchanges and identifications between you and the screen.[39] When you are in this bubble dancing to the rhythm of a digital binge, you get to be "dreamed-through" by algorithmic parasites that sneak into your organism. These little beasts enter your body and conquer even the most remote corners of your soul.[40]

So now parts of you literally dream the dreams of these machinic bugs—and they have planted a nice big waving flag in the midst of your psyche, marking their territory.[41]

. . .

Repetition: Changing what we pay attention to impacts what we can be affected by.[42]

. . .

That's how you end up there, moving your thumb up and down, up and down, up and down, with a half-open mouth and the posture of a grumpy teenager—openly affectable. But you are not playing with your own images, you are not rearticulating your relationship with the world, you are not in a creative flow, and there is no Sofía holding space for you. You are being rearticulated and dreamed-through by machinic assemblages that transform the data you produce into value across the infosphere.[43]

. . .

"What's happening now, Samuele?" Sofía asks.

I try to reply, but my voice doesn't come through. My body is a porous surface of contact floating through oceanic blueness. Something hits me and vanishes, something clings to me like a barnacle, something passes through me leaving a faint trace. Something—I can't even see. I squeeze my eyes shut.

. . .

The imagination of the patient under hypnosis is enhanced through the loosening of what Freud called the critical faculty of the ego, a loosening that allows the emergence of unconscious images coming from the patient's imagistic reservoir.[44] It's like tuning into the images populating our unconscious or connecting to an internal space that allows us to enter some sort of a dream world. Within this space, it becomes possible to reorganize our relationship with these images or to reinsert new images through guided and intentional visualizations.

This reorganization can happen because under hypnosis people are often still aware of themselves and their own thought processes—hypnotic trance seems indeed to be characterized by an entanglement between fuzzy relaxation and lucid awareness.[45] Hypnosis is not sleep, and it's not wakefulness either.[46]

This is why François Roustang defines hypnosis a form of *veille paradoxale*, a paradoxical wakefulness.[47]

. . .

Following what I write in chapter 3, if we understand the images populating our imagistic reservoir as unconscious *dispositifs*, we can consider how images have the hypnotic power to define our subjectivity through processes of identification. I wrote in chapter 1 about how identifying with something means to become like the object we identify with—and how an important type of identification happens through the incorporation of someone else's gaze.

In a similar sense, the images that users absorb when in a hypnotic state in front of the screen become magnetic attractors for potential identificatory processes. Have you ever spent so much time watching a TV show that you start dreaming about it, or even acquire some of the mannerisms of a character in the show?[48] It happens so easily because the screen enthralls you. It puts you very quickly into a hypnotic state, and it's like plugging your unconscious into a suggestive dream station that pumps images into your veins—and these imagistic *dispositifs* make you available to very specific orders of reality.[49] It's so easy because the screen's hypnotic inductions make you affectively available. You are in front of the screen, after all, to get your affective fix.

. . .

Flickering inside the bubble, I saw this image of us glued to a burning spiral of reciprocal accusations—we formed a loopy bundle of rage attached to this spiral on fire, and no one wanted to let go. You screamed, I screamed, we spiraled. In a continuously rotating motion—we burned.

. . .

Images have a particular capacity to affect us. The affect theorist Brian Massumi writes about the "primacy of the affective in image reception" to suggest that we perceive images affectively long before we can make sense of them through our conscious cognition.[50] Lisa Stevenson, who calls for an imagistic anthropology, writes that images have the capacity to "express without formulating" precisely because they resist transparent and discursive meaning.[51] This resistance, which makes images fundamentally opaque, might be the reason images can exert an affective pull over us.

Think, for example, about the clusters of images tethered to what Berlant calls the "good life." As I explored in chapter 2, the imaginary of the good life can hold captive your affective life, orient your expectations about what it should look like to be in a relationship, what it should look like to have access to the good life.[52] Cruel optimism entails a hypnotic relationship to our objects of attachment. It's not just that we desire the good life: We are hypnotized by its cluster of images.[53]

. . .

The things that affect you can have a hypnotic hold over you, which means that affect is influence. And this is how hypnosis too can be understood—as influence.[54] When we are in front of our screens, we are literally washed over by a restless bonanza of digital influencers: So why not drift aside from their influencing and influence ourselves instead? Why not try to learn how to play with images and to develop our own bubbly imagistic practices? An imagistic practice, as I understand it, allows us to be in touch with the images that populate our unconscious, to activate or reorganize our imagistic archives or, to use William Mazzarella's wider notion, our "mimetic archives."

Mazzarella defines the *mimetic archive* as something "embedded not only in the explicitly articulated forms commonly recognized as cultural discourses but also in built environments and material forms, in the concrete history of the senses and in the habits of our shared embodiment."[55] Mimetic archives can hold and fold within themselves sedimented images that have been lying dormant in our collective and individual unconscious.[56] Imagistic practices can activate or reactivate images that have been suppressed or forgotten, just as they can choregraph new imagistic compositions.

To tap into parallel, subversive, or transformative imagistic archives, we can engage with a wide range of practices. I am thinking, among other possibilities, about lucid dreaming, visualizations of all kinds, psychedelic experience, meditation, or spiritual rituals. My point here is that the images we hold within ourselves—conscious or unconscious—have the capacity to orient and shape our desires and expectations. And to learn how to play with images can lay the ground for a life slightly less territorialized by parasitic images that dream through us without our consent. If ever so slightly.

Of course, as I indirectly suggest in chapter 3, it's not a question of freedom from dominant imagistic *dispositifs* but rather about a movement of "liberation and capture" between *dispositifs*.[57]

. . .

After my father passed away in 2021—a rather violent and angry death—I developed an imagistic practice that I find so soft and warm. Toward the end of my morning routine, I imagine my father and my mother on the sides of a waterfall in the middle of a forest—my father is usually on the right and my mother on the left. The waterfall is on top of a small hill inside the forest, and it's surrounded by rocks. I go toward them until I see them close to me. Sometimes my parents are just there looking at me with the waterfall behind them. Sometimes my dad is dancing, which is nice to see because he was heavily disabled all his life. My mom is often dancing and laughing, which is kind of how she was until she died. Then I go toward the waterfall, and the water usually transforms into this bright light—a waterfall resting on an invisible luminosity.

My parents bless the water, and I take some of it into my hands and pour it over my head. The color of this light can change—some mornings it's blue, sometimes it's white, sometimes all the colors. Then I hug my mom and dad and tell them I love them—I hug them so tight that I bring them inside my chest. I incorporate them, I eat them up, like eating their spirit bodies through my chest.[58] And now they are inside, like spirit *dispositifs*, imagistic orienting devices.[59] The next morning, they will be back out again, by the waterfall, telling me that it's okay, that sometimes it's okay not to be okay, that I just need to rest within this circular movement, so I can let go and fall within the relaxing dance of being and not being.[60]

. . .

My hands still holding a sphere in front of my chest, I try to open my mouth to hear the vibration of my own voice, but I feel heavy and drowsy. I am pulled back toward the bubble, new images flickering across it. "Yes, Samuele sink into it, sink into these images." Sofía's voice carries the warmth of an elsewhere gliding across the air in between us.

"I see surfaces," I tell her, "horizontal planes cutting through the sphere. There are colors now, the images are colored, there is a liquid paint moving through the screens, words, writings. It's some fluid, a dark orange color falling through planes, like drops of color passing from plane to plane, now there is a word on one of the screens, now it's just colors."

"Yes, like this." Sofía encourages me. "Horizontal surfaces, of course, you often said you lived many vertical experiences here, in this metaphor you use often, yes, there is the need to horizontalize, in order to transmit it, no? They are expressive surfaces. . . . What's this color dropping through planes?"

I mumble something, saying that the color is turning into a vibration coming out of my chest, a sound, a frequency.

"Your voice?" Sofía tentatively whispers, "Now you are still assimilating what will afterward transform into a sound, a frequency, color surfaces, concepts, personal experiences. Good, very good."

. . .

The wide-funnel-mouth-state is fun. You could even keep pushing through and maybe reach other, deeper stages, but let's not get too psychedelic. You are in a state where you can see images, play with them. Things feel fuzzy, creative, and connected. It can be scary, but it's mostly beautiful when you relax into this state's movements.

You can't stay there all the time, however, because the world calls you back into presence. It narrows your focus again into its regimes of attention. So there is this movement, this coming and going between two stages or states of being. That's the oscillatory movement I am thinking about. It's a movement that is about latching onto something to let it go to latch onto it to let it go again.

. . .

Would you believe me if I told you that this whole book project started with the bubble image? A bunch of tiny little screens folded within a circular bubbly movement.

. . .

I didn't share the image I had of the bubble when under hypnosis to show you how much more exciting it would be to produce your own images, as opposed to scrolling through your algorithmic feeds. The point would rather be about developing new and collective forms of image work, ones that could move us away from the images produced by the scrolling society. I don't know what collective image work would look like because I need some help, or my images will always be as banal as a bubble coming out of my chest.

I am wondering, for example, what it would mean to curate our algorithmic feeds to avoid consuming all sorts of racist, ableist, and sexist content that promotes an unconscious assimilation of normative ideals of what a body should look like—this can be imagined as a collective practice that slowly erodes the dominant presence of some images over others.

Maybe we could get together with our circles of friends and share our feeds to discuss them and think about what these images are doing for us.[61] Would you be ashamed of your feed if your friends could see it? Or we could get together for a collective session of hypnotic visualizations and share the images that are bursting through our bodies to explore them together. Or something else that I am too trapped in my own loops to imagine.

. . .

I say this also thinking about how new forms of psychedelic capitalism tend to reproduce dominant imaginaries. Even psychedelics, after all, are context dependent.[62] And a good chunk of contemporary psychedelic image work seems indeed devoted to reinforcing specific values and anxieties about individual freedom, creativity, productivity, brain hacking, productivity, and also more productivity—from neocolonial ayahuasca tourism to microdosing LSD before hopping on the self-driving bus toward an open-floor office in Silicon Valley.[63]

. . .

And that's where the relative uselessness of the bubble image finds a soft spot in my thinking. A bubbly image about a circular movement, about a work of transformation that can't be understood in linear terms. About something that doesn't need to be particularly spectacular, miraculous, or sudden. The loopy bubble comes in and out, and I have to keep working with whatever is inside of it—some things leave the bubble, some stay.

It's a nonlinear process that doesn't need to have a quantifiable output. It's about staying with the bubble, attending to it, while transforming things, changing my relationship to them across time, rearticulating them. Slowly. The bubble is not completely outside me, like the transitional objects I wrote about in chapter 3. The bubble is just an image, but its morphing softness can envelop, affect, and refract a world filled to the brim with possibilities.[64]

. . .

"What are we doing here, Samuele?" Sofía smiles at me and then looks out the window. "Sometimes I wonder," she continues, "what are you going to do with all of this. . . ."

. . .

The fragments I draw from my hypno-archive also offer a refracted way to think about data and knowledge in the contemporary condition. In 2008, Chris Anderson provocatively proclaimed the end of theory, heralding the arrival of a new godly assemblage: Big Data.[65] *Dataism* promises a transparent and predictive knowledge of individual behaviors as much as social systems, viral transmissions, and cosmic events.[66] Despite innumerable algorithmic failures and infrastructural biases, data-logical thinking occupies a central position in the humanities and the social sciences as well.[67] Why go and talk to someone to ask them how they are doing when you can access their heart rate, generate a word cloud of their social media posts, or get to know how many milliseconds they focused on a section of the screen? Or why go talk to someone if you can watch them through a one-way mirror instead?[68]

. . .

It's not about being data-phobic. I write this knowing that my daily life is punctuated by interactions with data-driven platforms that define the way I get to know myself, understand my "progress," and measure my state of being. Most of my practices are based on a data-logical quantification of my existence that helps me stay afloat.[69]

But these types of data are just that, types of data, and they can't be the only input through which we get to know ourselves, our relationships, and our planetary condition.[70] What types of data emerge through lucid dreaming or hypnosis, for example? What can these modes, and the data they generate, tell us about our affective attachments?

Can hypnosis help us rethink our loops?

. . .

Here is a lateral quote that exceeds the context of this chapter but that launched me into its writing: "Precisely because the plane of immanence is prephilosophical and does not immediately take effect with concepts, it implies a sort of groping experimentation and its layout resorts to measures that are not very respectable, rational, or reasonable. These measures belong to the order of dreams, of pathological processes, esoteric experiences, drunkenness and excess. We head for the horizon, on the plane of immanence, and we return with bloodshot eyes, yet they are the eyes of the mind. Even Descartes had his dream. To think is always to follow the witch's flight."[71]

. . .

During some of my hypnosis sessions, the images that emerged seemed to have a very clear meaning for me and the work I was trying to do. But sometimes these experiences didn't produce much that could be mobilized, used, translated, transformed, analyzed. There were so many things inside that bubble that I couldn't see. For this type of data, the most manifest meaning might in fact be the least interesting.[72] Freud suggests that when we are interpreting unconscious images produced through dreaming, we have to accept that at the core of our dreams there is a dark vanishing point that destabilizes our attempts to make sense of them.[73] Freud calls this the dream's navel, "the spot where [the dream] reaches down into the unknown."[74] The opaque navel of the dream is in contrast with the ideals of transparency and legibility that characterizes dataism.[75]

. . .

The word *data* is the plural of the Latin *datum*, which is the past participle of the verb *dare*, to give. The Latin *datum* can thus be translated in English as "that which has been given." Our relationship to data could become so much more generative if we start thinking about them as gifts or presents.[76] The present (as gift) is a material vessel carrying the intention and *presence* of someone or something else—something that isn't enclosed within the vessel, or at least not fully captured by it.

That's the beautiful hermeneutics of gifts, which are never really what they are—the way we receive them really depends on what we assume they mean; and the closer we are with the person giving us the gift, the more meaning we attach to it.[77]

. . .

One day I gave you a piece of paper I found in the street, and you thought it was the most amazing thing I ever gave you—the other day I gave you that other thing I have been planning for a month, and you said it was obvious I didn't love you anymore.

. . .

The datum is something that has been packaged by someone for a specific purpose, which means it's not a neutral object. The datum is a present that could have infinitely different meanings depending on the context—who is giving it, who is receiving it, when and how. I say this because it could be important, in this historical moment, to receive digital data with the ambivalence you would feel when receiving a gift from someone whose intentions you mistrust. "Is this *really* for me?"

. . .

We could also ask the same question of our unconscious when we have strange dreams or images that we don't fully understand: Is this really for me? Because your unconscious also wants things for you, and the problem is that most of the times, what it wants are not your desires but someone else's. For example, the desires of those little algorithmic beasts I was talking about before, or the projected desires or affects of your partner, as I explored in the past chapters. That's what Jacques Lacan would say about this: Your desire, in fact, is not your own because it holds within itself the relational and symbolic order you have incorporated as you developed as a subject.[78]

. . .

A few weeks after my mother died in 2009, I dreamed about her calling me on my flip phone. In the dream, I was worried about my mom's state of health, but she kept telling me that she was doing very well—all immersed as she was in her fluffy celestial clouds over the Mediterranean Sea. The dream was so vivid that I still remember it as if it happened yesterday—her voice rising above the waves and reaching my ears from the belly of the dream. A few days after my dad died in 2021, I dreamed I was on a Zoom call with him and my sister. I was similarly asking about how he was doing, but I couldn't hear him clearly, and the video kept freezing. I don't remember much else about the dream, except this image of my frozen father inside a digital rectangle.[79]

. . .

Buenos Aires, Argentina. April 2014. I am sitting in Sofía's office with my eyes closed. We are talking about how, for the past few weeks, I have had a burning sensation on my left arm together with a tingling on the tip of my fingers.[80] After a short hypnotic induction, Sofía asks me to visualize myself in front of a mirror. I sink into my breathing pattern and imagine myself in my bedroom, in front of the mirror. I see my face. I am wearing a green shirt and a pair of jeans. I look at my arms reflected in the mirror, and I notice that my left arm is missing.

"Hmm, good, good, your left arm is missing. . . . What else?" Sofía asks.

I focus on my absent limb. The empty space replacing my arm suddenly catches fire. My ghost-arm-on-fire keeps burning, and my body progressively disappears from the mirror I am facing. I can only see my burning arm piercing through the mirror and reaching out.

"Hmm, hmm . . . very good," Sofía comments. "Maybe the arm is your connection to the real, or whatever you want to call it, affects and emotions, a connection with the sensory world. With the other arm, you write and codify. This burning arm connects you to things, and the other transforms them—maybe it writes? Yes, two parts, two hands, and one is on fire, good, very good."

Sofía lingers on a shared silence. "It's a very emotional image," she continues, "and it's also just an image. Maybe one hand writes and the other gathers through fire—the arm on fire connects you to the world, and these connections . . . they are data, they are impressions, sensations, emotions, that later will undergo a series of transformations. They will come out, but only after you have absorbed enough.

"You transform what you came here to absorb, and you are already doing it because this happens beyond your will—maybe there is an unconscious desire, maybe you have an anxiety about losing control over the process, not knowing where you are going.... Samuele, where are you now?"

. . .

In an essay about Hegel and animal magnetism, Jean-Luc Nancy writes that *affectedness* is "nothing but the possession of alteration as a property."[81] This means that when something affects us, it transforms us. Affectedness or affectability, as the capacity to alter oneself through an encounter with what is other, is one of the central properties of the living.[82] To resist change is to set aside, repress, or cancel out what has the capacity to affect us. To resist change is to keep surfing the wave of a hypnotic induction without entering a wider space of affectability. To resist change is to repress the fact that a part of our being is wired into this burning fire, one that knows more than we do.

. . .

"Good, good," Sofía continues, "let the arm burn, let it do its work, then when you have absorbed enough you will use the other arm, that side of you that decodes, organizes, articulates, writes, produces. But you are still here, you are still receiving it. Now just let it burn and be with your arm on fire. The moment of transformation will come, like it always does."

I am impatient—a bad patient without patience—I want to leave this hypnotic state and interrupt the visualization. I want to leave the room and the therapy session. Fieldwork, relationships, ideas, couples, loops, lost relationships, dead parents, gazes—I want to let them all go.

My left arm is burning. I can feel its pulsing heat. I bring my attention to my own impatience and breathe within it; I follow the fire's heat and let it pass through my arm, then across my neck and down my spine. A warm tingling expands across my back. The fire sucks out the light around itself and produces more darkness. The mirror is gone. The heat moves again from my left hand to my upper back and then reaches my right hand. I breathe deeply, slowly. I am not feeling too well.

I move restlessly on the chair.

"Samuele, you can open your eyes now if you want," Sofía soothes me.

My left arm is burning. I let myself slip into its dark and luminous fire.

I open my eyes.

OUTRO

I wrote the first draft of *Into the Loop* with the angry angst of a joyfully lost teenager running back home under the rain of a cold dawn while crying, laughing, or singing after having done something stupid, or something vital, or something like that. The pouring rain carrying the salt of tears to the corners of my mouth, running with the incoordination I gain when texturing sentences in my mind, or knitting conceptual pillows I will sink into once back home.

The last revision was undertaken with an aspirational desire to embrace movement through stillness, to smooth some of the sharp angles, to slow down my paranoid reactions to academic forms of thinking, and, overall, to write with a different breathing pattern. Maybe it's still dawn, but I am standing still in front of the window, holding a pose longer than I thought I could, and I start feeling a vital warmth that, from the bottom of my feet, wraps me into something I can't call mine.

Both writing modes, the laughing-crying-running-idiot and the wannabe-Daoist, have been, fundamentally, ways to voice a silent scream, one that tends toward the infinite motions of becoming pulsing behind the icy realization that some things, always one too many, have been lost—some let go, some the grip didn't hold, some abruptly disappeared, some violence took them, some love took them. I mourn them all, lovingly. I mourn them all with the loving awareness that their departure forced me to dance over the beats of decompositional transformations.

. . .

I wrote these pages indexing a constellation of missed encounters with what has been lost, I wrote to fill the voids in between us, I wrote to reach toward you with the fuzzy warmth of a question one asks just before falling asleep.

Notes

INTRODUCTION

1. This book's ethnographic materials were observed and recorded in Spanish. I have transcribed all my recordings directly from Spanish to English and modified spoken sentences to make them more readable to the English reader while retaining the meaning and tone of the speaker's words. I leave in brackets words that didn't find a happy translation. This project received Ethics Approval from UC Berkeley. All patients agreed to be observed and recorded during their therapy sessions.

2. Adapted from the *New Oxford American Dictionary*.

3. For a cosmic anthropology of systems and system theory, see Olson, *Into the Extreme*. On cybernetics, see Wiener, *Cybernetics*; for an intellectual and scientific history of the cybernetic era, see Heims, *The Cybernetics Group*; on the historical relationship between cybernetics and systemic family therapy, see Weinstein, *The Pathological Family*.

4. Weinstein, *The Pathological Family*, 6. Weinstein explores how in postwar America the family turned into a visual and performative object of study as well as a therapeutic site of intervention. In addition to systemic therapy, see, for example, the use of one-way mirrors in the Strange Situation Procedure experiment that grounds attachment theory (as in Ainsworth et al., *Patterns of Attachment*). I further discuss the Strange Situation Procedure in chapter 3.

5. The famous essay by Gregory Bateson, Don Jackson, and Jay Haley on the role of the "double bind" in schizophrenic symptom formation well represents how cybernetic theories of communication participated in the development of systemic therapy (see Bateson et al., "Toward a Theory of Schizophrenia"). The Mental Research Institute in Palo Alto, California, played a crucial role in the development of systemic therapy. More widely, the systemic model has played a particularly important role in the fields of family and couple therapy (see Weinstein, *The Pathological Family*).

6. See Bateson, "The Cybernetics of 'Self.'" Clifford Geertz has famously described the Western conception of the person—as "a bounded, unique, more or less integrated motivational and cognitive universe, a dynamic center of awareness, emotion, judgment and

action"—as "a rather peculiar idea within the context of world's cultures" ("From the Native's Point of View," 59).

7. Bateson, "The Cybernetics of 'Self,'" 331.

8. I am here resonating with the work of my dear friend and colleague Eduardo Kohn, who writes about the eco-logical "we" that emerges from whatever "I" we think we are (see Kohn, "Forest Forms and Ethical Life").

9. Bateson, "The Cybernetics of 'Self,'" 319.

10. Bateson even proposes to rethink the alcoholic's returns to the bottle as a surrender to a force that actually affords a more "correct" experience of a loop that exceeds the self ("The Cybernetics of 'Self,'" 313). I am here forcing a bit Bateson's own perspective considering his critical take on the very notion of "force" in favor of the notions of "difference" and "information" (see Bateson, "Pathologies of Epistemology").

11. In Collu, "#Zoombies," I write about an anthropology beneath, beyond, and despite the human, borrowing from Eduardo Kohn's anthropology beyond the human (see Kohn, *How Forests Think*).

12. For a recent exploration of cybernetics and behavioral loops, see, for example, Resch and Parzer, "Cybernetics and Behavioral Loops."

13. I am here thinking, among others, about Maggie Nelson, *The Argonauts*; Kathleen Stewart, *Ordinary Affects*; Lauren Berlant and Kathleen Stewart, *The Hundreds*; Susan Lepselter, *The Resonance of Unseen Things*; Lisa Stevenson, *Life Beside Itself*; Stefania Pandolfo, *Knot of the Soul*; Michael Taussig, *The Mastery of Non-Mastery*; Robert Desjarlais, *The Blind Man*. See also Anand Pandian and Stuart McLean's collection of experimental and literary anthropological writings, *Crumpled Paper Boat*. Before writing, I keep my typing fingers nourished with the poetic voices of authors like Valeria Luiselli, *Faces in the Crowd*; Emily Ogden, *On Not Knowing*; Mary Ruefle, *Madness, Rack, and Honey*; Elizabeth Hardwick, *Sleepless Nights*; and Joyelle McSweeney, *Death Styles*, among others.

14. This section animates a slightly different two hundred words cowritten with Eric Taggart. See Collu and Taggart, "Rest So Deep Now."

15. I am here thinking about Lisa Stevenson, who, after reading a draft of this manuscript, said, "Yes, but . . . is a loop a loop a loop?"

16. According to the World Health Organization, between 2015 and 2017 in Argentina there were about 226 psychologists for every 100,000 inhabitants. As a point of comparison, in the United States there were 30 psychologists per 100,000. Numbers are even higher in Buenos Aires, where there seem to be 1,572 psychotherapists for every 100,000 inhabitants. I take this information from Marsilli-Vargas's recent book on psychoanalytic genres of listening in Buenos Aires (*Genres of Listening*, 109).

17. The anthropologist Sergio Visacovsky writes about psychoanalysis in Argentina as a national "secular theodicy" often mobilized to understand individual and collective distress ("La constitución de un sentido práctico"). During Argentina's 2000–2001 economic crisis, for example, psychoanalysts were part of a public conversation, one that asked whether psychoanalysis could address the causes and consequences of the national economic crisis (see Plotkin and Visacovsky, "Los psicoanalistas y la crisis"). In "Armed Against Unhappiness," the anthropologist Sean Brotherton writes about psychoanalysis as a cultural "grammar."

18. See Plotkin (*Freud in the Pampas; Argentina on the Couch*). See also Dagfal, *Entre Paris y Buenos Aires*, on the impact of French psychoanalysis on Argentina; and Vezzetti, *Aventuras de Freud en el país de los argentinos*, on the history of psychoanalysis in Argentina. For an ethnography of Argentinean psychotherapeutic culture in Buenos Aires's marginalized areas, see María Epele's work ("Psychotherapy, Psychoanalysis and Urban Poverty in Argentina"; "Breaking Down"). See also Mariano Plotkin and Nicolás Viotti's exploration of the heterogeneous entanglement between secular and religious therapeutic practices in Buenos Aires ("Between Freud and Umbanda"). Psychotherapy is extensively present in Argentinean TV shows, reality TV, and movies. I am thinking, for example, among many others, about *Historias de Diván* (Juan José Jusid), a 2013 TV show based on the homonymous book by the Argentinean psychoanalyst Gabriel Rolón, who played an important role in bridging psychoanalysis with self-help culture (see Papalini, "Recetas para sobrevivir a las exigencias del neocapitalismo"). See also *Vulnerables* (dir. Daniel Barone and Adrián Suar), a 1999–2000 TV series on group therapy, or the 2012–14 Argentinean adaptation of the Israeli TV show *BeTipul* (dir. Ori Sivan) titled *En Terapia* (dir. Alejandro Maci).

19. As Plotkin points out in *Argentina on the Couch*, twelve years after the restoration of democracy in Argentina, Army Chief of Staff General Balsa made a public appearance on television and spoke about the past military dictatorship in terms of the nation's "unconscious traumas" (1).

20. I didn't convince him, not even a little bit.

21. On the role of family therapy and social psychology in Argentina see Macchioli, "Inicios de la terapia familiar en la Argentina."

22. See Vezzetti, "From the Psychiatric Hospital to the Street." As Vezzetti writes, "Although it is impossible to evaluate the real impact of this intervention on the life of the city, the experience reflected a shift from the private therapeutic to a public and popular psychoanalysis conceived and practiced directly over society" (141).

23. I am thinking here about the front page of an issue of the *Revista Ñ* I saw during fieldwork in 2013, which had the title "El psicoanálisis saca el diván a la calle" [Psychoanalysis takes the couch to the street]—the cover had a drawing of Freud and Lacan walking with a (psychoanalytic) couch in the street (with an ambulance in the background).

24. See Marsilli-Vargas, *Genres of Listening*, on multifamily structured psychoanalytic treatment.

25. The process of observing the observers and focusing on their therapeutic impact is part of what has been called second-order cybernetics in family therapy. See, for example, Smith and Karam, "Second-Order Cybernetics in Family Systems Theory."

26. I am here thinking about, and resonating with, recent works that explore the entanglement between media and psychotherapy. In particular, Hannah Zeavin's *The Distance Cure* shows how communication technologies—from letters to radio to the phone to algorithmic auto-intimacy—are, in fact, an integral part of the fantasies, promises, and accomplishment of different psychotherapeutic models. See also Jeremy Greene's *The Doctor Who Wasn't There* for a historical analysis of the relationship between communication technologies and mediated clinical encounters. More specifically, on the mediati-

zation of psychoanalysis in Buenos Aires, see Marsilli-Vargas, "The Offline and Online Mediatization of Psychoanalysis."

27. This seems different from therapy sessions filmed with the idea of making them as real as possible by hiding the presence of video cameras. I am thinking, for example, about the recent TV show *Couples Therapy* (Eli Despres, , Josh Kriegman, Elyse Steinberg) — see Schwartz, "The Therapist Remaking Our Love Lives on TV."

28. On refraction and anthropology, see Collu, "Refracting Affects."

29. See Collu, "#Zoombies"; Collu and Stillinger, "Like Buzzing in My Brain."

30. The therapeutic spaces and scenes I describe in the book might at times feel cut off or severed from Argentina's cultural and historical context, especially for an anthropological readership. This an intentional cut, and it's the result of an ambivalent relationship I have with the central role that context and culture need to play in anthropological descriptions and analysis. On the one hand, the refractive anthropology of the book tries to perform the phenomenological experience of "getting caught" (Favret-Saada, *Deadly Words*) in, or by, the rectangularized cuts of the screen when watching live therapy through all kinds of visual devices—cultural context thus flickers throughout the text as a mediatic, and refracted, absent presence. On the other hand, there are also other layers of reasoning behind my decision not to foreground cultural context as a main explanatory principle. One of them is related to a *vibe*, for lack of a better term, I got from Argentinean anthropologists, sociologists, and historians I met when I was in Buenos Aires. These academics consistently manifested a bitter distaste for ethnographers who, like me, would come from North American academies, spend short periods of time in Argentina, and then write books "about Argentina" based on relatively narrow sets of ethnographic materials. Most of these works, according to the academics I talked to, seemed characterized by a hermeneutic and ethnographic disconnect between what North American authors would write and the Argentinean lifeworld. An Argentinean sociologist once took me aside after a workshop to tell me how *not* to write my dissertation: "Most people come here from [North] American academia just to find what they already wanted to find when they wrote their grant applications." But even before beginning my research in Buenos Aires, a specific moment with a close friend from Cordoba shaped my overall hermeneutic mood on this matter. A couple of days after I landed in Argentina to start my research, I was telling my friend something about my research project while we were both walking back home at the crack of dawn after a night of *fernet con coca*. My friend suddenly turned to me and with the calm lucidity of a mother telling her son to tighten his scarf, she said, "Samuele, *no somos tus Indios* [we are not your Indians]." This friend of mine was referring to an explicitly colonial way in which North American researchers tend to objectify the Argentinean (and, more broadly, Latin American) context. These interactions, among other things, reinforced my desire to try to write not *about* Argentina but *from* Argentina, in ways that hopefully will still capture a local genre of experience, however laterally and refractedly.

31. I am thinking with Eve Kosofsky Sedgwick's "reparative" approach (in "Paranoid Reading and Reparative Reading"), as well as Kathleen Stewart's call to move away from "critique" understood as the academic habit "of snapping at the world as if the whole point of being and thinking is just to catch it in a lie" ("In the World That Affect Proposed," 196).

32. Berlant, "The Unfinished Business of Cruel Optimism."

33. I am borrowing Deleuze's expression about a "double movement of liberation and capture," which he uses in a different context in a book about Bergson, cinema, and the "time-image" (Deleuze, *Cinema 2*, 68).

CHAPTER 1. SEEING YOURSELF BEING SEEN

1. For a recent use of "seeing oneself seeing oneself," see Song, "Seeing Oneself Seeing Oneself." See also Lacan who, echoing Paul Valéry, writes, "I saw myself seeing myself" (*The Four Fundamental Concepts of Psychoanalysis*, 80); or Merleau-Ponty's use in *The Visible and the Invisible* of a similar expression, "touching myself touching" (9).

2. "The value of permanent recording of therapeutic experience in motion pictures is self-evident," writes Nathan Ackerman, a pioneering figure of systemic therapy, in *Treating the Troubled Family*, ix. Video recording was, in his view, "the only known method to date that provides a satisfactory permanent record of a Gestalt, a merging of the image of face, voice, emotion, and bodily expression" (ix). The development of "second-order cybernetics" and narrative approaches in systemic family therapy has complicated Ackerman's perspective through a constructionist understanding of visual technologies (see, for example, Anderson and Goolishian, "The Client Is the Expert"; Hoffman, "A Constructivist Position for Family Therapy"). For a detailed history of systemic family therapy, see Weinstein, *The Pathological Family*. See also Madanes, *Behind the One-Way Mirror*, on the benefits of being able to see families through the one-way mirror.

3. Let's call the TV show you are binging *Desperate Black Mirrors*. With your neck strained toward the screen and your upper back arched like a champion, there you are, eagerly savoring the show without actually perceiving the screen that is showing you the show. Also, spoiler alert: At the end of the *Desperate Black Mirrors* season finale, we will discover that N. is not dead, but her spirit is trapped inside a digital house of mirrors. On this topic, see what Bolter and Grusin write on transparent immediacy in *Remediation* (23–24).

4. And a nice allegory for the play of identifications haunting the ethnographer's relation with their field.

5. This might be why this type of mirror is also occasionally called a two-way mirror.

6. Merleau-Ponty thus writes that to see is to "have at distance," to experience a split between the viewer and what is seen ("Eye and Mind," 357). The development of perspective in the Renaissance well represents the mobilization of these objectivist features of vision (see Arasse, *Histoires de peintures*; Carbone, "Lo schermo, la tela, la finestra").

7. Because of its relationship with objectivist science and Western modernity, the centrality of vision has been deeply criticized for its complicity with colonial apparatuses of capture. See, for example, Howes, *Empire of the Senses*; Brennan and Jay, *Vision in Context*; Crary, *Techniques of the Observer*; Jay, *Downcast Eyes*; and Levin, *Sites of Vision*. This model of vision, as Michel de Certeau writes in "La folie de la vision," implies the "exaltation of a scopic and gnostic drive" where "the fiction of knowledge is related to this lust to be a viewpoint and nothing more" (92). Donna Haraway has sharply described in "Situated Knowledges" how this type of vision reproduces objectivist male-centric scien-

tific knowledge that should be challenged through situated, partial, and feminist forms of (optical) objectivity.

8. I am here thinking about Daisy Couture's brilliant master's thesis on somatoform disorders and the (im)possibility of medical uncertainty, titled "The Place Where the Ground Gives Way."

9. I am alluding to Merleau-Ponty's sentence in "Eye and Mind" about the "secret and feverish genesis of things in our body" (358). See also Merleau-Ponty's writings in *The Visible and the Invisible*. Christine Buci-Glucksmann provides a fabulous engagement with Merleau-Ponty, and Lacan's reformulation of Merleau-Ponty's ontology of vision, in *The Madness of Vision*. I am here also thinking with the anthropologist Robert Desjarlais, who writes in *The Blind Man* that "to perceive in the world, in any flow of time, implies a baroque- like panoply of optics, media, mediations; memories, associations, expectations; displacements and discontinuities; connections, forces, affective tonalities; blind spots and epiphanies.... Vision is riddled with hallucinatory valences" (189). On vision and madness, see also Michel de Certeau's poetic writing on the "folly of vision" ("La folie de la vision"). On the baroque as anthropological mode of knowing, see Mattijs van de Port, "Baroque as Tension."

10. I am also here thinking about experiments in "binocular rivalry" that show how humans can't consciously "see" two images at the same time when prompted with two stimuli (one presented to each eye). On this, see Thompson's description of binocular rivalry experiments in *Waking, Dreaming, Being* (28–34). See also Varela and Thompson, "Color Vision"; and Varela et al., *The Embodied Mind*.

11. The neuroscientist Anil Seth, for example, describes Adelson's Checkerboard illusion (*Being You*, 95). There is a checkerboard with two selected squares (A and B); it looks as if A is darker than B. However, the two squares, it turns out, are the same exact shade of gray—it can be useful to look up this image! This happens, Seth explains, because of our brain's predictions of, and adjustments to, the ambient shadows in the image. Seth uses this example, among many others, to build his argument about (conscious) perception as a controlled hallucination (198).

12. Daisy Couture, thank you for helping me writing better sentences in these sections and, widely, throughout this book. For careful editing in earlier versions of this chapter, thank you Jordan Hodgins and Eli Sheiner—your interventions are textured within this version.

13. Merleau-Ponty, "Eye and Mind," 371.

14. In the words of Robert Desjarlais, to see is to encounter phenomena that are phenomenic as much as phantasmatic. In *The Blind Man*, Desjarlais develops his ethnographic imagination in terms of a "ph*anomenology*," where phenomena are always already *ph*antasmatic. Keeping the *ph* in *phantasm*, Desjarlais points at the entanglement between fantasy and phenomenality (see also Collu, "The Datum").

15. The feverish mystery of transparently opaque vision.

16. Merleau-Ponty, *The Visible and the Invisible*, 150. Inspired by Merleau-Ponty, Lacan makes a similar point in *The Four Fundamental Concepts of Psychoanalysis*, drawing a diagram where the screen/image stands in between the subject and the gaze (91).

17. In *The Visible and the Invisible*, Merleau-Ponty describes reversibility as a potenti-

ality that is "always imminent but never realized" (147). Merleau-Ponty widely explored the entwining between the imaginary and our perception, describing how the visible enfolds within itself an imaginary dimension, an invisible flesh that affects our perception (see also Carbone, *The Flesh of Images*; Carbone, *Filosofia-schermi*; and Vasseleu, *Textures of Light*).

18. See also Collu, "A Therapy of Screens"; and Merleau-Ponty, *The Visible and the Invisible*.

19. I am thinking here about the importance of learning how to shrug this type of gaze off with a controlled movement of the shoulders. The movement should start from the shoulder blades and shouldn't be done too fast unless one is a skilled practitioner of the protective-gaze scapula shrug. On prophylactic and evil gazes, see below.

20. I am taking this idea from the media theorist Kaja Silverman, who writes in *The Threshold of the Visible World* about the camera as the primary place where the subject can "apprehend" the gaze (135).

21. When I write about the gaze, I am drawing especially from the French philosophical and psychoanalytic tradition that includes authors such as Jean-Paul Sartre, Maurice Merleau-Ponty, Jacques Lacan, Frantz Fanon, and Michel Foucault, among others. On the "motif of the gaze" in French theory see, for example, the fascinating work of the anthropologist Hoon Song in "Seeing Oneself Seeing Oneself" and *Pigeon Trouble*.

22. I am thinking about Sartre's famous "keyhole" example from *Being and Nothingness*, where the subject bends toward the keyhole and suddenly hears some steps (377). See also Jacques Lacan's reference to this example in *The Four Fundamental Concepts of Psychoanalysis* (84).

23. From a talk I gave on Zoom during the COVID-19 pandemic (see Collu, "Compulsive Synchronicity").

24. Freud, *Group Psychology*, 46–48.

25. I know it's kind of a strange image—imagine a part of your ego hammering against another part of your ego. I am referring here to what Freud calls the "ego-ideal" in his *Group Psychology*. I am also using the language of "parts" in reference to the Internal Family Systems model (see Schwartz and Sweezy, *Internal Family Systems Therapy*).

26. This identification will be, for Freud, the ground for the child's desire to take his father's place as his mother's loved object. I am using the masculine pronoun here to avoid erasing Freud's gendered articulation of his theory of identification, which is based on his description of the Oedipus complex (see Freud, *Group Psychology*, 46–53).

27. See Butler on performativity in *Gender Trouble*, and Tarde on imitation in *The Laws of Imitation*. Think about one of your relatives at dinner saying that you look so much like your father. Every time someone tells me something like this, I feel a burst of rage radiating through my chest, as if that comment could potentially erase my identity, my own difference from my father. Though I don't look like my father, there are, in fact, parts of me that are actually him; sometimes when I laugh, I feel his facial muscles animating mine.

28. Adam Phillips underlines the arbitrariness of the ego's identificatory processes in "Keeping It Moving," writing that the ego "is always dressing up for somewhere to go" (151). I am here also thinking in terms of developmental psychology and cognitive an-

thropology about the "thinking through other people's mind" model that accounts for the cognitive internalization of socially shared expectations (see Veissière et al., "Thinking Through Other Minds"). In chapter 2, I suggest that anything which has the capacity to affect us has the potential to become the object of an identification. This means that we can potentially identify with *anything* that manages to produce or induce a state change in our embodied psychic life.

29. I always love to return to Eric Taggart's rendition of the mirror stage: "Lacan's Mirror Stage: A full-length mirror—Lacan's of course—assembles all your messy senses into a clean and singular image: It's you!!! Sort of. Because it also makes you into an object. Displacing your senses into an imago, a kind of external first-avatar. Oh, and your (m) other is there too. Behind you in the mirror. Triangulating what you feel and what you see and what you see-feeling-you" (in Taggart, "Before U Ever Even Heard of Oedipus," 101).

30. Lacan, "The Mirror Stage." This process, for Lacan, belongs to the realm of the Imaginary.

31. As Kaja Silverman notes, in his first seminar, *Freud's Papers on Technique*, Lacan refers to the mirror stage as literally doing the work of a container, a vase (Silverman, *The Threshold of the Visible World*, 11).

32. Lacan, "The Mirror Stage," 76 (emphasis in original). "An image," Lacan continues, "that is seemingly predestined to have an effect at this phase, as witnessed by the use in analytic theory of antiquity's term, 'imago'" (76). Lacan calls this image an imago, referring to what in ancient Rome were death masks used during funerary rituals; this is also to underline the fact that during the mirror stage the infant introjects an alien object that turns the ego itself into an object rather than a subject.

33. While misrecognizing herself, however, the infant is also literally seeing her own reflected image (see Silverman, *The Threshold of the Visible World*, 11).

34. Merleau-Ponty, *The Visible and the Invisible*, 139.

35. Which, in turn, can fuel narcissistic depressive behaviors, which, in turn, fuel anger directed at people who "don't understand," an anger which is actually directed at myself, which, in turn, fuels . . .

36. Probably.

37. "A projection," Teresa Brennan writes, drawing from Melanie Klein, "is what I disown in myself and see in you; a projective identification is what I succeed in having you experience in yourself, although it comes from me in the first place" (*The Transmission of Affect*, 29). On projective identification, see also, among others, Odgen, *Subjects of Analysis*.

38. For the sake of simplicity, in this chapter when I say identification I also imply the possibility of projective identification.

39. See also Fanon's description of colonial atmospheres of violence in *The Wretched of the Earth*.

40. Fanon, *Black Skin, White Masks*, 89.

41. On abjection, see Julia Kristeva, *Powers of Horror*, and Judith Butler's critical reformulation of this notion in *Gender Trouble*.

42. I use the term *m/other* following the psychoanalytic suggestion that the mother is

not just the mother but also the child's first Other, one exceeding the specific biological mother.

43. See Žižek, *Organs Without Bodies*, on how the reflecting surface delimits and distributes an excess with respect to reflection itself. The excess, in this case, is an imagined unity. As I mention below, the breast of the mother, in its biocultural and adaptive reconfigurations toward the infant, can already be understood as a mirror. On the body of the mother as mirror or translator of the infant's own sensations, see, for example, Bion, *Experiences in Groups*.

44. The breast and the notification are two types of *feed* (see Taggart, "Before U Ever Even Heard of Oedipus").

45. On the male gaze, see, among others, Berger, *Ways of Seeing*; Mulvey, "Visual Pleasure and Narrative Cinema"; and Silverman, *The Threshold of the Visible World*.

46. See Al-Saji, "A Phenomenology of Hesitation." See also Young, "Throwing Like a Girl," for a phenomenological approach to feminine spatiality.

47. Al-Saji explores how white and male positionalities tend to embody an "ontological expansiveness" that assumes they are *always already* at home in the world (see "A Phenomenology of Hesitation," 149–50).

48. Al-Saji describes how in racialized and gendered ways of seeing, the subject of perception wears "visual blinders" that don't allow them to "see otherwise" ("A Phenomenology of Hesitation," 138–39).

49. This chapter went through multiple revisions with Leo Stillinger, who helped me to write and rewrite many things and especially to find a flow amid the collection of broken mirror fragments.

50. I am thinking here about *The Blind Man*, Robert Desjarlais's beautifully disturbing ode to the identificatory fantasies of anthropological voyeurism.

51. I further explore the concept of availability in terms of affects and hypnosis in chapters 2 and 4 respectively.

52. Maybe this play of gazes and identifications describes what could underlie a gaslighting dynamic. I will explore the temporal aspect of this reciprocal freezing in chapter 3.

53. Bateson describes this as a symmetrical "binary relationship" ("The Cybernetics of 'Self,'" 323).

54. The more she . . .

55. Bateson also considered the possibility of mixed and more complex binary relations implying an entanglement of complementary and symmetric loops (see Bateson, "The Cybernetics of 'Self,'" 322–23).

56. "These potentially pathological developments," Bateson writes, "are due to undamped or uncorrected positive feedback in the system and may . . . occur in either complementary or symmetrical systems" ("The Cybernetics of 'Self,'" 324). On schismogenesis, see *Naven*, Bateson's ethnographic work on New Guinea, as well as the more recent work of Graeber and Wengrow, *The Dawn of Everything*, where they make an interesting point about schismogenesis—a difference that started out very small (maybe Thiago was only slightly more forgetful than Paula) can eventually grow to massive proportions as the loop accentuates and accentuates it (56–57).

57. To say it with Bateson, these would be the "mental characteristics" of the system, an emergent mind exceeding the sum of its parts (see Bateson, "The Cybernetics of 'Self,'" 316).

58. Freud, *Group Psychology*, 47.

59. Freud, *Group Psychology*, 47.

60. It's a bit disgusting to think about it in this sense, but, following this metaphorical line of thinking, one could consider projective identification as eating something that the other person has already chewed on. On a more poetic note, here and throughout this chapter I am deeply inspired and beautifully haunted by Stefania Pandolfo's work on Freud's "emotional tie" in the context of spirit possession in Morocco, in *Knot of the Soul*. On cannibalism, identification, and the emotional tie, see also Borch-Jacobsen, *The Emotional Tie*; Mazzarella, "Holding the Frame/Playing the Game."

61. But also, agonistically, be*at* them.

62. This doesn't mean that the interruption of repetition produces a lasting change. Therapeutic transformation requires surrender, a surrender to the desire to keep that momentary interruption alive and give it space, give it time—day after day, moment after moment. The philosopher Alain Badiou talks about love as an event, one that erupts into our world and interrupts repetition (see *Being and Event* and *In Praise of Love*). Love, like therapeutic transformation, is an event that requires a certain fidelity if you want it to keep animating the present tense of your relationships. When I say fidelity, I mean it as a practice, not as a value.

63. In these types of microinteractions, I think the romantic couple shows its intrinsically cinematic face. Tied to the emergence of the bourgeois intimate sphere, the romantic couple form flourished within historical regimes of exposure and visibility. I am thinking here about how Eva Illouz suggests, in *Consuming the Romantic Utopia*, that we cannot separate romantic love from the emergence of cinematic structures of consumption. I am also thinking with Lauren Berlant's descriptions of how, through the constitution of intimate therapeutic publics, "the inwardness of the intimate is met by a corresponding publicity" (in Berlant, *Intimacy*, 1; see also *Cruel Optimism*). On the couple and family forms of publicity, see also Giddens, *The Transformation of Intimacy*; Habermas, *The Structural Transformation of the Public Sphere*; and Warner, *Publics and Counterpublics*.

64. On the role of visual devices in the context of therapy, see, among others, the work of Cheryl Mattingly, who addresses the therapeutic features of the video camera in the context of an ethnography pursued through videotaped sessions of occupational therapy (see Mattingly, "Emergent Narratives").

65. Benjamin, who both draws on and departs from Lacan's symbolic notion of the "third" (see Lacan, *Freud's Papers on Technique*) describes different typologies of thirdness; for example, what she calls the "rhythmic third" or the "moral third," which are types of thirdness she maps onto a feminist rereading of the mother-infant relationship (in Benjamin, "Beyond Doer and Done To"). See also Thomas Ogden on thirdness and the analytic third in *Subjects of Analysis*. I am in debt here and throughout this chapter to the work of William Mazzarella, who offers a compelling rearticulation of Benjamin's notion of thirdness (see Mazzarella, "Holding the Frame/Playing the Game").

66. Joan Copjec writes in relation to Lacan's notion of narcissism: "Since something always appears to be missing from any representation, narcissism cannot consist in finding satisfaction in one's own visual image. It must, rather, consist in the belief that one's own being exceeds the imperfections of its image. Narcissism, then, seeks the self beyond the self-image" (*Read My Desire*, 37).

67. During my research in Buenos Aires, I transcribed together with Elisa, a systemic family therapist, about fifty old tapes and DVDs that were part of small archives held in different therapeutic institutions across the city. The recordings weren't organized in any coherent way, and most of the time there was just a single therapy session recorded with the same patients. This scene is a transcription of a ten-minute-long fragment I found on a scratched DVD—the copy of an older VHS—titled "Jorge y Gala. Problems of Communication. Dr. Sánchez."

68. Maybe, though, because we will never know.

69. The Wiltwyck team in New York, among whom was Salvador Minuchin (one of the founding fathers of family therapy), was well aware of this process. "The consciousness of being observed," they wrote, "is an intermediate step in the process of introspection. *The participant observes in himself what he assumes the unseen observer is focusing on*" (Minuchin et al., *Families of the Slums*, 268–69).

70. Consider, for example, seventeenth-century magic lantern shows projecting images on a screen in front of audiences in the dark—the screen was kept wet to be more invisible to the audience, to "dissolve the boundary between the reality of the auditorium space and the world of fantasy and occult penetrating into it" (Huhtamo, "Elements of Screenology," 35). This screen was a wet surface in the darkness of vision, hiding its presence while revealing a world existing beyond the surface itself. Screens need a certain amount of darkness to both disappear and show. "The darkness of the theater required for the clarity of the performance," writes Merleau-Ponty in *Phenomenology of Perception* (103).

71. Italian philosopher Mauro Carbone, drawing from his close engagement with the work of Merleau-Ponty, proposes in *Filosofia-schermi* to consider the screen as a theme, a figure, or a form that is never fully "given" as it acquires concrete shapes depending on its historical manifestations (100).

72. Carbone, *Filosofia-schermi*, 99. On compulsive returns to the screen as a "devotional rectangle," see Collu, "#Zoombies."

73. Heidegger, *The Question Concerning Technology*, 166. That's how Martin Heidegger connects the word *theory* with the realm of vision. Heidegger describes theory as a way of seeing, an inspired clairvoyance that "pays heeds" to what comes to presence (*The Question Concerning Technology*, 164). The Latin translation of the Greek word *theoría* (theory) is *contemplatio* (contemplation). The verb *contemplari* means "to partition something off into a separate sector" (165). The work of theory, Heidegger seems to suggest, is a visual act of divination facilitated by the creation of a screen that delineates a privileged area in space and time. Different theories make us see different things, make us see differently. On this, see also the art historian Daniel Arasse's work on the "templum" in *Histoires de peintures*, 63–64. The rectangular cut that delimits a privileged space can also be found in Leon Battista Alberti's famous treatise *On Painting*, which marks the (conventional) origin of perspective in the European Renaissance. "On the surface on

which I am going to paint," Alberti writes, "I draw a rectangle of whatever size I want, which I regard as an open window through which the subject to be painted is seen" (55). Bringing to light the relation between perspective and mediums, Panofsky reminds us that the very word *perspective* means "seeing *through*" (*Perspective as Symbolic Form*, 27). On how the window screen demarcates the difference between the "I" and the world, thus entangling subjectivity and the cutting work of visual devices, see Carbone, *Filosofia-schermi*, 111; Wajcman, *Fenêtre*. On the difference between the window and the screen, see Carbone, "Lo schermo, la tela, la finestra."

74. In "Comprehending Screens," Vivian Sobchack considers the screen as an in-between, an interface, and a "permeable boundary" (92). Screens, Sobchack writes, are media that display what we see but also work like the boundary of a system, the concrete materialization of its limit (94). Creating a division between spaces, the screen distributes the here, the there, and their respective excesses; the screen captures what I call the "here-else" (see Collu, "Refracting Affects"; Collu and Stillinger, "Like Buzzing in My Brain"). Erkki Huhtamo's compelling "archeology of the screen" describes screens as "information surfaces" ("Elements of Screenology," 32); these surfaces create a frame around the world and animate what happens within it, catalyzing our attention.

75. The body itself works like a screen, as a surface of contact that has the capacity to affect and be affected (see Collu, "Refracting Affects"). Bruno Latour, among others, defines the body as an interface (*Reassembling the Social*, 206). See also Anna Caterina Dalmasso's phenomenological work on the body as a screen, *Le corps, c'est l'écran*.

76. I am referring to the first paragraph of the chapter.

77. Silverman, *The Threshold of the Visible World*, 196.

78. See Mulvey, "Visual Pleasure and Narrative Cinema."

79. See Silverman, *The Threshold of the Visible World*. Michael Warner's *Publics and Counterpublics* explores the ways in which publics are created through the screen, which can act as the "mediator of public discourse" (I am thankful to one of this book's anonymous reviewers for this phrasing). In this sense, the screen is also creating a historically located public through its capacity to act as a cultural mediator. In this chapter, I have drifted aside from the complex problem of distinguishing publics from audiences, as Warner does in suggesting that audiences seem to be more "concrete" than publics (see *Publics and Counterpublics*, 66–67).

80. Lacan, *The Four Fundamental Concepts of Psychoanalysis*, 72.

81. Copjec, *Read My Desire*, 36.

82. The one-way mirror, as I describe it in this chapter, could also materialize the Lacanian split between the subject (or the eye) and the gaze (Lacan, *The Four Fundamental Concepts of Psychoanalysis*). Indeed, for Lacan, even while being constituted through it, the subject never fully coincides with the gaze but is rather split from it. The split is like an indexical wound left behind by the cutting work of the screen. Following this orientation, in *Read My Desire* Joan Copjec troubles feminist readings in film theory of the "male gaze" that assume a coincidence between the eye and the gaze in psychoanalysis, accounts that don't take into account the constitutive split between the subject and the gaze that (in)forms it.

83. Parts of the sections addressing social media and the contemporary condition draw

from "A Scroll Through the Present," a short manifesto-essay joyously cowritten with Jean-Philippe Bombay (Bombay and Collu, "A Scroll Through the Present"). See Foucault, *Discipline and Punish*, on the panopticon.

84. Adapted from Bombay and Collu, "A Scroll Through the Present," 70. I am in resonance here with Byung-Chul Han's work on the digital panopticon in *Psychopolitics*. Michel Foucault famously described Jeremy Bentham's panopticon as the emblematic architecture of disciplinary societies. "The panopticon," Foucault writes in *Discipline and Punish*, "is a machine for dissociating the see/being seen dyad: in the peripheral ring, one is totally seen, without ever seeing; in the central tower, one sees everything without ever being seen" (201–2). This optical infrastructure allows an invisible surveillance and induces in the inmate "a state of conscious and permanent visibility that assures the automatic functioning of power" (201). In disciplinary societies, prisoners, students, soldiers, and citizens incorporate the gaze of power and thus obey without having to be constantly policed through the use of force—prisoners comply even if the tower is empty. However, authors like Hoon Song (*Pigeon Trouble*) and Joan Copjec (*Read My Desire*) suggest that the panoptic model of vision mostly implies an imagined transparency of the medium and a coincidence between the gaze of power and the subject constituted through it. Following the intensification of surveilling strategies after 9/11 (see Lyon, *Surveillance After September 11* and *The Culture of Surveillance*), surveillance studies also addressed the proliferation of "surveillant assemblages" as forms of power that cannot be attributed to one single "Orwellian Big Brother" (see Ericson and Haggerty, *The New Politics of Surveillance and Visibility*). On this, see also Collu, "A Therapy of Screens."

85. Adapted from Bombay and Collu, "A Scroll Through the Present," 71.

86. Evans-Pritchard, *Witchcraft, Oracles and Magic*, 1. On the anthropology of the evil eye, see, for example, De Martino, *The Land of Remorse* and *Magic*; and, more refractedly, Favret-Saada's ethnography of affects, witchcraft, and the unconscious in *Deadly Words* and *The Anti-Witch*.

87. I am thinking about Evans-Pritchard's descriptions in *Witchcraft, Oracles and Magic*, but also Lévi-Strauss's reference to "voodoo death" in "The Sorcerer and His Magic" (161–79). Maybe we could understand in this way the suicidality that can be traced back to posts, comments, likes, and dislike on social media that detrimentally impact the user's psychic life.

88. On screens, tweeting birds, planetary pandemics, and the #Hypnocene, see Collu, "#Zoombies." On "eat or be eaten," I am drawing here from Benjamin, "Beyond Doer and Done To," and Mazzarella, "Holding the Frame/Playing the Game."

89. Mazzarella, "Holding the Frame/Playing the Game," 188.

90. Mazzarella, "Holding the Frame/Playing the Game," 174.

91. Mazzarella, "Holding the Frame/Playing the Game," 183. For the sake of simplicity in this chapter I am not exploring the transferential and libidinal forces underlying, if not fueling, these processes. It must be noted, however, that transference might be what propels these processes. I explore the affective and energetic dimensions of transference and identification in chapter 2.

92. I am thankful to one of the anonymous reviewers of the book for helping me think about the generative question of address and addressability in this chapter and, more

widely, in the book. On addressability, I am here thinking with William Mazzarella, who has explored the contemporary blend of impersonal intimacy created by (the fantasy of a) perfect addressability of the not-so-autonomous subject, an addressability that is often in the second person and sustains a wide range of forms of power and extraction (see Mazzarella, *The Mana of Mass Society*). In this sense, my own use of the second-person address does attempt to animate an affective response in the reader through the creation of an improvised and impersonal intimacy, one which is about "us" but also about the constitutive screens, splits, and cuts in between.

93. This sentence draws from experiments in thinking with Eric Taggart (see also Collu and Taggart, "Rest So Deep Now"; and Taggart, "Remediating Attachment").

94. Evil eyes and prophylactic gazes are briefly discussed during a Q&A in Lacan's eleventh seminar (*The Four Fundamental Concepts of Psychoanalysis*, 118).

95. There is a gesture Italian kids (used to?) make when insulted by someone else, which involves saying *specchio riflesso buttati nel cesso* while extending both arms forward with crossed fingers on each hand, palms facing outward to create a symbolic mirror barrier that "reflects" insults back to the sender. The sentence could be loosely translated, "Reflecting mirror, [you] fall into the toilet," that is to say, "What you said will bounce back to you and flush you down the toilet."

96. This gaze also protects the patients in the therapy session. "We should all be able to see what happens in a therapy room," commented Romero, a therapist I interviewed in Buenos Aires. "You have no idea about the damage a single therapist can do to patients. They can do whatever . . . and they only respond to their supervisor if they have one." Romero described the visual technologies of systemic therapy in their capacity to provide democratic access, distribution, and responsibility. Interestingly, it is precisely with the return of democracy in Argentina that the systemic model, among other models, began circulating (see Collu, "A Therapy of Screens").

97. On self-development, expertise, and confessional technologies of the self, see, among others, Cole, "The Role of Confession in Reflective Practice."

98. See Huhtamo, "Elements of Screenology," 99.

99. Carbone, *Filosofia-schermi*, 113.

100. I am here also thinking with the media theorist Francesco Casetti, whose book *Screening Fears* explores the "projection/protection" complex in relation to visual *dispositifs*—from phantasmagoria to screen-based bubbles. See also Collu and Stillinger, "Like Buzzing in My Brain," on the "protection/projection" complex, Proustian portals, and social media scrolling.

101. The containing role of the screen is in resonance with Donald Winnicott's notion of holding environments, developed in *Playing and Reality*. On holding environments and therapeutic spaces, see chapter 2.

102. Yanina Gori was an essential thinking companion since the very beginnings of my intellectual development, so our conversations are always already present throughout the book. Among an infinity of other things, she also helped me deepen my understanding of the role of the gaze in Fanon, Lacan, and coupled forms of life. Indirectly, in this chapter I have been echoing and responding to what she wrote in a baroquely ficto-critical essay titled "Acute Melancholia."

103. Professor Z. had another point: The one-way mirror is, in fact, a rather disturbing device. Freud's notion of the uncanny can be useful here (see Freud, "The Uncanny"). Freud suggests that when we experience something as uncanny, we are perturbed because we are confronted with the reemergence of something that was familiar to us but that we have repressed and forgotten. The one-way mirror is an uncanny device, maybe because it brings into the present aspects of the visual realm that play an important role in our experience of the world, but that remain mostly unconscious and are rarely the object of our attention. See also Ravetto-Biagioli, *The Digital Uncanny*.

104. See what I write in the introduction about Argentina's therapeutic culture.

105. I mean, have you tried TikTok?

CHAPTER 2. ATMOSPHERIC CRISIS

1. During my research, I attended the team's meetings every week for one year. Together we observed around one hundred hours of live therapy.

2. As mentioned in the introduction, systemic therapists in observing rooms take notes, exchange comments about the unfolding therapy, and occasionally interrupt the session through an intercom to talk directly to the leading therapist. When they talk to the therapist through the intercom, they offer comments about something they think the therapist is missing, suggest specific questions to ask the couple, or call in to provoke an atmospheric shift in the unfolding session.

3. This chapter draws from a published article where I engage with the same therapy sessions with Micol, Enrique, and Simona (see Collu, "Refracting Affects").

4. As mentioned in the introduction, almost every session of systemic therapy includes a break, during which the leading therapist goes to the screening room and debriefs with the team about the ongoing therapy.

5. These six men, including Enrique, were all in the same age range (forty-three to fifty-four). Their wandering through the city reminds me of Michel de Certeau's urban walkers, "whose bodies follow the thicks and thins of an urban 'text' they write without being able to read it" (*The Practice of Everyday Life*, 93).

6. I am thinking about this as a reversal of Arlie Hochschild's description in *The Time Bind* of the gendered avoidance of coming back home from work to avoid "more work."

7. I owe to Ramzi Nimr the image of "taking hold," when during our seminar on affects he asked, "Yes, but what *takes hold*?"

8. Stewart, "Atmospheric Attunements," 452.

9. Anderson is citing Gernot Böhme, "Atmosphere as the Fundamental Concept," 114.

10. Anderson, "Affective Atmospheres," 78. Atmospheres might also be tethered to a wider "ecological niche" (see Rose et al., "Towards Neuroecosociality").

11. The freezing force of the death drive? I am thinking here about the anthropologist David Knight, whose ethnography *Vertiginous Life* discusses atmospheres in "post-crisis" Greece. I discuss the death drive at greater length in chapter 3.

12. Stewart, "Weak Theory in an Unfinished World," 72.

13. For a material and affective philosophy of becoming and transformation, see Barad,

Meeting the Universe Halfway. See also Bennett, *Vibrant Matter*; Deleuze, *Bergsonism*; Deleuze, *Pure Immanence*; Deleuze and Guattari, *A Thousand Plateaus*.

14. On the "affective turn" in the social sciences and critical theory, see Clough and Halley, *The Affective Turn*; and Gregg and Seigworth, *The Affect Theory Reader*. I am echoing the idea of a "leaky sense of self" from Manning, *Always More Than One* (1).

15. Deleuze, *Spinoza*, 123; also in Probyn, "Writing Shame," 77. In *The Strange Order of Things*, neuroscientist Antonio Damasio writes that the capacity to be affected belongs to all forms of life and that, in fact, the capacity to be affected underlies bacteriological life itself.

16. I am here thinking about Jaak Panksepp's affective neuroscience (see Panksepp, *Affective Neuroscience*; Davis and Panksepp, *The Emotional Foundations of Personality*; Davis and Montag, "Selected Principles of Pankseppian Affective Neuroscience"). See also Barrett, *How Emotions Are Made*, for a take on the science of emotions that brings together psychology and neuroscience while also making space for cultural constructivism; and Damasio, *Looking for Spinoza*, for an exploration of affect between philosophy and neuroscience. For a critique of the mobilization of neurobiology in the social sciences, see Leys, "The Turn to Affect"; Leys, *The Ascent of Affect*; and Frank and Wilson, "Like-Minded," for a response.

17. In "The Autonomy of Affect," Massumi writes that affective intensities bear a certain amount of potential—you are taken by a nervous excitement, and your hands are sweating more than usual, but you could just as well be anxious, happy, scared, impatient, joyful, curious, or all of them at once. In this sense, Massumi writes about affects as encapsulating an emergent potentiality, whereas emotions are "qualified affects" and "sociolinguistic qualification[s]" of affective intensities ("The Autonomy of Affect," 24). This view, interestingly, doesn't depart that radically from current applications of predictive models of the brain to the science of emotions (see Barrett, *How Emotions Are Made*).

18. Anderson, "Affective Atmospheres," 79.

19. I am here thinking about Sara Ahmed's essay "Happy Objects," which describes how the way things affect us shapes our moral understanding of them as good or bad objects.

20. I am here thinking about Paul Ekman's much-debated idea that we can identify universal basic emotions or affects through facial micro-expressions (see Ekman and Friesen, *Unmasking the Face*). In the second part of the sentence, I am referencing Deleuze and Guattari's idea that artists create "percepts" and "affects," whereas philosophers create "concepts" (*What Is Philosophy?*, 24).

21. Downward spirals were often triggered by anonymous reviewers commenting on drafts of my articles about anthropology and affects—these reviews were rather violent, angry, and affected. To cheer myself up, I often imagined this affected red-faced reviewer unleashing all sorts of affects while screaming through the keyboard that affect is not a thing.

22. For an exploration of affects in psychoanalysis, see, for example, Borch-Jacobsen's work, *The Emotional Tie*; for an exploration of more-than-human affects, see Angerer, *Desire After Affect*; Clough, *The User Unconscious*.

23. See Barrett, *How Emotions Are Made*; Davis and Panksepp, *The Emotional Foundations of Personality*.

24. Williams, *Marxism and Literature*, 132. Drifting aside from the attempt to distinguish fully formed and more conscious emotional states from affects, critical theorists like Ahmed (*The Cultural Politics of Emotions*; "Happy Objects"), Berlant (*Cruel Optimism*; *Desire/Love*), or Stewart (*Ordinary Affects*; "Atmospheric Attunements") have explored how affective structures of feeling underlie different forms of economic, political, and ordinary experience in our "historical present" (*Cruel Optimism*, 54).

25. *Take me to that room now, please.* I am taking the room example from Brennan, *The Transmission of Affect*, 1.

26. I am taking this example from Anderson, "Affective Atmospheres," 80.

27. Gregg and Seigworth, introduction to *The Affect Theory Reader*, 2.

28. Of course, to different scales and degrees.

29. See, on this, Massumi's "Notes on Translation" in the introduction to Deleuze and Guattari's *A Thousand Plateaus*, xvi; and Spinoza, *Ethics*, 70, part 3, post 2. On the distinction between *affectus* and *affectio* in relation to force, see also Watkins, "Desiring Recognition, Accumulating Affect," 269.

30. Affective impact leaves traces that can have radically different temporalities. I am oscillating here between Massumi's description of affect as virtual, as something that happens "too quickly to have happened" ("The Autonomy of Affect," 30) and my reading of Stefania Pandolfo's work on trauma understood as an affective knot that is never fully processed (*Knot of the Soul*).

31. Psychoanalytically, we could think of this as an amount of psychic energy that fuels an "object cathexis." In *The Language of Psychoanalysis*, Laplanche and Pontalis write that cathexis implies that "a certain amount of psychic energy is attached to an idea or to a group of ideas, to a part of the body, to an object, etc." (62). Understood in this way, affect is a type of psychic energy or force that maps onto what Freud more widely called *libido*, a life force that binds you to other people, objects, and environments (see Freud, *New Introductory Lectures on Psycho-Analysis*; Freud, *Group Psychology*). See also Borch-Jacobsen's description of libido and the "primal band" in *The Freudian Subject*. When I write in chapter 1 about Brenda and the process of seeing oneself being seen, for example, we can say that Brenda invested a certain amount of psychic energy, of affect, into the imagined gaze of her audience. This is where the force of the gaze comes from. It's the affective force we invest in it.

32. Just don't forget to stay hydrated.

33. Spinoza, *Ethics*, 70, part 3 D3, and post 1.

34. Usually in a moment like this I tend to overeat or to overdrink. It's almost as if I'm punishing myself for not being able to move away.

35. And this is also when I tend to overeat and overdrink—*it's a complex reality.*

36. Massumi, "The Autonomy of Affect," 16; on this, see also, Collu, "Refracting Affects," 291.

37. I am here thinking about the psychologist Silvan Tomkins and the priority he gives to the face as one of the primary sites of and for affective communication. Tomkins developed a very articulated "affect theory" that describes the human affective system as our "primary motivation system" (*Affect Imagery Consciousness*, 6), one that has the capacity to amplify or limit even our most hardwired instinctual drives, such as when distress

or excitement override a baby's hunger drive—on Tomkins and the drives, see also Frank and Wilson, *A Silvan Tomkins Handbook*. Affects, for Tomkins, are bodily forces that determine what we pay attention to, what we remember, and the way we know the world around us. Tomkins's work has been explored in detail by Eve Sedgwick, who mobilized it to rethink core aspects of critical theory and the social sciences (see Sedgwick and Frank, "Shame in the Cybernetic Fold"; Sedgwick, *Touching Feeling*).

38. Merleau-Ponty, *Phenomenology of Perception*.

39. Narrative, as Paul Ricoeur suggests, is the extraction of a configuration out of a potentially chaotic succession of events (see *Time and Narrative*, vols. 1 and 2); on the therapeutic impact of narratives and "emplotment," see Mattingly, *Healing Dramas and Clinical Plots*. On the therapeutic role of narrative and metaphor, see also, among others, Kirmayer, "The Cultural Diversity of Healing."

40. Berlant, *Cruel Optimism*, 2.

41. So why should the reader know more than Micol and me?

42. Among many others, for a sharp critique of heteronormative romantic love, see Kipnis, *Against Love*. See also Illouz, *Why Love Hurts* and *The End of Love* for a sociology of modern love. The romantic couple form is not a universal fact of nature but a culturally specific form that mostly belongs to Euro-American modernity. It is indeed through heterogeneous processes tied to modernity and to the rise of consumer capitalism that the promises of coupled intimacy have become central "transit points" of Western liberal democracies. I am here also thinking with Povinelli, *The Empire of Love*, about the "intimate event" as a critical mechanism of Western "liberalism" (17). In *The End of Love*, Eva Illouz also suggest that romantic love has developed through a secularization of a religious notion of love that rechanneled Christian ideals of love into the romantic couple form. As I was writing this book, the genealogical ties between psychology, romantic love, and democracy have been in the back of my mind—it could be generative to explore this connection further, especially considering the particular history of democracy in Argentina. Anthony Giddens, for example, has explored in *The Transformation of Intimacy* how modern democracies are entangled with the rise of the intimate and romantic sphere, which, in turn, is also tied to the expansion of the psychological disciplines. In *Saving the Modern Soul*, Eva Illouz more specifically writes about how the emergence of a Western modern self is tethered to the entanglement between romantic love and psychotherapy. See also Éric Smadja's sociohistorical work on the Western couple, *Le couple et son histoire*. For an exploration of private life in a non-Western setting, see, for example, *Private Life Under Socialism*, Yunxiang Yan's anthropology of intimacy and private life in a Chinese village. I refer here to modernity not only as a historical period that starts around the seventeenth century, but also a constellation of individual and collective imaginaries. These imaginaries can be related to the rise of industrial and consumer capitalism in the European and American colonial empires as well as to the fragmentation of religious worldviews through processes of secularization. Foucault famously described modernity as an ethos in "What Is Enlightenment?"

43. In *The End of Love*, Eva Illouz's analysis of "unloving" and late-modern "negative relations" seems to confirm the centrality of romantic love even in light of, despite, or because of its failures.

44. See also Illouz's work on consuming the "romantic utopia" and sociopsychological suffering (*Consuming the Romantic Utopia*; *Why Love Hurts*). When I write "contemporary society," I am referring to global assemblages that have been territorialized by a Western capitalism that comes with values such as romantic love.

45. As Giddens writes, the "pure relationship" refers to a "situation where a social relation is entered into for its own sake, for what can be derived by each person from a sustained association with another; and which is continued only insofar as it is thought by both parties to deliver enough satisfactions for each individual to stay within it" (*The Transformation of Intimacy*, 59).

46. The other day I was talking to a friend about the origin story of his current couple form: "You know," he told me with a patronizing flair, "when I turned twenty-nine, I said to myself, *I am almost thirty. I have a good job. It's time to find someone, buy a house, and settle down.* So, I got on a dating app, and I found someone. It was time, you know; I was almost thirty!" *Well . . . good luck, champion!*

47. See Berlant, *Cruel Optimism*.

48. I am here also thinking about Sara Ahmed's notion of "happy objects."

49. Berlant, *Cruel Optimism*, 1.

50. Cruel optimism, Berlant writes, entails developing an enduring attachment to "couples, families, political systems, institutions, markets and work," despite the abundant "evidence of their instability, fragility, and dear cost" (*Cruel Optimism*, 2).

51. Berlant, *Cruel Optimism*, 2 (emphasis added). They continue, "But, again, optimism is cruel when the object/scene that ignites a sense of possibility actually makes it impossible to attain the expansive transformation for which a person or a people risks striving; and, doubly, it is cruel insofar as the very pleasures of being inside a relation have become sustaining regardless of the content of the relation, such that a person or a world finds itself bound to a situation of profound threat that is, at the same time, profoundly confirming" (2).

52. Just write things out, share them, let them bump into feedback walls so they can transform, so they can exist beyond your narcissistic attachment to them and circulate beyond your paranoid fear of not being liked.

53. On "attempted solutions," I am thinking with the Argentinean systemic therapist Marcelo Ceberio ("Querer y no lograr"). For an overview of the notion of redundant attempted solutions in systemic therapy, see Vitry et al., "Redundant Attempted Solutions."

54. This sentence is from Collu, "Refracting Affects," 295.

55. I am here paraphrasing Ben Anderson, who writes, "Note how an atmosphere 'surrounds' a couple or one finds oneself 'enveloped' by an atmosphere" ("Affective Atmospheres," 80).

56. Anderson, "Affective Atmospheres," 80.

57. On the relationship between affects and mediums, see Collu, "Refracting Affects."

58. I am here also thinking about Sloterdijk's focus on forms and enclosures as the condition of possibility of affective relations. "Love stories," Sloterdijk writes, "are stories of form" (*Bubbles*, 12).

59. Anderson, "Affective Atmospheres," 80. Through William Mazzarella's engagement with Peter Sloterdijk in *The Mana of Mass Society*, I am here also thinking about the cou-

ple's constitutive resonance that gives their "bi-unity" or their being a pair an affective quality.

60. The Argentinean "middle class" is an ambiguous and "residual" category (Adamovsky et al., *Clases medias*, 115), as the majority of the Argentinean population recognizes itself as being part of it. Tied to nationalistic origin stories, the Argentinean middle class catalyzes a moral imaginary of white and "modern" migrants of European descent who "built" the country (see Visacovsky and Garguin, *Moralidades, economías e identidades de clase media*). The middle class emerged in the public discourse as the main protagonist of the 2001–2 crisis: on one side actively engaged in the *cacerolazo* (spontaneous street protests), on the other called out for its neoliberal practices of consumption that metonymically represented the "sins" of the nation (see Fava and Zenobi, "Moral, política y clase media").

61. For an anthropology of the Argentinean crisis and "post-crisis ecologies of investment," see D'Avella, *Concrete Dreams*; see also Muir, "The Currency of Failure"; Muir, "On Historical Exhaustion"; and Visacovsky, "'Hasta la proxima crisis.'" For an account of the economic collapse from a financial perspective, see Blustein, *And the Money Kept Rolling In*. For a feminist call to revisit gendered infrastructures, see the Argentinean economist Mercedes D'Alessandro, *Economía feminista*.

62. See, among others, D'Avella, "Ecologies of Investment," 174.

63. See Muir, "The Currency of Failure," 317. For a critical anthropology of "crisis," see Roitman, *Anti-Crisis*; Masco, "The Crisis in Crisis"; and Knight, *Vertiginous Life*.

64. See Bleichmar's *Dolor país y después*.

65. For a critique of the mobilization of psychoanalysis to understand the economic crisis in Argentina, see Plotkin and Visacovsky, "Los psicoanalistas y la crisis."

66. Brennan draws from studies on the "failure to thrive in neglected children" and especially on the comparison of two orphanages after World War II (see Brennan, *The Transmission of Affect*, 34–35).

67. See Brennan, *The Transmission of Affect*; and Jardine et al., *Living Attention*.

68. Too phallic a metaphor? The joy*stick* offers a quite literal image to think about the masturbatory side of this masculine position, who asks for attention without reciprocity.

69. And what about Haley and me watching "the girlfriend" watching "the boyfriend"?

70. I am here drawing from Eve Kosofsky Sedgwick's use of "positions," which she takes from Melanie Klein (Sedgwick, "Paranoid Reading and Reparative Reading," 128).

71. See Collu, "#Zoombies."

72. As I write in chapter 1, this is what in systemic therapy is understood as a complementary interaction, wherein the more Simona does something, the less Enrique does it (the more I try to get closer to you, the more you retreat). This is differentiated from a symmetrical interaction, wherein Simona's action would be matched by Enrique's actions (the more I scream, the more you scream).

73. "Circular causality focuses on the reciprocal relationship between two events. The perspective of reciprocal relationships stems from the foundations of cybernetics, which refers to the regulatory action where one part of the system impacts another. A reciprocal perspective moves away from the mechanical way of viewing systems (individualistic) toward a relational viewpoint with a focus on interactional patterns between contextual

factors that exist within families. The shift in conceptualization creates a circular process in which one part of the system influences other parts" (Kelledy and Lyons, "Circular Causality in Family Systems Theory," 431). Norbert Wiener—the mathematician who gave birth to cybernetics as the science of communication between humans and machines (see Wiener, *Cybernetics*)—and Gregory Bateson's application of cybernetics in the social sciences is at the origins of systemic therapy's understanding of circular causality (see Bateson, *A Sacred Unity*; Bateson, *Steps to an Ecology of Mind*; Heims, *The Cybernetics Group*).

74. As mentioned in the introduction and chapter 1, cybernetic theories of communication, which inspired systemic psychotherapy, look at how interactions between partners form larger systems with characteristics that exceed the sum of the individuals composing them.

75. Bateson describes the "mental properties" of cybernetic systems, writing that "*the mental characteristics of the system are immanent, not in some part, but in the system as a whole*" ("The Cybernetics of 'Self,'" 444, emphasis in original).

76. Thank you, Daisy Couture, for helping me with your writerly wisdom in these sections.

77. Brennan, *The Transmission of Affect*, 30. Brennan explores how affective dumping is part of a "foundational fantasy" that involves the infant's dumping of negative affects onto the body of the mother, which is identified by infants as the source of their discomfort.

78. Sara Ahmed describes the deeply gendered dimensions of "working tables" and who gets to write at them (*Queer Phenomenology*, 3–4).

79. Freedom is a content and app blocker.

80. Brennan considers how the affective relationship between "dumper" and "dumpee" characterizes asymmetrical axes of power and violence that are intrinsically colonial, racialized, and gendered (*The Transmission of Affect*).

81. Fanon, *Black Skin, White Masks*. See the section on Fanon in chapter 1.

82. Drawing from Fanon as much as Guattari, *Chaosmosis*; Foucault, *Technologies of the Self*; and Merleau-Ponty, *Phenomenology of Perception*, I imagine liberation phenomenology as a transformative process that implies a patient labor of de-subjectification accompanied by a hesitant acceptance of one's own positionality—hesitant even toward the position that allows one to think about de-subjectification. But I am not sure an honest liberation phenomenology can or should be fully articulated. So, for now, I can only try to practice intentional forms of hesitation, a zealous mistrust of my own affective tendencies. I write in terms of hesitation echoing Alia Al-Saji's call for political and temporal practices of hesitation that interrupt gendered and racialized regimes of perception (Al-Saji, "A Phenomenology of Hesitation").

83. Depression is introjected anger. "Frequently," Brennan writes, "affects deplete when they are introjected, when one carries the affective burden of another, either by a straightforward transfer or because the other's anger becomes your depression" (*The Transmission of Affect*, 6, see also 43). This discussion can be connected to what I write about projective identification in chapter 1.

84. I am here referring to the previous Anderson quote about "tones of feeling" filling the space "like a haze" (Anderson, "Affective Atmospheres," 80).

85. I am here thinking about Freud's description of the unconscious as a "cauldron full of seething excitations" (*New Introductory Lectures on Psycho-Analysis*, 73).

86. I am using the term *impersonal* in reference to the work of, and conversations with, Setrag Manoukian on the impersonal (see, for example, Manoukian, "A Vocabulary for the Impersonal").

87. Learning, for example, is a state-dependent cognitive faculty, and the affective state that we are in when we learn determines our capacity to absorb and memorize new information. Think about moments in your life when what you are reading is so boring and you are so bored that you cannot even finish a sentence, and you must start reading again because you were completely checked out; or think about the affective state of fear, urgency, and excitement that helped you power through hundreds of pages before a final exam. For Silvan Tomkins, affects have a certain autonomy because they are also able to amplify and build on themselves, as when joyful laughter makes you joyfully laugh because laughter activates a joyful affect and even when you read this sentence you might be smiling a little bit, just a little bit, only because you read about joyful laughter and maybe an image is taking shape in your body (see Tomkins, *Shame and Its Sisters*, 81–85; and Sedgwick and Frank, "Shame in the Cybernetic Fold").

88. See Proust, *Swann's Way*. In resonance with Proust, the philosopher Henri Bergson writes that "every perception is already memory" (*Matter and Memory*, 150).

89. Here I am thinking about Piera Aulagnier's notion of the "pictographic reservoir" (*The Violence of Interpretation*, 38), which I encountered for the first time in Stefania Pandolfo's work on "psychic carvings" and emotional ties (see Pandolfo, *Knot of the Soul*, 97). I am also alluding to Freud's suggestion that dreams, and more widely the unconscious, "think predominantly in visual images" (Freud, *The Interpretation of Dreams*, 79), an idea that grounds Lisa Stevenson's call for an imagistic anthropology in *Life Beside Itself*. For more on this, see chapter 4.

90. I am here using the language of activation and resonance, mobilizing a vocabulary I take from William Mazzarella's work, which describes the role of affective resonances and transferential activations in contemporary processes of subject formation (see Mazzarella, *The Mana of Mass Society*; Mazzarella, "Holding the Frame/Playing the Game").

91. And, following what I write in chapter 1, relationships that shaped your primary set of identifications. See Freud's text on transference ("Observations on Love in Transference," 341–53) and his classic case study on Dora, which explores a complex case of transference ("Fragment of an Analysis of Hysteria," 435–540). The transference/countertransference relationship is a fundamental aspect of the "therapeutic frame," Hannah Zeavin writes, and it implies "the projection of feelings for a primary historical object onto and from the analyst, which the analyst and the patient engage in a lived repetition (and hopefully working through)" (*The Distance Cure*, 16).

92. Winnicott, "Fear of Breakdown," 92; cited in Pandolfo, *Knot of the Soul*, 69.

93. "The point about transference," William Mazzarella writes, "is that it's where I repeat myself in my libidinal relations with others, but also, and for the same reason, where those patterns can not only be re-enacted but also, in the clinic, transformed" ("Holding the Frame/Playing the Game," 176).

94. Sloterdijk, *Bubbles*, 13.

95. I have elsewhere defined this temporal composition as the "here-else" (Collu, "Refracting Affects"; Collu and Stillinger, "Like Buzzing in My Brain").

96. I mean ecological here in systemic terms, as referring to a system of relations between humans, nonhumans, and the environment (see Bateson, *Steps to an Ecology of Mind*). I am grateful for my continuing conversations with Aidan Seale-Feldman on the "ecology of psychic life" (see Seale-Feldman and Collu, "Towards an Anthropology of Psychic Life").

97. Or maybe the cruel optimism of a system that builds itself around Simona and Enrique's cruel optimism. Or the cruel optimism of an ethnographer who looks at the cruel optimism of a system that wraps itself around Simona and Enrique's cruel optimism. Or the cruel optimism of a reader who keeps reading about the cruel optimism of an ethnographer who . . .

98. Here, I am thinking about Eduardo Kohn's work on psychedelic ego dissolution and the emergence of "new wholes" (in "Forest Forms and Ethical Life"); and about Bateson's descriptions of the surrender to the "mind" of a system ("The Cybernetics of 'Self,'" 309).

99. This is maybe a minor version of, or variation on, the anthropological "otherwise" (see McTighe and Raschig, "Introduction"; Povinelli, "Routes/Worlds"; Povinelli, *Geontologies*).

100. Developing this parallel further, I have suggested that we could reimagine affects as "late modern spirits" (Collu, "Refracting Affects," 293).

101. These therapeutic rituals often mobilize trancelike states that affect the participant. In a state of trance, we loosen our ties with our self-enclosed and bounded forms of being and become available to be affected by someone or something else. Trance can be imagined here as an affective and affected state of being. See, for example, Michel de Certeau's work on the Catholic exorcist Father Surin who, during the famous possession at Loudun in the mid-seventeenth century, takes into his own body the evil spirit possessing the Ursuline nun Jeanne des Anges, thus dispossessing her of the spirit (Certeau, *The Possession at Loudun*). Among the wide range of anthropological works on ritual, I am thinking about the "madness of the gods" amid the Thonga as described by Luc de Heusch (*Sacrifice in Africa*), where the possessed are liberated from the evil spirit by mimetically embodying the spirit itself. The spirit becomes present because it is channeled through the affective body of the possessed (see Borch-Jacobsen, *The Emotional Tie*). I have also in mind the classic work by Alfred Métraux on voodoo rituals (*Voodoo in Haiti*) and more recent anthropologies of mediumship and spirit possession in rural China (Ng, *A Time of Lost Gods*), Zanzibar (Motta, *Esprits fragiles*), and Morocco (Pandolfo, *Knot of the Soul*).

102. See, for example, Mattingly, *Healing Dramas and Clinical Plots*; Mattingly, "Emergent Narratives"; Carr, *Scripting Addiction*; Ochs and Capps, *Living Narrative*.

103. See Lévi-Strauss, "The Effectiveness of Symbols."

104. See Severi, "Memory, Reflexivity and Belief," for a rereading of the Kuna ritual.

105. "Empiricist anthropology," Jeanne Favret-Saada writes, "presupposes, among other things, the human subject's essential transparency to himself. Yet there is an essential opacity. It matters little what name is given to this opacity (e.g. the 'unconscious'): what

is important, in particular for an anthropology of therapies, is to be able to posit it, and place it at the heart of our analyses" (*The Anti-Witch*, 107). Affect is one possible name given to this opacity, and it can help us rethink current theories of therapeutic efficacy. On ritual healing, see also the work of Laurence Kirmayer, who develops a general theory of ritual healing through the exploration of the "placebo response" ("Unpacking the Placebo Response"). See also Dow, "Universal Aspects of Symbolic Healing"; and Scheff, *Catharsis in Healing, Ritual, and Drama.*

106. Durkheim, *The Elementary Forms of Religious Life*, 217. Similarly, Victor Turner's "rites of passage" are characterized by an affective "liminal phase" that allows for the creation of a potentially therapeutic *communitas* (Turner, *The Ritual Process*). See also Mazzarella, *The Mana of Mass Society*, for a description of the mana-like "vital energetics" running across the nervous system of human societies.

107. I have learned it watching sessions of therapy, but also by personally discharging, receiving, dumping, or refusing affects that couldn't be held. This chapter, and maybe even the whole book, develops in fact around a restless search for therapeutic holding space. I take the notion of holding space from Donald Winnicott's description of "holding" in maternal care (from "The Theory of the Parent-Infant Relationship"), and from Winnicott's point about how psychotherapy can offer a holding environment where patients and therapists can "play" with "transitional phenomena" (in *Playing and Reality*). My dear friend and colleague Eric Taggart, who is writing about the Strange Situation Procedure and the onto-generative aesthetics of attachments (see Taggart, "Before U Ever Even Heard of Oedipus"), had Winnicott's *Playing and Reality* shipped to my house while I was writing this chapter. This exceeds what I can explicitly explore in this chapter but, in one way or the other, what I describe here also points at the therapeutic role of transitional phenomena.

108. Contemporary forms of power and governance are indeed increasingly addressing and targeting the affective life of the population. Precisely because affects activate an autonomic reaction that bypasses conscious awareness, one of the main arenas of today's affective governance is tied to the compulsive use of screens. From neuro-marketing to emotional artificial intelligence, an increasing number of digital media platforms mobilize "affect theory" to target what Patricia Clough calls the "user unconscious" (Clough, *The User Unconscious*). On affective governance and digital media, see Boler and Davis, *Affective Politics of Digital Media*; and McStay, *Emotional AI*. When binge-watching, listening, or scrolling, what we consume is also increasingly affect based; for example, think about the Netflix category of "Feel Good" movies and TV shows, or the Spotify playlist "Walk Like a Badass"—today's genres are primarily affect based. On the erotics of affective governance, see Collu, "#Zoombies"; Mazzarella, *The Mana of Mass Society*; and Mazzarella, "Holding the Frame/Playing the Game."

CHAPTER 3. COMPULSIVE REPETITIONS

1. *Sniff-tap. Sniff-sniff, sniff-tap, tap.*

2. This makes me think about Merleau-Ponty, who writes about the obscurity necessary for the clarity of the spectacle in relation to the body as the background of/for action

(*Phenomenology of Perception*, 103). In this case, the bright light after the spectacle provides a new type of foggy obscurity.

3. Following what I write in chapter 1, Romina seems to be offering herself to the eye of an anonymous and potentially infinite gaze. I am underlining the performative aspect of Romina's "poses," as in a yoga pose or when one is posing for a photograph, to foreground the idea that Romina is never alone in this scene: The camera is recording, and "we" are watching. At the same time, I want to evoke the idea of a private spectacularization of one's own intimate exteriority. I am especially thinking about the ambivalence of the intimate sphere with Lauren Berlant, who writes on the ways institutions of intimacy are folded within contemporary therapeutic cultures, which, as witnessing genres, sustain clusters of public intimacy (*Intimacy*, 1).

4. Classic data analysis bingeing. On insistent returns to ethnographic scenes, I am thinking about Todd Meyers's *All That Was Not Her*, a book where returning, repeating, and reimagining are central to ethnographic ways of thinking.

5. I am following the idea that Freud's notion of the uncanny also refers to the perception of vital forces within the inanimate (see Freud, "The Uncanny"). The uncanny is, in this sense, the disturbing experience of seeing life in something "dead"—see Lydia Liu's *The Freudian Robot* for a discussion of the uncanny in relationship to machines and robots.

6. In my enthusiastic attachment to these few recorded minutes, I remember fantasizing about sampling Almibar's "Shall we leave it here?" and Romina's vanishing steps and mixing them with some dubstep electronic music.

7. This question references the title of W. J. T. Mitchell's reflection on the surplus value of images, *What Do Pictures Want?* Here I am also echoing Dziga Vertov's notion of the "kino-eye," which engages with optical *dispositifs* as sentient forms of life (*Kino-Eye*, 41). As Jean Epstein writes, the cognitive faculty of the "automatic eye" of the camera (the kino-eye) lies in its capacity to record, "think-out," express, and imagine the infinite movements of the real (*The Intelligence of a Machine*, 13).

8. As I write in an extensive footnote in the introduction, the therapeutic scenes I describe in this book can feel at times cut off from the Argentinean context. My sporadic reference to the "streets of the city" in the book tries to index my ambivalent relation to anthropological context. The streets of the city are indeed one of the book's few references to an ethnographic "outside." The ambiguous presence of that outside was often experienced while hearing the incessant textured murmurs of the city while watching live therapy sessions. Interestingly, the streets of Buenos Aires have clustered a wide range of historical intensities across decades. For example, the streets of the capital have been the site of recursive encounters between infrastructural crises and the joyful/desperate/violent/necessary street protests that have characterized different moments of Argentinean history (such as the *cacerolazo* protests of 2001 or 2012). The streets of the city thus capture for me the sonic indexing of an epistemological crisis of/about place and placing, a crisis about the role of the cultural in anthropological analysis. At a more personal level, the streets of the city emerge in the book also as the site of relational meltdowns, psychogeographic drifting, and existential crisis.

9. Recursive returns to a scene, an image, a sentence, can go in different ways. Some-

times the return allows you to keep encountering something new, something you didn't notice before. Sometimes the return wraps you into a confused cloud, and you don't even know why you are returning, but a tension-toward pushes you to return again and again. As Berlant suggests throughout *Desire/Love*, returns condense a desire to understand but also to control the scene, to structure a fantasy around it.

10. I am drawing from Lawrence Cohen's essay on the "scene of instruction" ("The Gay Guru"). From the first day I met him to the present moment, Lawrence Cohen, my dear mentor, never ceases to fold my minimalist brain within a baroque architecture of potentially infinite scenes of instructions.

11. Eliade, *Myth and Reality*, 30.

12. Eliade writes also about the relationship between myth and the "eternal return" (see *Myth and Reality* and *The Myth of the Eternal Return*). On ritual practices and "resonant activations," I am here also echoing William Mazzarella's work *The Mana of Mass Society*.

13. I am writing these sentences while reading Alia Al-Saji's essay "The Memory of Another Past."

14. I am citing Clifford Geertz's sentence about the human as "an animal suspended in webs of significance he himself has spun" ("Thick Description," 5). Thank you, Diana Allan, for reminding me of this sentence in a beautifully crafted document you wrote and kindly shared with me.

15. I am thinking here also about what I write in terms of "projective identification" loops in chapter 1.

16. See Williams, *Marxism and Literature*, on "structures of feeling" (128–35). I am thinking about *strictures*, evoking also what I wrote in terms of spaces of enclosure and atmospheres in chapter 2.

17. And the anthropologist's attention, and the reader's attention . . .

18. Here, I am thinking with Henri Lefebvre's attention to rhythm as a pulsating cadence *making* and *marking* sociorelational and embodied spaces (in *Rhythmanalysis*). At the same time, I approach rhythm as a "productive repetition" (Deleuze and Guattari, *A Thousand Plateaus*, 314) that emerges from, and summons a milieu. Deleuze and Guattari's rhythmic imagination suggests that there is a relationship between refrains (as rhythmic differential repetitions) and territories (*A Thousand Plateaus*, 326–27). What interests me in this context is to consider the relationship between the couple's refrains and the relational milieu that couple is "acting out" in front of the therapist and the camera. For an anthropological attunement to rhythmic lifeworlds, see *Reel World*, Anand Pandian's work with Tamil filmmakers. I am here thinking also with Leo Stillinger's beautifully written master's thesis, "Hiker's Midnight," which explores rhythm and long-distance walking.

19. I have learned the adjective *hollow* from my dearest friend and colleague Emily Ng, and up until recently I thought she wrote about hollowed temporalities, but, after checking with her, I realized she doesn't write about hollowed temporalities. Ng uses the "hollow" as a figure to describe the gravitational pulls around radical absences and within cosmological reconfigurations in the context of post-Mao mediumship in China (see Ng, *A Time of Lost Gods*, 28). #Forgetful#Hollowed#Friendship.

20. See Deleuze and Guattari on deterritorialization (*A Thousand Plateaus*).

21. On being at home and habitability, I am thinking with the phenomenological tradition in anthropology and critical theory. Among others, I am inspired by Ahmed, *Queer Phenomenology*; Csordas, *Embodiment and Experience*; Desjarlais, *Counterplay*; Merleau-Ponty, *Phenomenology of Perception*; Throop, *Suffering and Sentiment*; and Zigon, *Disappointment*. For a critical phenomenology of dwelling in the contemporary condition, see Jarrett Zigon and Jason Throop's edited collection of essays, "Dwelling in the Contemporary Condition." On dwelling and habitation, I am here also thinking with Zigon's ethics of dwelling developed in "An Ethics of Dwelling and a Politics of World-Building." For an introduction to critical phenomenology, see Weiss et al.'s edited volume, *50 Concepts for a Critical Phenomenology*.

22. The paragraph continues: "Perhaps the child skips as he sings, hastens or slows his pace. But the song itself is already a skip: it jumps from chaos to the beginnings of order in chaos and is in danger of breaking apart at any moment" (Deleuze and Guattari, "Of the Refrain," in *A Thousand Plateaus*, 311). Refrains and songs, Winnicott suggests, can also function as "transitional objects" (*Playing and Reality*, 3)—see what I write below in this chapter on transitional objects. Like a haunting refrain that keeps coming back through different channels, I have encountered and reencountered this quote from Deleuze and Guattari in Yanina Gori's email on "Exiting the Blues" (2017), conversations with Haley Baird on refrains and rhythms (2018), Setrag Manoukian's class Poetry of Anthropology (2019), and a conversation with Jason Throop and Setrag Manoukian about reencountering this quote across citational refractions (2024).

23. On the "free energy principle" and the "predictive brain," see Carhart-Harris and Friston, "The Default-Mode, Ego-Functions and Free-Energy"; Friston, "The Free-Energy Principle"; Holmes, *The Brain Has a Mind of Its Own*; Seth, *Being You*. I am referring to a neuroscientific framework that understands the brain as an inference machine: "This framework assumes that the brain uses internal hierarchical models to predict its sensory input and suggests that neuronal activity (and synaptic connections) try to minimize the ensuing prediction error or (Helmholtz) free energy. This free-energy is a measure of surprise and is essentially the amount of prediction-error" (Carhart-Harris and Friston, "The Default-Mode, Ego-Functions and Free-Energy," 1267).

24. That sticky can of maple syrup can with drips on its bottom that drives me crazy because I *always* clean it up, and I have to scratch the solidified syrup with the sponge, and then the sugary texture sticks to the sponge, and it irritates me—so maybe that's why I never find it. I just don't want to see it. Bayesian brain hypothesis meets repressive hypothesis meets domestic *always-ness*.

25. Bombay and Collu, "A Scroll Through the Present," 90. This section and several others in this chapter that address the user's relationship with social media quote a piece cowritten with Jean-Philippe Bombay for the Montreal-based *Stasis* collective. We wrote the piece in a cheerfully angry ranting mood, finishing each other's sentences and typing as fast as we could. That piece was a turning point in my relationship with writing, so I am deeply grateful to J.-P. for allowing that experimentation. On users and screens, I am also drawing from two other pieces I have written (see Collu, #Zombies; Collu and Stillinger, "Like Buzzing in My Brain").

26. The evil twin of Winnicott's "good enough" mother? The "really good mother,"

the one who feeds you the feed before you even want it. "There is a reason they call it the *feed*," Eric Taggart often tells me.

27. See William James on fringes and suffusion (*The Principles of Psychology*, 258). Here I am echoing Agamben's description of the "couch potato" and the de-subjectified television viewer ("What Is an Apparatus?," 21).

28. Freud, *Beyond the Pleasure Principle*, 7.

29. In this chapter I alternate between the plural "death drives" (to follow more closely Freud's phrasing) with the singular "death drive" for the sake of flow and legibility.

30. Freud, *Beyond the Pleasure Principle*, 14–15.

31. Freud, *Beyond the Pleasure Principle*, 15. The good little boy, Freud tells us, sometimes draws even greater pleasure from playing only the first part of the game—the object of attachment being *just gone* (at least temporarily).

32. I am referring to Tony Robbins, the ambivalent guilty pleasure for an anthropologist like me raised by a Protestant pastor. Another version of his refrain is *repetition is the mother of all skills*.

33. It's the animated gazes that make the chairs spectral. Barthes writes about the eidolon of an image, which is emitted by the object in the photograph, a spectacular ghost, a spectrum. The spectrum "retains, through its root, a relation to 'spectacle' and adds to it that rather terrible thing which is there in every photograph: the return of the dead" (Barthes, *Camera Lucida*, 9). In this case, the deadly spectrum is vitalized through the (always already cinematographic) injection of time. So maybe it's a temporal movement that animates the inanimate and makes it spectral? This image can also be tied back to the reversibility of vision I explored in chapter 1.

34. The focal point is the point where waves/rays intersect after being reflected or refracted and the point from which diverging rays or waves appear to proceed. In this image there is something about how the two gazes intersect at a focal point, which acts as an absent third that makes the two gazes come together—the therapeutic setting's *jouissance*? Following what I write in chapter 1, the absent presence of the therapist's chair in this image is a third that gives life to the dyad.

35. I am citing the opening image of Sedgwick's essay on learning, pedagogy, death, and Buddhism, "Pedagogy of Buddhism" (in *Touching Feeling*, 153).

36. I am indirectly citing the phenomenological anthropologist Thomas Csordas, who has written about the body as the "existential ground of culture" (in "Embodiment as a Paradigm for Anthropology," 5; see also Csordas, *Embodiment and Experience*).

37. I am thinking about the standing desk extravaganza—and I must admit that I am a standing desk enthusiast. Especially for tasks that seem bureaucratic but that also have a depressingly existential dimension to them like tax filing, writing all sorts of reports, cover letters, or grant applications—I need an aggressively energetic posture to get through them without spiraling bio-existentially in a downward motion.

38. Ahmed, *Queer Phenomenology*, 1. Sara Ahmed's work widely describes dominant orientations toward heteronormative object choice. In this book, Ahmed also uses a "sitting device" as a scene of instruction, when she writes about writing tables and how the (white male) philosopher's table orients regimes of gendered productivity.

39. The notion of availability, the way I am using it, is similar to the notion of af-

fordance (see Gibson, *The Ecological Approach to Visual Perception*; Ramstead et al., "Cultural Affordances"). Ahmed also uses this notion in a similar way (e.g., *Queer Phenomenology*, 38).

40. Agamben, "What Is an Apparatus?" In the English translation, Agamben's Italian term *dispositivo* is translated as "apparatus," but I prefer to use the French term *dispositif* to keep the etymological relationship of this word with the Latin noun *dispositio* (arrangement) and the verb *disponere* (to arrange, to distribute)—the Latin root also connects to the French être disposé (to be available), which captures well the relationship between *dispositifs* and regimes of availability. The French etymology also keeps alive the connection with Michel Foucault's work on the *dispositif* (see also Collu, "A Therapy of Screens").

41. Agamben, "What Is an Apparatus?," 14.

42. Agamben, "What Is an Apparatus?," 14.

43. The subject, Byung-Chul Han writes, is the one who "has been cast down" (*Psychopolitics*, 1).

44. And if you are oriented toward something different, you can easily become what Sara Ahmed calls an "affect alien" (in "Happy Objects," 30).

45. When I teach about the *dispositif*, I usually explain it exploring a continuum that goes from Bourdieu's *habitus* to Foucault's technologies of the self to engage with the different degrees of consciousness afforded by different subjectifying *dispositifs*.

46. Yes! To think about *dispositifs* is an endless game—"literally anything"—and yes, it depends on which *dispositif* you are focusing on, and yes, you can only look at *dispositifs* through other *dispositifs*, and yes, it sounds a little flaky when there are words that you can use to capture and describe basically anything. Just like the word *anything*. But isn't it also so beautiful to embrace an unashamed degree of simplification, especially when it's done in the name of communicating something, of animating a thought, of making us see our own self through a different angle, through a different . . . *dispositif*?

47. I am thinking about the classic work of the cultural and linguistic anthropologist Edward Sapir—see the new edition of Sapir's *Selected Writings*; see also Duranti, *Linguistic Anthropology*.

48. On cultural affordances, see Ramstead et al., "Cultural Affordances."

49. I am citing the lyrics of Wet Leg's song "Chaise Longue" (2021).

50. For example, I wish I was writing in a standing position right now—but the chair, the chair sucks you in.

51. An intersubjective bubble animated by Maurice Blanchot's "space of literature" (in *The Space of Literature*).

52. Taggart, "Before U Ever Even Heard of Oedipus" and "Remediating Attachment."

53. The Strange Situation Procedure involves eight episodes/moments: (1) mother, baby, and experimenter; (2) mother and baby alone; (3) a stranger joins the mother and infant; (4) mother leaves baby and stranger alone; (5) mother returns and stranger leaves; (6) mother leaves and infant left completely alone; (7) stranger returns; (8) mother returns and stranger leaves. In his doctoral dissertation, "Remediating Attachment," Taggart addresses how this experiment has been compulsively repeated for decades, thus becoming the researcher's own *fort/da* object. The different attachment styles slightly

change their names across literatures, but the four main categories are secure attachment, anxious-ambivalent attachment, anxious-avoidant attachment, and disorganized attachment (see Ainsworth et al., *Patterns of Attachment*).

54. Taggart, "Before U Ever Even Heard of Oedipus," 105. In this sense, Taggart explores the "re/mediation" as a psychic drive that organizes processes of subjectification (in "Remediating Attachment"). The re/mediation drive foregrounds the role that different objects have had in psychoanalytic theories of subject formation—from Freud's wooden reel to Lacan's mirror, to Winnicott's blankets and puppets ("Before U Ever Even Heard of Oedipus," 100–101). On re/mediation and affective infrastructures, I am here also thinking with, and about, Yanina Gori's work on how community art in Cuba re/mediates social crisis, providing the ground for newly generative affective infrastructures (see Gori, "Re/Mediating Revolution").

55. See also the peek-a-boo game. For a short nonfiction piece on the couple form's *fort/da*, see Collu and Taggart, "Rest So Deep Now."

56. Winnicott, *Playing and Reality*, 3.

57. Winnicott, *Playing and Reality*, 18.

58. Winnicott also describes sounds, babbling, and musical notes as transitional objects (see *Playing and Reality*, 5). If you are reading this note, this is dedicated to you, Eloisa, and Softy Bunny. As Haley Baird commented when reading this section, this way to understand the transitional object erases the possibility of letting the object be its own thing, to imagine the animatedness of the object. On this idea, see the paragraphs at the end of this chapter. Thank you, Haley Baird, as always, for constantly inspiring my thinking and my being.

59. Winnicott, *Playing and Reality*, 70.

60. While I acknowledge the different intellectual histories behind the different terms, here I am using *self*, *identity*, and *subjectivity* with a certain looseness to make my point, which is mostly about the relationship between *dispositifs* and what they produce (be it a self, an identity, or a subject). On the making of the modern self, see Taylor, *Sources of the Self*; Rose, *Governing the Soul*. On subjectivity, see Biehl et al., *Subjectivity*; Butler, *Gender Trouble*; Foucault, *The Hermeneutics of the Subject*. On cultural identity, see Amselle, *Mestizo Logics*; Gupta and Ferguson, *Culture, Power, Place*.

61. Marcuse, *Eros and Civilization*.

62. I am here thinking about Natasha Dow Schüll's work on gambling addiction in Las Vegas, *Addiction by Design*, and her descriptions of how the repetitive gestures of gamblers at the slot machines put them in what they call the "zone" (30).

63. Ultimate in the sense of "central, critical" but also "final" if one is to take this apocalyptically.

64. Here, I am thinking about friends who have, at least once, destroyed their phone by throwing it against the wall or on the floor. I have such a narcissistic attachment to digital and technological prostheses that even in the most incandescent moments I would rather hurt myself than damage my phone or laptop.

65. "Contemporary addiction, so the digital behaviorist suggests, is fueled by unexpected or intermittent reward: we return to the same because we don't know how different it will be, because it gives our neural pathways a dopamine slap. However, we are

addicted to a very restricted kind of uncertainty. How many texts will I get? How different is the world now in respect to five seconds ago? How many times did you check in the past minutes?" (Bombay and Collu, "A Scroll Through the Present," 76). On digital addiction, see also Alter, *Irresistible*; Newport, *Digital Minimalism*; Price, *How to Break Up with Your Phone*.

66. Bombay and Collu, "A Scroll Through the Present," 82.

67. This sentence makes me think about a song Haley played for me recently, Ian Dury's "Hit Me with Your Rhythm Stick" (1978).

68. Or, as Byung-Chul Han writes, the "global synagogue ... of the Digital" (*Psychopolitics*, 12).

69. "Both the smartphone and the rosary," the quote continues, "serve the purpose of self-monitoring and control. Power operates more effectively when it delegates surveillance to discrete individuals" (Han, *Psychopolitics*, 12).

70. Bombay and Collu, "A Scroll Through the Present," 82.

71. This is where the mythical present of the romantic couple form meets the predictive brain hypothesis meets the future perfect of algorithmic *dispositifs*.

72. On screens and trance, see Collu, "#Zoombies"; and Collu and Stillinger, "Like Buzzing in My Brain."

73. As Berlant writes about cruel optimism: "What's cruel about these attachments, and not merely inconvenient or tragic, is that the subjects who have x in their lives might not well endure the loss of their object or scene of desire, even though its presence threatens their well-being; because whatever the *content* of the attachment is, the continuity of the form of it provides something of the continuity of the subject's sense of what it means to keep on living on and to look forward to being in the world" (*Cruel Optimism*, 24).

74. Throughout this chapter, Deleuze's *Difference and Repetition* has been insistently whispering to my ears and haunting my typing fingers. I just didn't return to that book enough times to feel I can foreground my engagement with it.

75. More of this in chapter 4.

76. Looking for the remote control to control the volume of the patient who is feeling controlled.

77. If you follow a possible reading of Lacan's notion of the unconscious, a software is, in fact, running through us. Among others, Lydia Liu explores in depth how Lacan's "cybernetic unconscious" considered the capacity of probabilistic forces to animate the human and its "machinic" behaviors (in *The Freudian Robot*).

78. I have been told many times of similar scenes where the couple stages their fights only in the presence of the therapist. "The funniest part is to witness their fights for the whole session and then see them walk out hand in hand, as if nothing happened," Marisa, a couple therapist, once commented. In another situation, I have watched a videotaped session where a therapist, Milena, was completely left out by the couple, who kept cutting her off throughout the session. Milena, to break up the couple's arguments, took a break to go behind the one-way mirror (although she knew that no one was watching the session). In the video, the couple literally fall silent the very moment Milena leaves the room. These small events make explicit the spectacular dimension of the couple form during couple therapy, as well as the intimate publicity at the core of this relational structure of desire.

79. This is an example of what I write in chapter 2 in terms of atmospheres radiating from couples.

80. What I am writing here about Freud's theory of the *death drives* is a temporary simplification of a complex theory presented in a book (*Beyond the Pleasure Principle*) filled to the brim with twists and turns and contradictory propositions. Giving more weight to one passage of that book rather than another could easily flip upside down what I am saying here. In fact, the homeostatic tendency of the death drive, according to Freud, ends up being mostly in service of the pleasure principle itself, which seems to contradict what Freud initially set out to do in the book; that is, to describe forces "beyond" the pleasure principle (see Freud, *Beyond the Pleasure Principle*, 59). The Lacanian tradition would indeed understand Freud's death drive *as* the pleasure principle and posit a different non-homeostatic death drive running after a tensile excess which is *really* beyond the pleasure principle—on this, see for example Alenka Zupančič's *What Is Sex?*, 94–106. I write this footnote while doing the final edits of the book and after a full year spent with my friends and colleagues at McGill to read and reread *Beyond the Pleasure Principle* in the context of the "Beyond the Anthropology Principle" reading group I organized with Setrag Manoukian.

81. Freud, *Beyond the Pleasure Principle*, 36.

82. If you hold a *wuji* stance long enough, you might even hear its pulse.

83. In the partial and specific reading I am offering here, the death drive is a conservative force that holds the ego together. Following Lacan, however, this approach to the death drive doesn't account for the tendency of the death drive to circle around a constitutive negativity, a movement which seems to potentially characterize all drives. On this, see for example Lacan's diagram about the double loop of the drive in *The Four Fundamental Concepts of Psychoanalysis*, 178.

More widely, I am here regretfully drifting aside from a wide range of works that engage with the death drive from a social, historical, and cultural perspective. The work of Stefania Pandolfo, for example, offers a masterful description of the temporality of the death drive as it haunts, sustains, and remediates historical trauma (Pandolfo, *Knot of the Soul*). I am here also thinking about Herbert Marcuse's Marxist reading of the complex relation between Eros and Thanatos from a historical and potentially revolutionary standpoint (Marcuse, *Eros and Civilization*). While the reader might expect that an anthropologist would at least make an attempt to offer a historical or cultural reading of the death drive, this is not the point I am trying to make in this chapter. However, this doesn't mean that the historical context is absent or irrelevant, that it doesn't, in fact, haunt what I say about the death drive, what I say in the empty spaces breathing between my words.

84. Ether(net)?

85. "The 'I' that I am not yet is already here, present in my present, which is always already territorialized by an upcoming algorithmic future. In the era of the digital uncanny an anticipated version of ourselves nibbles its way through our bellies. We are what we are going to be in a few nanoseconds. We identify with the point of view of an algorithm that sees us as what we will 'have been.' We belong to the future anterior. 'Samuele, we thought you would . . .' Click. I am the loop that feeds me with my future self" (Bombay and Collu, "A Scroll Through the Present," 90–91).

86. I find the Bayesian brain hypothesis quite generative because the understanding of the brain as a "predictive machine" is today used to develop artificial neural networks that work like a predictive brain. So predictive algorithms work like a brain, which works like a predictive algorithm—an almost seamless continuum between human and cybernetic loops of anticipation and prediction.

87. You never know what's going to come and hunt you down. So you surround yourself with transitional objects and homing devices that you keep returning to, so you can stabilize and sing the refrains of a scared little child. When I am on my binge train, after a few hours I become so scared to stop watching, to stop clicking, to just . . . stop. I am scared of not existing anymore once I turn off the light. I am a scared little child that wants the light always on, I need a warm, flickering, and predictive feed to keep singing songs that feed me fragments of my own self. "The über-eats of digital cannibalism" (Bombay and Collu, "A Scroll Through the Present," 91).

88. I am taking this expression from Al-Saji's essay on racialized ways of seeing and "ankylosed" forms of perception that anticipate and limit our visual range (see Al-Saji, "A Phenomenology of Hesitation").

89. This is what I call the fundamental arbitrariness of perceived immediacy (see also what I write in chapter 1 on the relationship between vision and the imagination).

90. Sometimes I am scared to play a specific music genre because I don't want the algorithm to think that that's what I will want tomorrow, so I prefer not to listen to what I would want to listen in that moment in order to avoid having to listen to it tomorrow.

91. "When the subject is de-psychologized—indeed, de-voided (*ent-leert*)—it opens onto a mode of existence that still has no name: an unwritten future" (Han, *Psychopolitics*, 79).

92. This could be possible if the screen was also a 3D printer or something.

93. Add "Slap Premium" to your "Binge-On" plan for only five million Crypto-Binge coins! But it's a type of cryptocurrency you can earn only when you binge. You accumulate fifty Crypto-Binge coins for every uninterrupted hour of bingeing.

94. I take the expression "experiment of experience" from the Italian anthropologist Leonardo Piasere (in *L'etnografo imperfetto*).

95. The first time I heard about the situationists was from my father, when I was about twelve years old. I was listening with fascination to my dad's stories about the situationists in Milano. One was about how my father was part of a group who threw a Molotov cocktail on stage to interrupt a concert where Carlos Santana was playing. "We are the situation! Fuck imperialist American music! Let's create interruptions!" I am not sure about the details and, more importantly, the accuracy of this family lore, but from a few Google searches it looks like something like that actually happened in Milan in the late 1970s.

96. I am here using the term *electric* in reference to Émile Durkheim's description of mana (in *The Elementary Forms of Religious Life*, 217).

97. Durkheim, *The Elementary Forms of Religious Life*, 213.

98. "The fascination and the power of ritual is that it at once activates and routinizes encounter" (Mazzarella, *The Mana of Mass Society*, 7). I am here also borrowing from Mazzarella's descriptions of how the collective forces of society are activated in ritualized

resonant encounters shaping contemporary subjectivity—from politics to neuromarketing (*The Mana of Mass Society*).

99. I am referring to what I write in chapter 2, "You can only scream, *I don't know what else, but not this.*"

100. I am here thinking about "loosening" the grip on the object, echoing Berlant's writing about "loosening the object" as a way to "unlearn its objectness" (*On the Inconvenience of Other People*, 28).

101. "Freedom is felt when passing from one way of living to another—until this too turns out to be a form of coercion. Then, liberation gives way to renewed subjugation. Such is the destiny of the *subject*" (Han, *Psychopolitics*, 1).

CHAPTER 4. OSCILLATIONS

1. Yanina Gori and I undertook some pretty wild trance work during that period—some traces of these experiences are contained in a paper Yanina wrote titled "Acute Melancholia: Through My Pharmakon" and a paper I wrote titled "From Symbolic to Mimetic Efficacy: Anthropological Reflections on Hypnosis, Mystical Experience, and the Affective Tie." In Berkeley, Stefania Pandolfo was the propelling force behind our thinking about hypnosis.

2. I owe my desire to experiment with all sorts of spiritual practices to my parents and their spiritual nomadism. I grew up in a Pentecostal church (my father was the pastor) and had early experiences with people speaking in tongues, dropping on the floor filled with the Holy Spirit, or being possessed by a demon. My bachelor's degree research brought me to a Buddhist monastery in Cambodia, where I studied tutelary spirits living inside a Buddha statue (Collu, "L'assenza presente di Buddha"). This grounds my interests in de-secularizing (or reenchanting) critical and analytical vocabularies (see Collu, "Refracting Affects"; Collu, "#Zoombies").

3. I used some of this footage in my doctoral dissertation to explore the relationship between hypnosis and the process of ethnographic research. In the dissertation, I engage with some of the images I describe here to sketch out a "refractive," rather than reflexive, anthropology—a refractive anthropology which starts from the presupposition that the ethnographer is always already opaque to themselves (see Collu, "Refractive Cogito"; Collu, "Refracting Affects").

4. Haley Baird's movement practices, her performative concept work, and her literal yet literary oscillations are the ongoing inspiration for this chapter's imagery and vocabulary—especially in relation to oscillations, rhythms, trembling, and emergent difference within oceanic entanglements. I borrow this chapter's title from her.

5. See Roustang, *Qu'est-ce que l'hypnose?*, 60; see also Roustang, *Il suffit d'un geste*. The very possibility of sitting down, occupying space, and finding ease within it of course presupposes an environment that affords the spatialization of your being, that allows you to be at home. Racialized and gendered social structures can make it impossible to be comfortable in one's own environment, where only some bodies have the privilege of "ontological expansiveness" (see Al-Saji, "A Phenomenology of Hesitation"; Sullivan, *Revealing Whiteness*).

6. In this chapter, I am writing about Western hypnosis but, of course, many aspects of hypnosis resonate with a wide range of contemplative and meditative traditions—from Daoism to Christianity to Buddhism to secular variations of mindfulness meditation. Many of these traditions have long preceded what today we call hypnosis, a term popularized by James Braid in the first half of the nineteenth century.

7. Merleau-Ponty, "Eye and Mind," 358.

8. Here Sofía uses a nice assonance in Spanish: *lo que viste* (what you saw), *lo que viviste* (what you lived).

9. Milton Erickson's work became especially known after Jay Haley published *Uncommon Therapy*, a book describing Erickson's approach to therapeutic change. Milton Erickson is not to be confused with Erik Erikson, who was a developmental psychologist and psychoanalyst (1939–94).

10. As I have explored in the previous chapters, the systemic perspective considers how the patient's problems are tethered to interactive loops that mostly exceed individual volition and consciousness. Short-circuiting might be one way to visualize the interruption of these loops; see chapter 2's description of an environmental catharsis that exceeds Micol, Simona, and Enrique; and chapter 3's image of the "buzzing interruption."

11. Jay Haley describes a classic trance induction of a participant during a lecture who tells Milton Erickson, "You may be able to hypnotize other people, but you can't hypnotize me!" Erickson then invites the subject to the lecture platform, asks him to sit down, and says to him, "I want you to stay awake, wider and wider awake, wider and wider awake." The subject promptly went into a trance (from Haley, "An Interactional Explanation of Hypnosis," 52). Erickson's hypnotic suggestions have influenced the development of multiple therapeutic models and traditions, from clinical hypnosis (Yapko, *Essentials of Hypnosis*; Yapko, *Trancework*) to strategic therapy (Madanes, *Behind the One-Way Mirror*; Nardone and Watzlawick, *Brief Strategic Therapy*) to neurolinguistic programming (Bandler et al., *Reframing*).

12. This principle is at the core of many Ericksonian techniques, such as paradoxical suggestions that ask patients to intentionally perform a symptom that would usually arise beyond their volition. The therapists I have observed could, for example, ask couples in therapy who were fighting too much to schedule their fights every night at 5 P.M. This simple and indirect suggestion can create unexpected unconscious responses that interrupt the repetition of the symptom. On the uses of paradoxes as therapeutic technique, see the work of the Milan Group (Palazzoli et al., *Paradox and Counterparadox*) and also Nardone and Watzlawick (*Brief Strategic Therapy*). Of course, the mobilization of unconscious processes is at the core of a wide range of therapeutic models that preceded and followed Milton Erickson's work (see Ellenberger, *The Discovery of the Unconscious*).

13. On this, see a systemic therapy classic titled, precisely, *Change* (Watzlawick et al.).

14. As I write later in this chapter, I resonate with Lisa Stevenson's call for an "anthropology through the image" (*Life Beside Itself*, 14), one that develops imagistic forms of thinking that drift aside from "discursive modes of knowing" (10).

15. See Yapko, *Trancework*.

16. Elkins et al., "Advancing Research and Practice," 382. The hypnotherapist Michael Yapko, commenting on this description, offers his own working definition of hypnosis as

a "focused experience of attentional absorption that invites people to respond experientially on multiple levels in order to amplify and utilize their personal resources" (*Trancework*, 8). See also Cardeña et al., "The Neurophenomenology of Neutral Hypnosis"; and Roustang, *Qu'est-ce que l'hypnose?*

17. In a slightly modified version, this section also appears in Collu, "#Zoombies," 205.

18. See Roustang, *Qu'est-ce que l'hypnose?*, 59. See also Yapko, *Trancework*, 69; and Yapko, *Essentials of Hypnosis*, 124.

19. See what I write in chapter 2 about affects and memories. Markovic and Thompson offer a compelling neurophenomenological discussion about states of absorption and imaginative involvement ("Hypnosis and Meditation," 83). Taken as a cognitive skill, hypnosis can't be considered an "altered state of consciousness" (see Veissière, "Varieties of Tulpa Experiences," 67; Raz, "Anatomy of Attentional Networks"). "The 'specialness' of hypnosis," the psychiatrist Laurence Kirmayer writes, "probably inheres not in any unique cognitive process but in the way common cognitive skills (including focused attention, absorption, imagination, and affective state-dependent dissociation) are combined to yield hypnotic behavior and experience" ("Hypnosis and the Limits of Socialpsychological Reductionism," 521).

20. I am thinking about Victor Turner's notion of liminality (*limen* means "threshold" in Latin) that describes a space characterized by the loosening of a person's temporal and symbolic structure—during the rites of passage described by Turner, participants become "liminal *personae* (threshold people)," who "are neither here nor there; they are betwixt and between the positions assigned and arrayed by law, custom, convention, and ceremonial" (*The Ritual Process*, 95). On dispossession rituals, I am thinking, for example, about the "madness of the gods" amid the Thonga as described by Luc de Heusch (*Sacrifice in Africa*), where the possessed are liberated from the evil spirit mimetically embodying the spirit itself (see also Collu, "Refracting Affects"). See also Ernesto De Martino's description of southern Italian tarantism (*The Land of Remorse*).

21. Luhrmann, *How God Becomes Real*, 71.

22. Luhrmann, *How God Becomes Real*, 70.

23. See Nakamura and Csikszentmihalyi, "The Concept of Flow." Experiences like "mind wanderings" are being explored in relation to an increased activity in the default mode network (DMN), a network of brain regions that activate when we are not engaged in demanding tasks requiring our attention. The DMN seems to be able to make connections that you can't make when you are actively engaged in the world around you. But it's still unclear to me if hypnotic states actually increase or decrease the activity in the DMN—see Deeley et al., "Modulating the Default Mode Network Using Hypnosis"; Jiang et al., "Brain Activity and Functional Connectivity Associated with Hypnosis"; Landry et al., "Brain Correlates of Hypnosis." From what I understand, hypnosis modifies or deactivates at least part of the DMN activity—this would be coherent with the idea that the DMN is the network of connections composing our "ego" (see Carhart-Harris and Friston, "The Default-Mode, Ego-Functions and Free-Energy"). In hypnosis research there is a debate about whether we should consider hypnosis a state or if it should be considered a psychological trait (see Cardeña et al., "The Neurophenomenology of Neutral Hypnosis"; Cardeña, "Hypnos and Psyche")—this debate exceeds the scope of this chap-

ter. However, it should be noted that I here tend to consider hypnosis as a state. It also remains an open question whether we should understand hypnosis as an altered state of consciousness or as an ordinary state of attention. In this chapter I tend to oscillate between these two positions.

24. Sloterdijk, *Bubbles*, 207.

25. See chapters 1 and 2.

26. I am referring to Freud's description of how the loved object can become a substitute of and for what he calls the "ego ideal" (see Freud, *Group Psychology*, 58–59; see also the second chapter, on affects that "spill over" and "take hold").

27. Mazzarella, *The Mana of Mass Society*, 5.

28. Mazzarella, *The Mana of Mass Society*, 5.

29. "Resonant encounters," Mazzarella writes, "are *erotic* in the ancient sense explored by Anne Carson: on the one hand, 'this heightened sense of one's own personality ("I am more myself than ever before!")', and, on the other hand a loss of self experienced as a crisis of physical and emotional integrity; Sappho called eros the 'melter of limbs'" (*The Mana of Mass Society*, 5).

30. I am here resonating with Peter Sloterdijk's philosophical genealogy of the face and the "interfacial sphere" (in *Bubbles*, 139–205).

31. This double-funnel model also implies that the opening is not infinite but still as wide as the formally possible range of psychocultural affordances.

32. On this, see, for example, Yapko's description of common misconceptions about hypnosis (*Trancework*, 8–9).

33. Franz Mesmer (1734–1815) well represents the tensions between the development of Western science and the progressive exclusion of phenomena that can't be accounted for by modern empiricist *dispositifs*. Mesmer, a German physicist who established himself in France, gathered a large following with his theory and practice of "animal magnetism" (the antecedent of what will later be called hypnosis). His unusual methods seemed to have extraordinary healing results. In 1784, the king of France, Louis XVI, appointed a commission—which included members of the Royal Academy of Science such as the French chemist Antoine Lavoisier and the American Ambassador Benjamin Franklin—to verify Mesmer's theory of a "magnetic fluid" connecting all living beings. His theories were discredited by the commission and thus relegated to the realm of superstition and charlatanism. The historian of psychoanalysis Henri Ellenberger offers a detailed history of Mesmer's antecedents and the relationship between animal magnetism and modern hypnosis (in *The Discovery of the Unconscious*); see also Chertok and Stengers's work on the relationship between hypnosis, science, and psychoanalysis (*A Critique of Psychoanalytic Reason*). Today, a growing body of scientific experiments and research is redefining our understanding of hypnotic phenomena through the scientific *dispositifs* of our present—from fMRIs to neurophenomenology. I am thinking, for example, about the recent development of the contemplative sciences (Raz and Lifshitz, *Hypnosis and Meditation*; Thompson, *Waking, Dreaming, Being*). Michael Lifshitz's eclectic neuroscientific work on meditation, hypnosis, and tulpamancy (see Lifshitz et al., "Absorption and Spiritual Experience") has deeply impacted my understanding of hypnosis, which had been mostly based on philosophical and anthropological works. More widely, the engag-

ing conversations at the Division of Transcultural Psychiatry at McGill with, among others, Laurence Kirmayer, Samuel Veissière, Elizaveta Solomonova, and Michael Lifshitz (again) have reframed my understanding of hypnosis (see, for example, Kirmayer, "Hypnosis and the Limits of Socialpsychological Reductionism"; Kirmayer, "Social Constructions of Hypnosis").

34. This idea could resonate with Teresa Brennan's reframing of attention as an affective (rather than exclusively cognitive) process (Brennan, *The Transmission of Affect*, 41).

35. Here, I am thinking about Ernest Rossi, a psychotherapist who closely worked with Milton Erickson. Rossi describes the "wave nature" of human consciousness, which includes different regimes of attention throughout the day and becomes highly suggestible during specific "windows" (see Rossi, *The Psychobiology of Gene Expression*; see also Greenfield, *Spirits with Scalpels*, 188–89).

36. See Tanya Luhrmann's work on absorption, *When God Becomes Real*, and also Lifshitz et al., "Absorption and Spiritual Experience."

37. Echoing Fredric Jameson's point about the waning of affect (*Postmodernism*, 10), maybe this represents the waning of peripheral awareness. I am also thinking about the hypnotic induction in terms of the "suppression of bottom-up prediction-errors" if we understand our brain as a composition of different layers and levels that tend to supress and reduce the entropy of lower levels (see Carhart-Harris and Friston, "The Default-Mode, Ego-Functions and Free-Energy"). On algorithmic governance and the digital unconscious, see Clough, *The User Unconscious*; Han, *Psychopolitics*; and O'Neil, *Weapons of Math Destruction*.

38. In my current research, where I record participants (between nineteen and twenty-four years old) while they are scrolling on their own TikTok account, many participants get quite upset with "the algorithm" when they are fed something they don't like. This seems, precisely, to be related to the fact that undesired content snaps them out of the feed flow (see Collu and Stillinger, "Like Buzzing in My Brain").

39. On this, see Collu and Stillinger, "Like Buzzing in My Brain." See also Mazzarella, *The Mana of Mass Society*, on constitutive resonance and addressability.

40. We are getting domesticated by living algorithms that think much faster than we do. Thinking about Mesmer's use of the term together with Hegel's writings, we should understand the Zoombie state we get into in terms of "animal magnetism" (see Hegel, *Le Magnétisme Animal*; on Zoombies see Collu, "#Zoombies"). We must indeed rethink the role of hypnosis in the human animal, because we are now being domesticated by living forms of intelligence that overpower us. And they transform us into salivating Pavlovian memes. I am thinking here about how experimental psychology's experiments on mice and intermittent reward have been used to design "addictive" digital platforms—on this see Martin, *Experiments of the Mind*. I am also thinking about James Lovelock's last book, *Novacene*, and the role of AI cyborgs as an emergent geological force.

41. Byung-Chul Han writes that "the capitalism of *Like* [social media] should come with a warning label: *Protect me from what I want*" (*Psychopolitics*, 15). I am echoing here Deleuze and Guattari's writing about territorialization and desiring-machines (*A Thousand Plateaus*).

42. On culture's capacity to shape shared registers of attention, see Samuel Veissière

("Varieties of Tulpa Experiences"). On culture and ecologies of attention, see Citton, *The Ecology of Attention*.

43. Thanks to Haley and Hugo for thinking with me about this during one warm summer night, over gin and tonics and a slightly too dry pork poke I made. On that occasion, Haley, you also helped me think about hypnosis, culture, and predictive processing. I am also thinking about rearticulation after a conversation with Jeremiah Scalia on biosemiotics and articulatory movement.

44. I am evoking here again Piera Aulagner's notion of the "pictographic reservoir" (*The Violence of Interpretation*, 38) in experiences that foreground primary unconscious processes. See also Pandolfo, *Knot of the Soul*, 97, on pictograms and psychic reservoirs. While Freud's "discovery of the unconscious" was deeply rooted in experiments with hypnosis, the father of psychoanalysis moved away from the therapeutic use of hypnosis, favoring the technique of free association. Freud explained free association as the attainment of a psychic state that "bears some analogy to the state before falling asleep—and no doubt also to hypnosis" (*The Interpretation of Dreams*, 127). On the couch, the patient is asked to say anything that comes to mind without any restriction, thus suppressing her critical faculty and learning how to observe the emergence of psychic images. In this state, the patient can intentionally follow the involuntary appearance of images, thus transforming the involuntary ideas into voluntary ones. Borch-Jacobsen explores in depth the continuities between free association, transference, and hypnosis (in *The Freudian Subject* and *The Emotional Tie*); see also Ellenberger, *The Discovery of the Unconscious*.

45. See Yapko, *Trancework*. As Borch-Jacobsen writes, this form of lucid awareness distinguishes, quite clearly, hypnotic experience from other trancelike experiences such as spirit possession (*The Emotional Tie*, 100–101).

46. I have been in conversation with the sleep and dream scientist Elizaveta Solomonova to understand to what extent hypnosis is different from sleep (in all its stages). The debate is still wide open, as it really depends how we define the thresholds between awareness, consciousness, and sleep. Sleepers, for example, are to an extent aware of their environment and incorporate environmental feedback while sleeping and can even be considered conscious during states like lucid dreaming (see Solomonova and Carr, "Incorporation of External Stimuli into Dream Content").

47. Roustang, *Qu'est-ce que l'hypnose?*, 18. In *Influence*, Roustang also writes, "It's the persistence of a certain degree and a certain form of vigilance that paradoxically offers hypnosis to the possibility of its description" (83, my translation).

48. This probably happened to many fans of the TV show *Succession*: After binge-watching four seasons of *Succession* in a few weeks, it became hard for me not to tell every single person I met to just simply "Fuck off!"

49. See Berardi, "The Image Dispositif."

50. Massumi, "The Autonomy of Affect," 24.

51. Stevenson, *Life Beside Itself*, 12. Stevenson is here citing Foucault, "Dream, Imagination and Existence," 36. The work of my dear friends and colleagues Lisa Stevenson and Diana Allan at McGill's Critical Media Lab is an endless source of inspiration. Among many other things, I am compelled by their different ways to develop imagistic anthro-

pologies that go beyond visual images—see, for example, Allan on "sounding sense" (in "Not the Songs but the Singing") and Stevenson on "sounding death" (in "Sounding Death, Saying Something").

52. I explore Berlant's notion of the "good life" in chapter 2. In my doctoral dissertation, I called the cluster of images orienting our romantic relationships the couple-image (Collu, "Refractive Cogito").

53. Thank you, Leo Stillinger, for this sentence and many other sentence fixes in this chapter and, more widely, in this book.

54. I am thinking, for example, about the title of François Roustang's book on hypnosis, *Influence*. My dear friend and colleague Nicola Di Croce translates in Italian the body's capacity to "affect and be affected" as the body's capacity to "influence and be influenced" (see Di Croce, "Le trasformazioni del commercio nell'atmosfera urbana").

55. Mazzarella, *The Mana of Mass Society*, 8.

56. In a similar vein, Lauren Berlant writes about "a history of impacts held in reserve" (*Cruel Optimism*, 84).

57. As in the introduction, I am here borrowing Deleuze's expression "double movement of liberation and capture" (*Cinema 2*, 68).

58. See chapter 1 on the oral drive and identification.

59. See chapter 3 on *dispositifs*.

60. My late father, when possessed by a sudden tenderness bracketing his omnivorous rage, often recalled with love the time Haley told him that "it's okay not to be okay."

61. Just like Freud's dreams, our social media feed should indeed be understood as another "royal road to the unconscious" (see Freud, *The Interpretation of Dreams*, 604). This is precisely what we are trying to do at McGill's Scrolling Societies Lab, where we collectively share, analyze, and comment on the video recordings of participants scrolling through their TikTok feed (see Collu and Stillinger, "Like Buzzing in My Brain").

62. Through ethnographic research in a shamanic center in the Peruvian Amazon, the anthropologist David Dupuis has shown how psychedelic experiences are deeply shaped by social and cultural context ("The Socialization of Hallucinations). See also Olson et al., "Tripping on Nothing," on placebo psychedelics and the impact of context-related expectations; and Dupuis and Veissière on psychedelics as "active super-placebos" (in "Culture, Context, and Ethics").

63. This is not a hyperbolic image; even Gwyneth Paltrow flew her team to Jamaica to do magic mushrooms in the first episode of *The Goop Lab* (Paltrow et al., "The Healing Trip"). In contrast, I am thinking about Eduardo Kohn's work with Manari Ushigua, who is a political and spiritual leader of the Sápara Nation in the Ecuadorian Amazon. Kohn and Ushigua mobilize psychedelic image work as well as dream work to develop alternative responses to our planetary crisis—from working with spirits to developing a cosmopolitical diplomacy. Kohn's visionary work has been an endless source of inspiration while writing this book (see Kohn, *How Forests Think*; and Kohn, "Forest Forms and Ethical Life").

64. In *Bubbles*, Peter Sloterdijk, whose work I am indirectly echoing across this chapter, offers a creative reading of interpersonal subject formation through the image of the bubble as a shared hypnotic and transferential space.

65. Anderson, "The End of Theory."

66. David Brooks wrote about "data-ism" in a *New York Times* opinion piece, which he opens by saying, "If you asked me to describe the rising philosophy of the day, I'd say it is data-ism" ("The Philosophy of Data"). The physicist and complex networks theorist Alessandro Vespignani has explored how "big data" can't offer a transparent representation of reality, describing data as intrinsically social artifacts (in *L'algoritmo e l'oracolo*).

67. Just to cite an "older" example, think about the parable of Google Flu Trends (see Lazer et al., "The Parable of Google Flu"). See also O'Neil's work on racialized algorithm infrastructures, *Weapons of Math Destruction*. In relation to the social sciences and humanities, I am thinking, for example, about the growing development of digital humanities programs or computational social sciences.

68. See also Byung-Chul Han's critique of dataism and the digital unconscious (*Psychopolitics*, 55–76).

69. For an anthropology of wearable technologies, see the work of Natasha Dow Schüll, "Data for Life." On "technologies of the self," see Foucault, *The Hermeneutics of the Subject*. Sometimes I think that after a few days without quantified "technologies of the self," I would find myself on the floor of some bar in Caracas without knowing what happened. (The imaginary of Caracas emerges from my absorption of an Italian Rum Pampero TV ad, which ended by saying "Rum Pampero, the rum drunk in the worst bars of Caracas." Caracas and alcoholic perdition will be always connected in my unconscious.)

70. On the planetary, see Chakrabarty, *The Climate of History in a Planetary Age*.

71. Deleuze and Guattari, *What Is Philosophy?*, 41.

72. On dream interpretation and the difference between manifest and latent content, see Freud, *The Interpretation of Dreams*.

73. Freud, *The Interpretation of Dreams*, 135.

74. Freud, *The Interpretation of Dreams*, 528. Here I am also thinking about the navel through Stefania Pandolfo's image of the "knot," a psychic signifier incarnating the trace of the symbolic Other (in *Knot of the Soul*).

75. Datafied forms of self-knowledge have become so important that if I go for a run without my smartwatch, it's as if I didn't go. See Schüll, "Data for Life," on datafied self-knowledge.

76. I take this also from an inspiring conversation with the anthropologist Matthew McCoy at UCLA. Innumerable conceptual adventures and drifts with Yanina Gori have also impacted my understanding of the gift as a concept space. I have thought about the datum with great fun and intellectual effervescence at UC Berkeley with Ned Dostaler—in 2017 we organized a roundtable titled "The Datum: Phenomenic Gifts, Phantasmatic Dispositifs" (American Anthropological Association, Washington, DC) to engage with the fantasies of, and about, the empirical in anthropology; I have also written about the datum and vision in a review of Robert Desjarlais's *The Blind Man* (Collu, "The Datum"). In the belly of the data-logical beast, the time has come for anthropology to ask again the question that made this discipline so useless, narcissistically trapped, and deeply original at the same time. What is data, or better, what gets to count as data and under which conditions? The anthropologist Jarrett Zigon also writes about the "relationality

of the datum as gift" to rethink the role of digital data and to propose a revised phenomenological ethics of hospitality in a data-centric society (in *How Is It Between Us?*, 74, 91).

77. Gift and exchange systems have been deeply central to anthropological thinking. I am here thinking about Marcel Mauss's essay on the gift (see Mauss, *The Gift*; see also Strathern, *The Gender of the Gift*; and Zigon, *How Is It Between Us?*).

78. See Lacan's Seminar XI (in *The Four Fundamental Concepts of Psychoanalysis*). On the inscription of the other's desire, see also Pandolfo, *Knot of the Soul*.

79. This dream also appears in Collu, "#Zoombies," 211.

80. The burning arm resonates with Freud's "dream of the burning child," where a father who has just lost his child dreams about the boy standing close and telling him, "Father don't you see that I am burning?" (Freud, *The Interpretation of Dreams*, 513). In this scene it seems I am talking to the m/other therapist while saying, "Sofía, can't you see that my arm is burning?" In biomedical cosmology, this neuropathic symptom is often plugged into the constellation of somatoform disorders, conversion syndromes, spinal cord injuries, or psychosomatic disorders—for a recent ethnography of somatoform disorders, see Daisy Couture, "The Place Where the Ground Gives Way." This is also a common symptom for people with the Chiari malformation, amid whom I did ethnographic research on their experience of chronic suffering (Collu, "Essere-nel-Chiari").

81. Nancy, *The Birth to Presence*, 18.

82. See Henry, *The Genealogy of Psychoanalysis*, on auto-affection, and Damasio, *The Strange Order of Things*, on affects and the biological development of life-forms.

Bibliography

Ackerman, Nathan Ward. *Treating the Troubled Family*. New York: Basic Books, 1966.

Adamovsky, Ezequiel, Sergio Eduardo Visacovsky, and Patricia Beatriz Vargas. *Clases medias: Nuevos enfoques desde la sociología, la historia y la antropología*. Buenos Aires: Ariel, 2014.

Agamben, Giorgio. "What Is an Apparatus?" In *What Is an Apparatus? And Other Essays*, 1–24. Stanford, CA: Stanford University Press, 2009.

Ahmed, Sara. *The Cultural Politics of Emotion*. London: Routledge, 2004.

Ahmed, Sara. "Happy Objects." In *The Affect Theory Reader*, edited by Melissa Gregg and Gregory J. Seigworth, 29–51. Durham, NC: Duke University Press, 2010.

Ahmed, Sara. *Queer Phenomenology: Orientations, Objects, Others*. Durham, NC: Duke University Press, 2006.

Ainsworth, Mary D. Salter, Mary C. Blehar, Everett Waters, and Sally N. Wall. *Patterns of Attachment: A Psychological Study of the Strange Situation*. New York: Psychology Press, 2015.

Alberti, Leon Battista. *On Painting and On Sculpture: The Latin Texts of De Pictura and De Statua*. London: Phaidon, 1972.

Allan, Diana. "Not the Songs but the Singing: Sounding Sense in Colonial Films from British Mandate Palestine." *Social Research: An International Quarterly* 89, no. 4 (2022): 1107–33.

Al-Saji, Alia. "The Memory of Another Past: Bergson, Deleuze and a New Theory of Time." *Continental Philosophy Review* 37, no. 2 (2004): 203–39. https://doi.org/10.1007/s11007-005-5560-5.

Al-Saji, Alia. "A Phenomenology of Hesitation: Interrupting Racializing Habits of Seeing." In *Living Alterities: Phenomenology, Embodiment, and Race*, edited by Emily Lee, 133–72. Albany: SUNY Press, 2014.

Alter, Adam. *Irresistible: The Rise of Addictive Technology and the Business of Keeping Us Hooked*. New York: Penguin, 2017.

Amselle, Jean-Loup. *Mestizo Logics: Anthropology of Identity in Africa and Elsewhere*. Stanford, CA: Stanford University Press, 1998.

Anderson, Ben. "Affective Atmospheres." *Emotion, Space and Society* 2, no. 2 (2009): 77–81. https://doi.org/10.1016/j.emospa.2009.08.005.

Anderson, Chris. "The End of Theory: The Data Deluge Makes the Scientific Method Obsolete." *Wired*, June 23, 2008. https://www.wired.com/2008/06/pb-theory/.

Anderson, Harlene, and Harold Goolishian. "The Client Is the Expert: A Not-Knowing Approach to Therapy." In *Therapy as Social Construction*, edited by Sheila McNamee and Kenneth J. Gergen, 24–39. Newbury Park, CA: Sage, 1992.

Angerer, Marie-Luise. *Desire After Affect*. Lanham, MD: Rowman and Littlefield, 2014.

Arasse, Daniel. *Histoires de peintures*. Paris: Gallimard, 2004.

Aulagnier, Piera. *The Violence of Interpretation: From Pictogram to Statement*. London: Routledge, 2001.

Badiou, Alain. *Being and Event*. London: A&C Black, 2007.

Badiou, Alain. *In Praise of Love*. London: Profile, 2012.

Bandler, Richard, John Grinder, and Steve Andreas. *Reframing: Neuro-Linguistic Programming and the Transformation of Meaning*. Moab, UT: Real People Press, 1982.

Barad, Karen. *Meeting the Universe Halfway: Quantum Physics and the Entanglement of Matter and Meaning*. Durham, NC: Duke University Press, 2007.

Barrett, Lisa Feldman. *How Emotions Are Made: The Secret Life of the Brain*. New York: Houghton Mifflin Harcourt, 2017.

Barthes, Roland. *Camera Lucida: Reflections on Photography*. New York: Macmillan, 1981.

Bateson, Gregory. "The Cybernetics of 'Self': A Theory of Alcoholism." In *Steps to an Ecology of Mind: Collected Essays in Anthropology, Psychiatry, Evolution, and Epistemology*, 309–37. Chicago: University of Chicago Press, 2000.

Bateson, Gregory. *Naven: A Survey of the Problems Suggested by a Composite Picture of the Culture of a New Guinea Tribe Drawn from Three Points of View*. 2nd ed. Stanford, CA: Stanford University Press, 1958.

Bateson, Gregory. "Pathologies of Epistemology." In *Steps to an Ecology of Mind: Collected Essays in Anthropology, Psychiatry, Evolution, and Epistemology*, 486–95. Chicago: University of Chicago Press, 2000.

Bateson, Gregory. *A Sacred Unity: Further Steps to an Ecology of Mind*. New York: HarperCollins, 1991.

Bateson, Gregory. *Steps to an Ecology of Mind: Collected Essays in Anthropology, Psychiatry, Evolution, and Epistemology*. Chicago: University of Chicago Press, 2000.

Bateson, Gregory, Don D. Jackson, Jay Haley, and John Weakland. "Toward a Theory of Schizophrenia." *Behavioral Science* 1, no. 4 (1956): 251–64. https://doi.org/10.1002/bs.3830010402.

Benjamin, Jessica. "Beyond Doer and Done To: An Intersubjective View of Thirdness." *Psychoanalytic Quarterly* 73, no. 1 (January 1, 2004): 5–46. https://doi.org/10.1002/j.2167-4086.2004.tb00151.x.

Bennett, Jane. *Vibrant Matter: A Political Ecology of Things*. Durham, NC: Duke University Press, 2010.

Berardi, Franco. "The Image Dispositif." *Cultural Studies Review* 11, no. 2 (2013): 64–68. https://doi.org/10.5130/csr.v11i2.3657.

Berger, John. *Ways of Seeing*. 1972. Reprint, London: Penguin Classic, 2008.

Bergson, Henri. *Matter and Memory*. Translated by N. M. Paul and W. S. Palmer. Rev. ed. New York: Zone, 1991.

Berlant, Lauren. *Cruel Optimism*. Durham, NC: Duke University Press, 2011.

Berlant, Lauren. *Desire/Love*. New York: Punctum, 2012.

Berlant, Lauren, ed. *Intimacy*. Chicago: University of Chicago Press, 2000.

Berlant, Lauren. *On the Inconvenience of Other People*. Durham, NC: Duke University Press, 2022.

Berlant, Lauren. "The Unfinished Business of Cruel Optimism: Crisis, Affect, Sentimentality." University of Toronto's Bonham Centre for Sexual Diversity Studies. Lynch Lecture, November 19, 2020.

Berlant, Lauren, and Kathleen Stewart. *The Hundreds*. Durham, NC: Duke University Press, 2019.

Biehl, João, Byron Good, and Arthur Kleinman. *Subjectivity: Ethnographic Investigations*. Berkeley: University of California Press, 2007.

Bion, W. R. *Experiences in Groups: And Other Papers*. London: Routledge, 2003.

Blanchot, Maurice. *The Space of Literature: A Translation of "l'Espace Littéraire."* Lincoln: University of Nebraska Press, 2015.

Bleichmar, Silvia. *Dolor país y después . . .* Buenos Aires: Libros del Zorzal, 2007.

Blustein, Paul. *And the Money Kept Rolling In (and Out): Wall Street, the IMF, and the Bankrupting of Argentina*. New York: PublicAffairs, 2006.

Böhme, Gernot. "Atmosphere as the Fundamental Concept of a New Aesthetics." *Thesis Eleven* 36, no. 1 (1993): 113–26. https://doi.org/10.1177/072551369303600107.

Boler, Megan, and Elizabeth Davis. *Affective Politics of Digital Media: Propaganda by Other Means*. London: Routledge, 2021.

Bolter, Jay David, and Richard Grusin. *Remediation: Understanding New Media*. Cambridge, MA: MIT Press, 1999.

Bombay, Jean-Philippe, and Samuele Collu. "A Scroll Through the Present." In *Soigner La Technologie? Cahier D'Enquêtes*, edited by Collectif Stasis, 70–103. Montreal: GRIP-UQAM, 2020.

Borch-Jacobsen, Mikkel. *The Emotional Tie: Psychoanalysis, Mimesis, and Affect*. Stanford, CA: Stanford University Press, 1993.

Borch-Jacobsen, Mikkel. *The Freudian Subject*. Stanford, CA: Stanford University Press, 1988.

Brennan, Teresa. *The Transmission of Affect*. Ithaca, NY: Cornell University Press, 2004.

Brennan, Teresa, and Martin Jay. *Vision in Context: Historical and Contemporary Perspectives on Sight*. London: Routledge, 1996.

Brooks, David. "The Philosophy of Data." *New York Times*, February 5, 2013. https://www.nytimes.com/2013/02/05/opinion/brooks-the-philosophy-of-data.html.

Brotherton, P. Sean. "Armed Against Unhappiness: Psychoanalytic Grammars in Buenos Aires." *Medical Anthropology Quarterly* 34, no. 1 (2020): 99–118. https://doi.org/10.1111/maq.12552.

Buci-Glucksmann, Christine. *The Madness of Vision: On Baroque Aesthetics*. Athens: Ohio University Press, 2013.

Butler, Judith. *Gender Trouble: Feminism and the Subversion of Identity*. London: Routledge, 2011.

Carbone, Mauro. *Filosofia-schermi: Dal cinema alla rivoluzione digitale*. Milano: Cortina Raffaello, 2016.

Carbone, Mauro. *The Flesh of Images: Merleau-Ponty Between Painting and Cinema*. Albany: SUNY Press, 2015.

Carbone, Mauro. "Lo schermo, la tela, la finestra (e altre superfici quadrangolari normalmente verticali)." *Rivista di estetica*, no. 55 (March 1, 2014): 21–34. https://doi.org/10.4000/estetica.921.

Cardeña, Etzel. "Hypnos and Psyche: How Hypnosis Has Contributed to the Study of Consciousness." *Psychology of Consciousness: Theory, Research, and Practice* 1, no. 2 (2014): 123–38.

Cardeña, Etzel, Peter Jönsson, Devin B. Terhune, and David Marcusson-Clavertz. "The Neurophenomenology of Neutral Hypnosis." *Cortex* 49, no. 2 (2013): 375–85. https://doi.org/10.1016/j.cortex.2012.04.001.

Carhart-Harris, R. L., and K. J. Friston. "The Default-Mode, Ego-Functions and Free-Energy: A Neurobiological Account of Freudian Ideas." *Brain* 133, no. 4 (2010): 1265–83. https://doi.org/10.1093/brain/awq010.

Carr, E. Summerson. *Scripting Addiction: The Politics of Therapeutic Talk and American Sobriety*. Princeton, NJ: Princeton University Press, 2010.

Casetti, Francesco. *Screening Fears: On Protective Media*. Princeton, NJ: Princeton University Press, 2023.

Ceberio, Marcelo Rodriguez. "Querer y no lograr: Soluciones intentadas fallidas." *Revista REDES*, no. 35 (2017): 99–116.

Certeau, Michel de. "La folie de la vision." *Esprit* (1940–), no. 66 (1982): 89–99.

Certeau, Michel de. *The Possession at Loudun*. Chicago: University of Chicago Press, 1970.

Certeau, Michel de. *The Practice of Everyday Life*. Berkeley: University of California Press, 1988.

Chakrabarty, Dipesh. *The Climate of History in a Planetary Age*. Chicago: University of Chicago Press, 2021.

Chertok, Léon, and Isabelle Stengers. *A Critique of Psychoanalytic Reason: Hypnosis as a Scientific Problem from Lavoisier to Lacan*. Stanford, CA: Stanford University Press, 1992.

Citton, Yves. *The Ecology of Attention*. Hoboken, NJ: John Wiley and Sons, 2017.

Clough, Patricia Ticineto. *The User Unconscious: On Affect, Media, and Measure*. Minneapolis: University of Minnesota Press, 2018.

Clough, Patricia Ticineto, and Jean Halley, eds. *The Affective Turn: Theorizing the Social*. Durham, NC: Duke University Press, 2007.

Cohen, Lawrence. "The Gay Guru: Fallibility, Unworldliness, and the Scene of Instruction." In *The Guru in South Asia: New Interdisciplinary Perspectives*, edited by Jacob Copeman and Aya Ikegame, 97–112. London: Routledge, 2012. https://doi.org/10.4324/9780203116258-5.

Cole, Mark. "The Role of Confession in Reflective Practice: Monitored Continuing Professional Development (CPD) in Health Care and the Paradox of Professional Autonomy." In *Theorizing Surveillance: The Panopticon and Beyond*, edited by David Lyon, 206–29. London: Routledge, 2006.

Collu, Samuele. "Compulsive Synchronicity: The Zoomification of Everyday Life." Paper presented at the Social Science Perspectives on the "New Normal," Transcultural Psychiatry Division, McGill University, 2020.

Collu, Samuele. "The Datum: Theory and the Feverish Madness of Vision." Visual and New Media Review, *Fieldsights*, June 4, 2019. https://culanth.org/fieldsights/the-datum-theory-and-the-feverish-madness-of-vision.

Collu, Samuele. "Essere-nel-Chiari: Corpi sofferenti, narrazioni e processi diagnostici." Master's thesis, Università di Bologna, 2009.

Collu, Samuele. "From Symbolic to Mimetic Efficacy: Anthropological Reflections on Hypnosis, Mystical Experience, and the Affective Tie." Unpublished manuscript, University of California, Berkeley, 2013.

Collu, Samuele. "L'assenza presente di Buddha: Statue e persone nel monastero cambogiano di K." Bachelor's thesis, Università di Bologna, 2006.

Collu, Samuele. "Refracting Affects: Affect, Psychotherapy, and Spirit Dis-Possession." *Culture, Medicine, and Psychiatry* 43, no. 2 (2019): 290–314. https://doi.org/10.1007/s11013-018-9616-5.

Collu, Samuele. "Refractive Cogito: An Ethnography of Relational Imagination." PhD diss., University of California, Berkeley, 2016.

Collu, Samuele. "A Therapy of Screens: Psychotherapy and the Visual Apparatus." *Anthropological Quarterly* 93, no. 4 (2020): 729–53. https://doi.org/10.1353/anq.2020.0065.

Collu, Samuele. "#Zoombies: Cybernetic Trance in Pandemic Times." In *Planetary Health Humanities and Pandemics*, edited by Heike Härting and Heather Meek, 199–217. London: Routledge, 2024.

Collu, Samuele, and Leo Stillinger. "Like Buzzing in My Brain: A Psychopolitical Phenomenology of TikTok." In *Négociations affectives: Expériences sensibles, réflexivités et enjeux de pouvoir*, edited by Arnaud Halloy and Paul Codja. Cahiers d'Anthropologie Sociale. Paris: Éditions de l'Herne, 2025.

Collu, Samuele, and Eric Taggart. "Rest So Deep Now." *Anthropology and Humanism* 48, no. 2 (2023): 435–36. https://doi.org/10.1111/anhu.12484.

Copjec, Joan. *Read My Desire: Lacan Against the Historicists*. Cambridge, MA: MIT Press, 1994.

Couture, Daisy. "The Place Where the Ground Gives Way: Somatoform Disorders and the (Im)Possibility of Medical Uncertainty." Master's thesis, McGill University, 2023. https://escholarship.mcgill.ca/concern/theses/ms35tf58f.

Crary, Jonathan. *Techniques of the Observer: On Vision and Modernity in the Nineteenth Century*. Cambridge, MA: MIT Press, 1990.

Csordas, Thomas J. *Embodiment and Experience: The Existential Ground of Culture and Self*. Cambridge: Cambridge University Press, 1994.

Csordas, Thomas J. "Embodiment as a Paradigm for Anthropology." *Ethos* 18, no. 1 (1990): 5–47. https://doi.org/10.1525/eth.1990.18.1.02a00010.

Dagfal, Alejandro. *Entre Paris y Buenos Aires*. Buenos Aires: Paidós, 2009.

D'Alessandro, Mercedes. *Economía feminista: Economía y feminismo unidos para revolu-
cionar ideas y estereotipos del presente*. Barcelona: Penguin Random House Grupo Editorial España, 2018.

Dalmasso, Anna Caterina. *Le corps, c'est l'écran*. Milan: Mimesis, 2018.

Damasio, Antonio. *Looking for Spinoza: Joy, Sorrow, and the Feeling Brain*. New York:
Random House, 2003.

Damasio, Antonio. *The Strange Order of Things: Life, Feeling, and the Making of Cultures*. New York: Vintage, 2019.

D'Avella, Nicholas. *Concrete Dreams: Practice, Value, and Built Environments in Post-
Crisis Buenos Aires*. Durham, NC: Duke University Press, 2019.

D'Avella, Nicholas. "Ecologies of Investment: Crisis Histories and Brick Futures in Argentina." *Cultural Anthropology* 29, no. 1 (2014): 173–99. https://doi.org/10.14506
/ca29.1.10.

Davis, Kenneth L., and Christian Montag. "Selected Principles of Pankseppian Affective
Neuroscience." *Frontiers in Neuroscience* 12 (2019). https://www.frontiersin.org
/article/10.3389/fnins.2018.01025.

Davis, Kenneth L., and Jaak Panksepp. *The Emotional Foundations of Personality: A Neurobiological and Evolutionary Approach*. New York: W. W. Norton, 2018.

Deeley, Quinton, David A. Oakley, Brian Toone, Vincent Giampietro, Michael J. Bram-
mer, Steven C. R. Williams, and Peter W. Halligan. "Modulating the Default Mode
Network Using Hypnosis." *International Journal of Clinical and Experimental Hypnosis* 60, no. 2 (2012): 206–28. https://doi.org/10.1080/00207144.2012.648070.

Deleuze, Gilles. *Bergsonism*. Translated by Hugh Tomlinson and Barbara Habberjam.
New York: Zone, 1990.

Deleuze, Gilles. *Cinema 2: The Time-Image*. Translated by Hugh Tomlinson and Robert
Galeta. Minneapolis: University of Minnesota Press, 1989.

Deleuze, Gilles. *Difference and Repetition*. Translated by Paul Patton. New York: Columbia University Press, 1994.

Deleuze, Gilles. *Pure Immanence: Essays on a Life*. Translated by Anne Boyman. New
York: Zone, 2001.

Deleuze, Gilles. *Spinoza: Practical Philosophy*. Translated by Robert Hurley. San Francisco: City Lights, 2001.

Deleuze, Gilles, and Félix Guattari. *A Thousand Plateaus: Capitalism and Schizophrenia*.
Translated by Brian Massumi. Minneapolis: University of Minnesota Press, 1987.

Deleuze, Gilles, and Félix Guattari. *What Is Philosophy?* Translated by Hugh Tomlinson
and Graham Burchell. New York: Columbia University Press, 1994.

De Martino, Ernesto. *The Land of Remorse: A Study of Southern Italian Tarantism*.
Translated by Dorothy Louise Zinn. London: Free Association, 2005.

De Martino, Ernesto. *Magic: A Theory from the South*. Translated by Dorothy Louise
Zinn. London: Hau, 2015.

Desjarlais, Robert. *The Blind Man: A Phantasmography*. New York: Fordham University
Press, 2018.

Desjarlais, Robert. *Counterplay: An Anthropologist at the Chessboard*. Berkeley: University of California Press, 2011.

Di Croce, Nicola. "Le trasformazioni del commercio nell'atmosfera urbana: Ambiente sonoro e attrattività dello spazio pubblico nel centro storico di Mestre." *Archivio di Studi Urbani e Regionali*, March 5–26, 2021. https://doi.org/10.3280/ASUR2021-130001.

Dow, James. "Universal Aspects of Symbolic Healing: A Theoretical Synthesis." *American Anthropologist* 88, no. 1 (1986): 56–69.

Dupuis, David. "The Socialization of Hallucinations: Cultural Priors, Social Interactions and Contextual Factors in the Use of Psychedelics." *Transcultural Psychiatry* 59, no. 5 (2022). https://doi.org/10.1177/13634615211036388.

Dupuis, David, and Samuel Veissière. "Culture, Context, and Ethics in the Therapeutic Use of Hallucinogens: Psychedelics as Active Super-Placebos?" *Transcultural Psychiatry* 59, no. 5 (2022): 571–78. https://doi.org/10.1177/13634615221131465.

Duranti, Alessandro. *Linguistic Anthropology: A Reader*. Hoboken, NJ: John Wiley and Sons, 2009.

Durkheim, Émile. *The Elementary Forms of Religious Life*. Translated by Karen E. Fields. New York: Free Press, 1995.

Ekman, Paul, and Wallace V. Friesen. *Unmasking the Face: A Guide to Recognizing Emotions from Facial Clues*. Cambridge, MA: Malor, 2003.

Eliade, Mircea. *Myth and Reality*. New York: Harper and Row, 1963.

Eliade, Mircea. *The Myth of the Eternal Return: Or, Cosmos and History*. Princeton, NJ: Princeton University Press, 1971.

Elkins, Gary R., Arreed F. Barabasz, James R. Council, and David Spiegel. "Advancing Research and Practice: The Revised APA Division 30 Definition of Hypnosis." *American Journal of Clinical Hypnosis* 57, no. 4 (2015): 378–85. https://doi.org/10.1080/00029157.2015.1011465.

Ellenberger, Henri F. *The Discovery of the Unconscious: The History and Evolution of Dynamic Psychiatry*. New York: Basic Books, 1970.

Emerson, Hannah. *The Kissing of Kissing*. Minneapolis: Milkweed Editions, 2022.

Epele, María E. "'Breaking Down': Afflictions and Treatments During Times of Crisis in Buenos Aires." *Culture, Medicine, and Psychiatry* 46 (2022): 761–78. https://doi.org/10.1007/s11013-021-09748-z.

Epele, María E. "Psychotherapy, Psychoanalysis and Urban Poverty in Argentina." *Anthropology and Medicine* 23, no. 3 (2016): 244–58. https://doi.org/10.1080/13648470.2016.1180664.

Epstein, Jean. *The Intelligence of a Machine*. Minneapolis: University of Minnesota Press, 2014.

Ericson, Richard Victor, and Kevin D. Haggerty, eds. *The New Politics of Surveillance and Visibility*. Toronto: University of Toronto Press, 2006.

Evans-Pritchard, E. E. *Witchcraft, Oracles and Magic Among the Azande*. Abridged ed. Oxford: Oxford University Press, 1976.

Fanon, Frantz. *Black Skin, White Masks*. New York: Grove Press, 2008.

Fanon, Frantz. *The Wretched of the Earth*. New York: Grove Press, 2007.

Fava, Ricardo, and Diego Zenobi. "Moral, política y clase media: Intelectuales y saberes en tiempos de crisis." In *Moralidades, economías e identidades de clase media: Estudios históricos y etnográficos*, 217–46. Buenos Aires: Editorial Antropofagia, 2014.

Favret-Saada, Jeanne. *The Anti-Witch*. Chicago: Hau, 2015.

Favret-Saada, Jeanne. *Deadly Words: Witchcraft in the Bocage*. Cambridge: Cambridge University Press, 1981.

Foucault, Michel. *Discipline and Punish: The Birth of the Prison*. Translated by Alan Sheridan. New York: Vintage, 1995.

Foucault, Michel. "Dream, Imagination and Existence: An Introduction to Ludwig Binswanger's *Dream and Existence*." In *Dream and Existence*, edited by Keith Hoeller, 29–78. Atlantic Highlands, NJ: Humanities Press, 1993.

Foucault, Michel. *The Hermeneutics of the Subject: Lectures at the Collège de France 1981–1982*. Translated by Graham Burchell. London: Picador, 2005.

Foucault, Michel. *Technologies of the Self: A Seminar with Michel Foucault*. Edited by Luther H. Martin, Huck Gutman, and Patrick H. Hutton. Cambridge, MA: University of Massachusetts Press, 1988.

Foucault, Michel. "What Is Enlightenment?" In *Ethics: Subjectivity and Truth*, vol. 1, 303–20. Essential Works of Michel Foucault, 1954–1984. New York: New Press, 1997.

Frank, Adam J., and Elizabeth A. Wilson. "Like-Minded." *Critical Inquiry* 38, no. 4 (2012): 870–77.

Frank, Adam J., and Elizabeth A. Wilson. *A Silvan Tomkins Handbook: Foundations for Affect Theory*. Minneapolis: University of Minnesota Press, 2020.

Freud, Sigmund. *Beyond the Pleasure Principle*. In *The Revised Standard Edition of the Complete Psychological Works of Sigmund Freud*, vol. 18. Lanham, MD: Rowman and Littlefield, 2024.

Freud, Sigmund. "Fragment of an Analysis of Hysteria (Dora)." In *The Penguin Freud Reader*, edited by Adam Phillips, 435–540. London: Penguin Classics, 2006.

Freud, Sigmund. *Group Psychology and the Analysis of the Ego*. Rev. ed. New York: W. W. Norton, 1990.

Freud, Sigmund. *The Interpretation of Dreams: The Complete and Definitive Text*. Translated by James Strachey. New York: Basic Books, 2010.

Freud, Sigmund. *New Introductory Lectures on Psycho-Analysis*. In *The Standard Edition of the Complete Psychological Works of Sigmund Freud*, edited by James Strachey, vol. 22. London: Hogarth and the Institute of Psycho-Analysis, 1964.

Freud, Sigmund. "Observations on Love in Transference." In *The Penguin Freud Reader*, edited by Adam Phillips, 341–53. London: Penguin Classics, 2006.

Freud, Sigmund. *The Penguin Freud Reader*. Edited by Adam Phillips. London: Penguin Classics, 2006.

Freud, Sigmund. "The Uncanny." In *The Standard Edition of the Complete Psychological Works of Sigmund Freud*, edited by James Strachey, vol. 17, 219–52. London: Hogarth, 1919.

Friston, Karl. "The Free-Energy Principle: A Unified Brain Theory?" *Nature Reviews Neuroscience* 11, no. 2 (2010): 127–38. https://doi.org/10.1038/nrn2787.

Geertz, Clifford. "'From the Native's Point of View': On the Nature of Anthropological Understanding." In *Local Knowledge: Further Essays in Interpretive Anthropology*, 55–70. New York: Basic Books, 1983.

Geertz, Clifford. "Thick Description: Toward an Interpretive Theory of Culture." In *The Interpretation of Cultures*, 3–30. New York: Basic Books, 1973.

Gibson, James J. *The Ecological Approach to Visual Perception*. New York: Psychology Press, 2013.

Giddens, Anthony. *The Transformation of Intimacy: Sexuality, Love, and Eroticism in Modern Societies*. Stanford, CA: Stanford University Press, 1992.

Gori, Yanina. "Acute Melancholia: Through My Pharmakon." Unpublished manuscript, University of California, Berkeley, 2013.

Gori, Yanina. "Re/Mediating Revolution: Cultivating Solidarity in a Queer Cuban Community." University of California, Los Angeles, 2021. https://escholarship.org /uc/item/84f334v9.

Graeber, David, and David Wengrow. *The Dawn of Everything: A New History of Humanity*. New York: Farrar, Straus and Giroux, 2021.

Greene, Jeremy A. *The Doctor Who Wasn't There: Technology, History, and the Limits of Telehealth*. Chicago: University of Chicago Press, 2022.

Greenfield, Sidney M. *Spirits with Scalpels: The Cultural Biology of Religious Healing in Brazil*. Walnut Creek, CA: Left Coast Press, 2008.

Gregg, Melissa, and Gregory J. Seigworth, eds. *The Affect Theory Reader*. Durham, NC: Duke University Press, 2010.

Guattari, Félix. *Chaosmosis: An Ethico-Aesthetic Paradigm*. Bloomington: Indiana University Press, 1995.

Gupta, Akhil, and James Ferguson. *Culture, Power, Place: Explorations in Critical Anthropology*. Durham, NC: Duke University Press, 1997.

Habermas, Jürgen. *The Structural Transformation of the Public Sphere: An Inquiry into a Category of Bourgeois Society*. Cambridge, MA: MIT Press, 1991.

Haley, Jay. "An Interactional Explanation of Hypnosis." *American Journal of Clinical Hypnosis* 1 (1958): 41–57. https://doi.org/10.1080/00029157.1958.10734336.

Haley, Jay. *Uncommon Therapy: The Psychiatric Techniques of Milton H. Erickson, M.D.* New York: W. W. Norton, 1973.

Han, Byung-Chul. *Psychopolitics: Neoliberalism and New Technologies of Power*. New York: Verso, 2017.

Haraway, Donna. "Situated Knowledges: The Science Question in Feminism and the Privilege of Partial Perspective." *Feminist Studies* 14, no. 3 (1988): 575–99. https://doi .org/10.2307/3178066.

Hardwick, Elizabeth. *Sleepless Nights*. New York: New York Review Books, 2011.

Hegel, Georg Wilhelm Friedrich. *Le Magnétisme Animal: Naissance de l'Hypnose*. Translated by François Roustang. Paris: Presses Universitaires de France, 2005.

Heidegger, Martin. *The Question Concerning Technology, and Other Essays*. New York: HarperCollins, 1977.

Heims, Steve J. *The Cybernetics Group*. Cambridge, MA: MIT Press, 1991.

Henry, Michel. *The Genealogy of Psychoanalysis*. Translated by Douglas Brick. Stanford, CA: Stanford University Press, 1993.

Heusch, Luc de. *Sacrifice in Africa: A Structuralist Approach*. Manchester, UK: Manchester University Press, 1985.

Hochschild, Arlie Russell. *The Time Bind: When Work Becomes Home and Home Becomes Work*. New York: Macmillan, 1997.

Hoffman, Lynn. "A Constructivist Position for Family Therapy." *Irish Journal of Psychology* 9, no. 1 (1988): 110–29. https://doi.org/10.1080/03033910.1988.10557709.

Holmes, Jeremy. *The Brain Has a Mind of Its Own: Attachment, Neurobiology, and the New Science of Psychotherapy*. London: Confer, 2020.

Howes, David. *Empire of the Senses: The Sensual Culture Reader*. Oxford: Berg, 2005.

Huhtamo, Erkki. "Elements of Screenology: Toward an Archeology of the Screen." *ICONICS: International Studies of Modern Image* 7 (2004): 31–82.

Illouz, Eva. *Consuming the Romantic Utopia: Love and the Cultural Contradictions of Capitalism*. Berkeley: University of California Press, 1997.

Illouz, Eva. *The End of Love: A Sociology of Negative Relations*. Oxford: Oxford University Press, 2019.

Illouz, Eva. *Saving the Modern Soul: Therapy, Emotions, and the Culture of Self-Help*. Berkeley: University of California Press, 2008.

Illouz, Eva. *Why Love Hurts: A Sociological Explanation*. Cambridge: Polity, 2012.

James, William. *The Principles of Psychology*. Cambridge, MA: Harvard University Press, 1981.

Jameson, Fredric. *Postmodernism, or, The Cultural Logic of Late Capitalism*. Durham, NC: Duke University Press, 1991.

Jardine, Alice A., Shannon Lundeen, and Kelly Oliver. *Living Attention: On Teresa Brennan*. Albany: SUNY Press, 2012.

Jay, Martin. *Downcast Eyes: The Denigration of Vision in Twentieth-Century French Thought*. Berkeley: University of California Press, 1993.

Jiang, Heidi, Matthew P. White, Michael D. Greicius, Lynn C. Waelde, and David Spiegel. "Brain Activity and Functional Connectivity Associated with Hypnosis." *Cerebral Cortex* 27, no. 8 (2017): 4083–93. https://doi.org/10.1093/cercor/bhw220.

Kelledy, Lisa, and Brandon Lyons. "Circular Causality in Family Systems Theory." In *Encyclopedia of Couple and Family Therapy*, edited by Jay L. Lebow, Anthony L. Chambers, and Douglas C. Breunlin, 431–34. Cham: Springer International, 2019. https://doi.org/10.1007/978-3-319-49425-8_248.

Kipnis, Laura. *Against Love: A Polemic*. New York: Vintage, 2004.

Kirmayer, Laurence J. "The Cultural Diversity of Healing: Meaning, Metaphor, and Mechanism." *British Medical Bulletin* 69, no. 1 (2004): 33–48. https://doi.org/10.1093/bmb/ldh006.

Kirmayer, Laurence J. "Hypnosis and the Limits of Socialpsychological Reductionism." *Behavioral and Brain Sciences* 10, no. 3 (1987): 521. https://doi.org/10.1017/S0140525X00023876.

Kirmayer, Laurence J. "Social Constructions of Hypnosis." *International Journal of Clinical and Experimental Hypnosis* 40, no. 4 (1992): 276–300. https://doi.org/10.1080/00207149208409662.

Kirmayer, Laurence J. "Unpacking the Placebo Response: Insights from Ethnographic Studies of Healing." In *Placebo Talks: Modern Perspectives on Placebo in Society*, edited by Amir Raz and Cory Harris, 119–43. Oxford: Oxford University Press, 2016.

Knight, Daniel M. *Vertiginous Life: An Anthropology of Time and the Unforeseen*. New York: Berghahn, 2021.

Kohn, Eduardo. "Forest Forms and Ethical Life." *Environmental Humanities* 14, no. 2 (2022): 401–18. https://doi.org/10.1215/22011919-9712478.

Kohn, Eduardo. *How Forests Think: Toward an Anthropology Beyond the Human*. Berkeley: University of California Press, 2013.

Kristeva, Julia. *Powers of Horror: An Essay on Abjection*. Reissue ed. New York: Columbia University Press, 2024.

Lacan, Jacques. *The Four Fundamental Concepts of Psychoanalysis*. Edited by Jacques-Alain Miller. Translated by Alan Sheridan. New York: W. W. Norton, 1998.

Lacan, Jacques. "The Mirror Stage as Formative of the Function as Revealed in Psychoanalytic Experience." In *Ecrits*, 75–81. New York: W. W. Norton, 2002.

Lacan, Jacques. *Freud's Papers on Technique, 1953–1954: The Seminar of Jacques Lacan, Book I*. New York: W. W. Norton, 1991.

Landry, Mathieu, Michael Lifshitz, and Amir Raz. "Brain Correlates of Hypnosis: A Systematic Review and Meta-Analytic Exploration." *Neuroscience and Biobehavioral Reviews* 81 (October 2017): 75–98. https://doi.org/10.1016/j.neubiorev.2017.02.020.

Laplanche, Jean, and Jean-Bertrand Pontalis. *The Language of Psychoanalysis*. London: Karnac, 1988.

Latour, Bruno. *Reassembling the Social: An Introduction to Actor-Network-Theory*. Oxford: Oxford University Press, 2005.

Lazer, David, Ryan Kennedy, Gary King, and Alessandro Vespignani. "The Parable of Google Flu: Traps in Big Data Analysis." *Science* 343, no. 6176 (2014): 1203–5. https://doi.org/10.1126/science.1248506.

Lefebvre, Henri. *Rhythmanalysis: Space, Time and Everyday Life*. London: Bloomsbury, 2013.

Lepselter, Susan. *The Resonance of Unseen Things: Poetics, Power, Captivity, and UFOs in the American Uncanny*. Ann Arbor: University of Michigan Press, 2016.

Levin, David Michael, ed. *Sites of Vision: The Discursive Construction of Sight in the History of Philosophy*. Cambridge, MA: MIT Press, 1999.

Lévi-Strauss, Claude. "The Effectiveness of Symbols." In *Structural Anthropology*, 198–204. New York: Basic Books, 2008.

Lévi-Strauss, Claude. "The Sorcerer and His Magic." In *Structural Anthropology*, 161–79. New York: Basic Books, 2008.

Leys, Ruth. *The Ascent of Affect: Genealogy and Critique*. Chicago: University of Chicago Press, 2017.

Leys, Ruth. "The Turn to Affect: A Critique." *Critical Inquiry* 37 (2011): 434–72.

Lifshitz, Michael, Michiel van Elk, and T. M. Luhrmann. "Absorption and Spiritual Experience: A Review of Evidence and Potential Mechanisms." *Consciousness and Cognition* 73 (2019): 102760. https://doi.org/10.1016/j.concog.2019.05.008.

Liu, Lydia H. *The Freudian Robot: Digital Media and the Future of the Unconscious*. Chicago: University of Chicago Press, 2010.

Lovelock, James. *Novacene: The Coming Age of Hyperintelligence*. Cambridge, MA: MIT Press, 2019.

Luhrmann, T. M. *How God Becomes Real: Kindling the Presence of Invisible Others.* Princeton, NJ: Princeton University Press, 2020.

Luiselli, Valeria. *Faces in the Crowd.* Minneapolis: Coffee House Press, 2014.

Lyon, David. *The Culture of Surveillance: Watching as a Way of Life.* Cambridge: Polity Press, 2018.

Lyon, David. *Surveillance After September 11.* Cambridge: Polity, 2003.

Lyon, David, Kirstie Ball, and Kevin D. Haggerty. *Routledge Handbook of Surveillance Studies.* London: Routledge, 2012.

Macchioli, Florencia. "Inicios de la terapia familiar en la Argentina, 1960–1979." *Estudos e Pesquisas em Psicologia* 12, no. 1 (2012): 274–87.

Madanes, Cloé. *Behind the One-Way Mirror: Advances in the Practice of Strategic Therapy.* San Francisco: Jossey-Bass, 1984.

Mahmood, Saba. *Politics of Piety: The Islamic Revival and the Feminist Subject.* Princeton, NJ: Princeton University Press, 2012.

Manning, Erin. *Always More Than One: Individuation's Dance.* Durham, NC: Duke University Press, 2013.

Manoukian, Setrag. "A Vocabulary for the Impersonal: A Notebook from Shiraz." In *Manifestos for World Thought,* edited by Lucian Stone and Jason Bahbak Mohaghegh, 155–69. London: Rowman and Littlefield International, 2017.

Marcuse, Herbert. *Eros and Civilization: A Philosophical Inquiry into Freud.* London: Routledge, 1956.

Markovic, Jelena, and Evan Thompson. "Hypnosis and Meditation: A Neurophenomenological Comparison." In *Hypnosis and Meditation: Towards an Integrative Science of Conscious Planes,* edited by Amir Raz and Michael Lifshitz, 79–106. New York: Oxford University Press, 2016.

Marsilli-Vargas, Xochitl. *Genres of Listening: An Ethnography of Psychoanalysis in Buenos Aires.* Durham, NC: Duke University Press, 2022.

Marsilli-Vargas, Xochitl. "The Offline and Online Mediatization of Psychoanalysis in Buenos Aires." *Signs and Society* 4, no. 1 (2016): 135–53. https://doi.org/10.1086/685822.

Martin, Emily. *Experiments of the Mind: From the Cognitive Psychology Lab to the World of Facebook and Twitter.* Princeton, NJ: Princeton University Press, 2022.

Masco, Joseph. "The Crisis in Crisis." *Current Anthropology* 58, no. S15 (2016): S65–76. https://doi.org/10.1086/688695.

Massumi, Brian. "The Autonomy of Affect." In *Parables for the Virtual: Movement, Affect, Sensation,* 23–45. Durham, NC: Duke University Press, 2002.

Mattingly, Cheryl. "Emergent Narratives." In *Narrative and the Cultural Construction of Illness and Healing,* edited by Cheryl Mattingly and Linda C. Garro, 181–211. Berkeley: University of California Press, 2001.

Mattingly, Cheryl. *Healing Dramas and Clinical Plots: The Narrative Structure of Experience.* Cambridge: Cambridge University Press, 1998.

Mauss, Marcel. *The Gift: The Form and Reason for Exchange in Archaic Societies.* New York: W. W. Norton, 2000.

Mazzarella, William. "Holding the Frame/Playing the Game: Transference as Political Potentiality." *Problemi International* 60, no. 11–12 (2022): 171–91.

Mazzarella, William. *The Mana of Mass Society*. Chicago: University of Chicago Press, 2017.

McStay, Andrew. *Emotional AI: The Rise of Empathic Media*. London: Sage, 2018.

McSweeney, Joyelle. *Death Styles*. Boston: Little, Brown, 2024.

McTighe, Laura, and Megan Raschig. "Introduction: An Otherwise Anthropology." Theorizing the Contemporary, *Fieldsights*, July 31, 2019. https://culanth.org /fieldsights/introduction-an-otherwise-anthropology.

Merleau-Ponty, Maurice. "Eye and Mind." In *The Merleau-Ponty Reader*, 351–78. Evanston, IL: Northwestern University Press, 2007.

Merleau-Ponty, Maurice. *Phenomenology of Perception*. London: Routledge, 2012.

Merleau-Ponty, Maurice. *The Visible and the Invisible: Followed by Working Notes*. Evanston, IL: Northwestern University Press, 1968.

Métraux, Alfred. *Voodoo in Haiti*. Gifkendorf, Germany: Merlin-Verlag, 1994.

Meyers, Todd. *All That Was Not Her*. Durham, NC: Duke University Press, 2022.

Minuchin, Salvador, Braulio Montalvo, Bernard G. Gurney, Bernice L. Rosman, and Florence Schumer. *Families of the Slums*. New York: Basic Books, 1967.

Mitchell, W. J. T. *What Do Pictures Want? The Lives and Loves of Images*. Chicago: University of Chicago Press, 2005.

Motta, Marco. *Esprits fragiles: Réparer les liens ordinaires à Zanzibar*. Lausanne: BSN Press, 2019.

Muir, Sarah. "The Currency of Failure: Money and Middle-Class Critique in Post-Crisis Buenos Aires." *Cultural Anthropology* 30, no. 2 (2015): 310–35. https://doi.org/10 .14506/ca30.2.10.

Muir, Sarah. "On Historical Exhaustion: Argentine Critique in an Era of 'Total Corruption.'" *Comparative Studies in Society and History* 58, no. 1 (2016): 129–58. https://doi .org/10.1017/S0010417515000596.

Mulvey, Laura. "Visual Pleasure and Narrative Cinema." *Screen* 16, no. 3 (1975): 6–18.

Nakamura, Jeanne, and Mihaly Csikszentmihalyi. "The Concept of Flow." In *Flow and the Foundations of Positive Psychology: The Collected Works of Mihaly Csikszentmihalyi*, edited by Mihaly Csikszentmihalyi, 239–63. Dordrecht: Springer Netherlands, 2014. https://doi.org/10.1007/978-94-017-9088-8_16.

Nancy, Jean-Luc. *The Birth to Presence*. Stanford, CA: Stanford University Press, 1993.

Nardone, Giorgio, and Paul Watzlawick. *Brief Strategic Therapy: Philosophy, Techniques, and Research*. Lanham, MD: Jason Aronson, 2005.

Nelson, Maggie. *The Argonauts*. Minneapolis: Graywolf Press, 2015.

Newport, Cal. *Digital Minimalism: Choosing a Focused Life in a Noisy World*. London: Penguin, 2019.

Ng, Emily. *A Time of Lost Gods: Madness, Mediumship, and the Ghost After Mao*. Oakland: University of California Press, 2020.

Ochs, Elinor, and Lisa Capps. *Living Narrative: Creating Lives in Everyday Storytelling*. Cambridge, MA: Harvard University Press, 2002.

Ogden, Emily. *On Not Knowing: How to Love and Other Essays*. Chicago: University of Chicago Press, 2022.

Ogden, Thomas H. *Subjects of Analysis*. Northvale, NJ: Jason Aronson, 1994.

Olson, Jay A., Léah Suissa-Rocheleau, Michael Lifshitz, Amir Raz, and Samuel P. L. Veissière. "Tripping on Nothing: Placebo Psychedelics and Contextual Factors." *Psychopharmacology* 237, no. 5 (2020): 1371–82. https://doi.org/10.1007/s00213 -020-05464-5.

Olson, Valerie. *Into the Extreme: U.S. Environmental Systems and Politics Beyond Earth*. Minneapolis: University of Minnesota Press, 2018.

O'Neil, Cathy. *Weapons of Math Destruction: How Big Data Increases Inequality and Threatens Democracy*. New York: Crown, 2017.

Palazzoli, Mara Selvini, Luigi Boscolo, Gianfranco Cecchin, and Giuliana Prata. *Paradox and Counterparadox: A New Model in the Therapy of the Family in Schizophrenic Transaction*. Translated by Elisabeth V. Burt. New York: Jason Aronson, 1985.

Paltrow, Gwyneth, Elise Loehnen, Andrew Fried, Shauna Minoprio, and Dane Lillegard. "The Healing Trip." *The Goop Lab*, episode 1, January 24, 2020. Netflix.

Pandian, Anand. *Reel World: An Anthropology of Creation*. Durham, NC: Duke University Press, 2015.

Pandian, Anand, and Stuart J. McLean. *Crumpled Paper Boat: Experiments in Ethnographic Writing*. Durham, NC: Duke University Press, 2017.

Pandolfo, Stefania. *Knot of the Soul: Madness, Psychoanalysis, Islam*. Chicago: University of Chicago Press, 2018.

Panksepp, Jaak. *Affective Neuroscience: The Foundations of Human and Animal Emotions*. Oxford: Oxford University Press, 2004.

Panofsky, Erwin. *Perspective as Symbolic Form*. New York: Zone, 1991.

Papalini, Vanina Andrea. "Recetas para sobrevivir a las exigencias del neocapitalismo (O de cómo la autoayuda se volvió parte de nuestro sentido común)." *Nueva Sociedad* 245 (June 2013): 163–77.

Phillips, Adam. "Keeping It Moving: Commentary on Judith Butler's 'Melancholy Gender / Refused Identification.'" In *The Psychic Life of Power*, by Judith Butler, 151–59. Stanford, CA: Stanford University Press, 1997.

Piasere, Leonardo. *L'etnografo imperfetto: Esperienza e cognizione in antropologia*. Bari: Laterza, 2002.

Plotkin, Mariano. *Argentina on the Couch: Psychiatry, State, and Society, 1880 to the Present*. Edited by Mariano Plotkin. Albuquerque: University of New Mexico Press, 2003.

Plotkin, Mariano Ben. *Freud in the Pampas: The Emergence and Development of a Psychoanalytic Culture in Argentina*. Stanford, CA: Stanford University Press, 2002.

Plotkin, Mariano Ben, and Nicolás Viotti. "Between Freud and Umbanda: Therapeutic Constellations in Buenos Aires, Argentina." In *The Routledge International Handbook of Global Therapeutic Cultures*, edited by Daniel Nehring, Ole Jacob Madsen, Edgar Cabanas, China Mills, and Dylan Kerrigan, 257–67. London: Routledge, 2020.

Plotkin, Mariano Ben, and Sergio E. Visacovsky. "Los psicoanalistas y la crisis, la crisis del psicoanálisis." *Cahiers de LIRICO*, no. 4 (2008): 149–63. https://doi.org/10.4000 /lirico.462.

Port, Mattijs van de. "Baroque as Tension: Introducing Turbulence and Turmoil into the Academic Text." In *Modes of Knowing: Resources from the Baroque*, edited by John Law and Evelyn Ruppert, 165–96. Manchester, UK: Mattering Press, 2016.

Povinelli, Elizabeth A. *The Empire of Love: Toward a Theory of Intimacy, Genealogy, and Carnality*. Durham, NC: Duke University Press, 2006.

Povinelli, Elizabeth A. *Geontologies: A Requiem to Late Liberalism*. Durham, NC: Duke University Press, 2016.

Povinelli, Elizabeth A. "Routes/Worlds." *E-Flux Journal*, no. 27 (blog), 2011. https://www.e-flux.com/journal/27/67991/routes-worlds/.

Price, Catherine. *How to Break Up with Your Phone: The 30-Day Plan to Take Back Your Life*. New York: Ten Speed Press, 2018.

Probyn, Elspeth. "Writing Shame." In *The Affect Theory Reader*, edited by Melissa Gregg and Gregory J. Seigworth, 71–90. Durham, NC: Duke University Press, 2010.

Proust, Marcel. *Swann's Way: In Search of Lost Time*, vol. 1. New Haven, CT: Yale University Press, 2013.

Ramstead, Maxwell J. D., Samuel P. L. Veissière, and Laurence J. Kirmayer. "Cultural Affordances: Scaffolding Local Worlds Through Shared Intentionality and Regimes of Attention." *Frontiers in Psychology* 7 (2016). https://www.frontiersin.org/article/10.3389/fpsyg.2016.01090.

Ravetto-Biagioli, Kriss. *The Digital Uncanny*. Oxford: Oxford University Press, 2019.

Raz, Amir. "Anatomy of Attentional Networks." *Anatomical Record Part B: The New Anatomist* 281B, no. 1 (2004): 21–36. https://doi.org/10.1002/ar.b.20035.

Raz, Amir, and Michael Lifshitz. *Hypnosis and Meditation: Towards an Integrative Science of Conscious Planes*. Oxford: Oxford University Press, 2016.

Resch, Franz, and Peter Parzer. "Cybernetics and Behavioral Loops." In *Adolescent Risk Behavior and Self-Regulation: A Cybernetic Perspective*, edited by Franz Resch and Peter Parzer, 71–80. Cham: Springer International, 2021. https://doi.org/10.1007/978-3-030-69955-0_8.

Ricoeur, Paul. *Time and Narrative*, vol. 1. Chicago: University of Chicago Press, 1984.

Ricoeur, Paul. *Time and Narrative*, vol. 2. Chicago: University of Chicago Press, 1990.

Roitman, Janet. *Anti-Crisis*. Durham, NC: Duke University Press, 2014.

Rolón, Gabriel. *Historias de diván*. Buenos Aires: Planeta Argentina, 2011.

Rose, Nikolas S. *Governing the Soul: The Shaping of the Private Self*. London: Free Association, 1999.

Rose, Nikolas, Rasmus Birk, and Nick Manning. "Towards Neuroecosociality: Mental Health in Adversity." *Theory, Culture and Society* 39, no. 3 (2021). https://doi.org/10.1177/0263276420981614.

Rossi, Ernest Lawrence. *The Psychobiology of Gene Expression: Neuroscience and Neurogenesis in Hypnosis and the Healing Arts*. New York: W. W. Norton, 2002.

Roustang, François. *Il suffit d'un geste*. Paris: O. Jacob, 2004.

Roustang, François. *Influence*. Paris: Éditions de Minuit, 1990.

Roustang, François. *Qu'est-ce que l'hypnose?* Critique ed. Paris: Éditions de Minuit, 1994.

Ruefle, Mary. *Madness, Rack, and Honey: Collected Lectures*. Seattle: Wave, 2023.

Sapir, Edward. *Selected Writings of Edward Sapir in Language, Culture and Personality*. Berkeley: University of California Press, 2021.

Sartre, Jean-Paul. *Being and Nothingness*. New York: Simon and Schuster, 2018.

Scheff, Thomas. *Catharsis in Healing, Ritual, and Drama*. Lincoln, NE: iUniverse, 2001.

Schüll, Natasha Dow. *Addiction by Design: Machine Gambling in Las Vegas*. Princeton, NJ: Princeton University Press, 2012.

Schüll, Natasha Dow. "Data for Life: Wearable Technology and the Design of Self-Care." *BioSocieties* 11, no. 3 (2016): 317–33. https://doi.org/10.1057/biosoc.2015.47.

Schwartz, Alexandra. "The Therapist Remaking Our Love Lives on TV." *New Yorker*, May 16, 2022. https://www.newyorker.com/magazine/2022/05/23/couples -therapy-showtime-orna-guralnik.

Schwartz, Richard C., and Martha Sweezy. *Internal Family Systems Therapy*. New York: Guilford, 2020.

Scott, James C. *Weapons of the Weak: Everyday Forms of Peasant Resistance*. New Haven, CT: Yale University Press, 1985.

Seale-Feldman, Aidan, and Samuele Collu. "Towards an Anthropology of Psychic Life." Unpublished manuscript.

Sedgwick, Eve Kosofsky. "Paranoid Reading and Reparative Reading, or, You're So Paranoid, You Probably Think This Essay Is About You." In *Touching Feeling: Affect, Pedagogy, Performativity*, 123–51. Durham, NC: Duke University Press, 2003.

Sedgwick, Eve Kosofsky. *Touching Feeling: Affect, Pedagogy, Performativity*. Durham, NC: Duke University Press, 2003.

Sedgwick, Eve Kosofsky, and Adam Frank. "Shame in the Cybernetic Fold: Reading Silvan Tomkins." In *Shame and Its Sisters: A Silvan Tomkins Reader*, edited by Eve Kosofsky Sedgwick and Adam Frank, 1–31. Durham, NC: Duke University Press, 1995.

Seth, Anil. *Being You: A New Science of Consciousness*. New York: Penguin, 2021.

Severi, Carlo. "Memory, Reflexivity and Belief: Reflections on the Ritual Use of Language." *Social Anthropology* 10, no. 1 (2002): 23–40. https://doi.org/10.1017/S0964028202000034.

Silverman, Kaja. *The Threshold of the Visible World*. London: Routledge, 1996.

Sloterdijk, Peter. *Bubbles: Spheres Volume I: Microspherology*. Translated by Wieland Hoban. Los Angeles: Semiotext(e), 2011.

Smadja, Éric. *Le couple et son histoire*. Paris: Humensis, 2011.

Smith, Miranda, and Eli Karam. "Second-Order Cybernetics in Family Systems Theory." In *Encyclopedia of Couple and Family Therapy*, edited by Jay Lebow, Anthony Chambers, and Douglas C. Breunlin, 1–2. Cham: Springer International, 2018. https://doi .org/10.1007/978-3-319-15877-8_308-1.

Sobchack, Vivian. "Comprehending Screens: A Meditation *in Medias Res*." *Rivista Di Estetica*, no. 55 (March 1, 2014): 87–101. https://doi.org/10.4000/estetica.959.

Solomonova, Elizaveta, and Michelle Carr. "Incorporation of External Stimuli into Dream Content." In *Dreams: Understanding Biology, Psychology, and Culture*, edited by Katja Valli and Robert J. Hoss, 1:213–18. Santa Barbara, CA: Greenwood ABC–CLIO, 2019.

Song, Hoon. *Pigeon Trouble: Bestiary Biopolitics in a Deindustrialized America*. Philadelphia: University of Pennsylvania Press, 2011.

Song, Hoon. "Seeing Oneself Seeing Oneself: White Nihilism in Ethnography and Theory." *Ethnos* 71, no. 4 (2006): 470–88. https://doi.org/10.1080/00141840601050676.

Spinoza, Benedict de. *Ethics*. Translated by Edwin Curley. London: Penguin Classics, 1996.

Stevenson, Lisa. *Life Beside Itself: Imagining Care in the Canadian Arctic*. Berkeley: University of California Press, 2014.

Stevenson, Lisa. "Sounding Death, Saying Something." *Social Text* 35, no. 1 (130) (2017): 59–78. https://doi.org/10.1215/01642472-3727996.

Stewart, Kathleen. "Atmospheric Attunements." *Environment and Planning D: Society and Space* 29, no. 3 (2011): 445–53. https://doi.org/10.1068/d9109.

Stewart, Kathleen. "In the World That Affect Proposed." *Cultural Anthropology* 32, no. 2 (2017): 192–98. https://doi.org/10.14506/ca32.2.03.

Stewart, Kathleen. *Ordinary Affects*. Durham, NC: Duke University Press, 2007.

Stewart, Kathleen. "Weak Theory in an Unfinished World." *Journal of Folklore Research* 45, no. 1 (2008): 71–82.

Stillinger, Leo. "Hiker's Midnight: Rhythms of Transformation on the Appalachian Trail." Master's thesis, McGill University, 2024. https://escholarship.mcgill.ca/concern/theses/6108vh985.

Strathern, Marilyn. *The Gender of the Gift: Problems with Women and Problems with Society in Melanesia*. Berkeley: University of California Press, 1990.

Sullivan, Shannon. *Revealing Whiteness: The Unconscious Habits of Racial Privilege*. Bloomington: Indiana University Press, 2006.

Taggart, Eric. "Before U Ever Even Heard of Oedipus: Remediating Attachment and the Strange Situation Procedure." In *Nothing Personal?!? Essays on Affect, Gender and Queerness*, edited by Omar Kasmani, Matthias Lüthjohann, Sophie Nikoleit, and Jean-Baptiste Pettier, 97–105. Berlin: B_Books, 2022.

Taggart, Eric. "Remediating Attachment: The Strange Situation Procedure as a Techno-primal Mise-en-Scène for Social Theory." PhD diss., University of California, Davis, 2023.

Tarde, Gabriel de. *The Laws of Imitation*. Lexington, KY: BiblioBazaar, 2009.

Taussig, Michael. *The Mastery of Non-Mastery in the Age of Meltdown*. Chicago: University of Chicago Press, 2020.

Taylor, Charles. *Sources of the Self: The Making of the Modern Identity*. Cambridge: Cambridge University Press, 1989.

Thompson, Evan. *Waking, Dreaming, Being: Self and Consciousness in Neuroscience, Meditation, and Philosophy*. New York: Columbia University Press, 2014.

Throop, Jason. *Suffering and Sentiment: Exploring the Vicissitudes of Experience and Pain in Yap*. Berkeley: University of California Press, 2010.

Tomkins, Silvan. *Affect Imagery Consciousness*, vol. 3, *The Negative Affects: Anger and Fear*. New York: Springer, 1991.

Tomkins, Silvan. *Shame and Its Sisters: A Silvan Tomkins Reader*. Edited by Eve Kosofsky Sedgwick and Adam Frank. Durham, NC: Duke University Press, 1995.

Turner, Victor. *The Ritual Process: Structure and Anti-Structure.* Piscataway, NJ: Transaction, 1995.

Varela, Francisco J., and Evan Thompson. "Color Vision: A Case Study in the Foundations of Cognitive Science." *Revue de Synthèse* 111, no. 1–2 (1990): 129–38. https://doi.org/10.1007/bf03181032.

Varela, Francisco J., Evan Thompson, and Eleanor Rosch. *The Embodied Mind: Cognitive Science and Human Experience.* Cambridge, MA: MIT Press, 2016.

Vasseleu, Cathryn. *Textures of Light: Vision and Touch in Irigaray, Levinas and Merleau-Ponty.* London: Routledge, 1998.

Veissière, Samuel. "Varieties of Tulpa Experiences: The Hypnotic Nature of Human Sociality, Personhood, and Interphenomenality." In *Hypnosis and Meditation: Towards an Integrative Science of Conscious Planes*, edited by Amir Raz and Michael Lifshitz. Oxford: Oxford University Press, 2016.

Veissière, Samuel P. L., Axel Constant, Maxwell J. D. Ramstead, Karl J. Friston, and Laurence J. Kirmayer. "Thinking Through Other Minds: A Variational Approach to Cognition and Culture." *Behavioral and Brain Sciences* 43 (January 2020): e90. https://doi.org/10.1017/S0140525X19001213.

Vertov, Dziga. *Kino-Eye: The Writings of Dziga Vertov.* Berkeley: University of California Press, 1984.

Vespignani, Alessandro. *L'algoritmo e l'oracolo: Come la scienza predice il futuro e ci aiuta a cambiarlo.* Milan: Il Saggiatore, 2019.

Vezzetti, Hugo. *Aventuras de Freud en el país de los argentinos: De José Ingenieros a Enrique Pichón-Rivière.* Buenos Aires: Paidós, 1996.

Vezzetti, Hugo. "From the Psychiatric Hospital to the Street: Enrique Pichon Rivière and the Diffusion of Psychoanalysis in Argentina." In *Argentina on the Couch: Psychiatry, State, and Society, 1880 to the Present*, 141–74. Albuquerque: University of New Mexico Press, 2003.

Visacovsky, Sergio. "'Hasta la proxima crisis': Historia cíclica, virtudes genealógicas y la identidad de clase media entre los afectados por la debacle financiera en la Argentina (2001–2002)." *CIDE Documentos de Trabajo* 43 (2010).

Visacovsky, Sergio. "La constitución de un sentido práctico del malestar cotidiano y el lugar del psicoanálisis en la Argentina." *Cuicuilco* 16, no. 45 (2009): 51–78.

Visacovsky, Sergio Eduardo, and Enrique Garguin. *Moralidades, economías e identidades de clase media: Estudios históricos y etnográficos.* Buenos Aires: Editorial Antropofagia, 2009.

Vitry, Grégoire, Claude de Scorraille, and Michael F. Hoyt. "Redundant Attempted Solutions: 50 Years of Theory, Evolution, and New Supporting Data." *Australian and New Zealand Journal of Family Therapy* 42, no. 2 (2021): 174–87. https://doi.org/10.1002/anzf.1448.

Wajcman, Gérard. *Fenêtre: Chroniques du regard et de l'intime.* Paris: Editions Verdier, 2004.

Warner, Michael. *Publics and Counterpublics.* New York: Zone, 2002.

Watkins, Megan. "Desiring Recognition, Accumulating Affect." In *The Affect Theory Reader*, edited by Melissa Gregg and Gregory J. Seigworth, 269–85. Durham, NC: Duke University Press, 2010.

Watzlawick, Paul, John H. Weakland, and Richard Fisch. *Change: Principles of Problem Formation and Problem Resolution.* New York: W. W. Norton, 1974.

Weinstein, Deborah. *The Pathological Family: Postwar America and the Rise of Family Therapy.* Ithaca, NY: Cornell University Press, 2013.

Weiss, Gail, Gayle Salamon, and Ann V. Murphy. *50 Concepts for a Critical Phenomenology.* Evanston, IL: Northwestern University Press, 2019.

Wiener, Norbert. *Cybernetics, or Control and Communication in the Animal and the Machine.* Cambridge, MA: MIT Press, 1961.

Williams, Raymond. *Marxism and Literature.* New York: Oxford University Press, 1977.

Winnicott, D. W. "Fear of Breakdown." In *Psycho-Analytic Explorations,* edited by Clare Winnicott, Ray Sheperd, and Madeleine Davis, 87–96. Cambridge, MA: Harvard University Press, 1989.

Winnicott, D. W. *Playing and Reality.* London: Routledge, 2005.

Winnicott, D. W. "The Theory of the Parent-Infant Relationship." *International Journal of Psycho-Analysis* 41 (December 1960): 585–95.

Yan, Yunxiang. *Private Life Under Socialism: Love, Intimacy, and Family Change in a Chinese Village, 1949–1999.* Stanford, CA: Stanford University Press, 2003.

Yapko, Michael D. *Essentials of Hypnosis.* Levittown, PA: Brunner/Mazel, 1995.

Yapko, Michael D. *Trancework: An Introduction to the Practice of Clinical Hypnosis.* London: Routledge, 2019.

Young, Iris Marion. "Throwing Like a Girl: A Phenomenology of Feminine Body Comportment Motility and Spatiality." *Human Studies* 3, no. 1 (1980): 137–56. https://doi.org/10.1007/BF02331805.

Zeavin, Hannah. *The Distance Cure: A History of Teletherapy.* Cambridge, MA: MIT Press, 2021.

Zigon, Jarrett. *Disappointment: Toward a Critical Hermeneutics of Worldbuilding.* New York: Fordham University Press, 2018.

Zigon, Jarrett. "An Ethics of Dwelling and a Politics of World-Building: A Critical Response to Ordinary Ethics." *Journal of the Royal Anthropological Institute* 20, no. 4 (2014): 746–64. https://doi.org/10.1111/1467-9655.12133.

Zigon, Jarrett. *How Is It Between Us? Relational Ethics and Care for the World.* HAU Essays in Ethnographic Theory. Chicago: HAU, 2024. https://press.uchicago.edu/ucp/books/book/distributed/H/bo215808296.html.

Zigon, Jarrett, and C. Jason Throop, eds. "Dwelling in the Contemporary Condition." Special issue, *Puncta* 5, no. 2 (2022).

Žižek, Slavoj. *Organs Without Bodies: Deleuze and Consequences.* London: Routledge, 2003.

Zupančič, Alenka. *What Is Sex?* Cambridge, MA: MIT Press, 2017.

Index

AA (Alcoholics Anonymous), 5
abjection, 26
Ackerman, Nathan, 139n2
affect: definitions, 51–52, 54; *affectedness*
(Nancy), 132; atmospheres and, 51, 55, 59,
69, 96; attachments and, 13, 57, 82; attention as, 172n34; autonomy of, 156n87;
as bodily force, 151n37; the body and, 51,
52–53; capacity to act and, 53–54, 55; capacity to be affected, 150n15; (dis)charges, 76,
77; children and, 63; crisis and, 76; cruel
optimism as, 58, 60; dumping (Brennan),
66, 67–68, 155n80; dumps, 13, 155n80; energy and, 66; exhaustion and, 63; the face
and, 151n37; femininity and, 63, 64, 67;
gender and, 63, 64, 67, 71; holding and,
149n7; images and, 124; intensities, 150n17;
joy, 52; loops and, 53; masculinity and,
63, 64, 67; memory and, 71; neuroscience
and, 51–52; as opacity, 158n105; openness,
108; present and, 56; relations and, 153n58;
repetition and, 13, 55, 97; scholarship on
(broadly), 51–52; transmission, 12, 63, 66,
73, 115, 118
affordances, 43, 93, 171n31
Agamben, Giorgio, 92, 162n27, 163n40
Ahmed, Sara, 92, 150n19, 153n48, 155n78,
162n38, 163n39, 163n44
Alberti, Leon Battista, 145n73
alcohol: alcoholism, 136n10; being buzzed, 77;
consumption, 115. *See also* drinking
Alcoholics Anonymous (AA), 5

alcoholism, 5
algorithms: attachments and, 94; Big Data
and, 128–29; bubbles and, 122–23; desire
and, 130; *dispositifs* (algorithmic), 165n71;
domestication through, 172n40; frustration at, 45; governance and, 122; imagined,
89; influencing, 127; knowledge (and mis-
understandings) of us, 89, 104, 105, 167n90,
172n38; predictive, 167n86; screens and, 45
Alicia, 55
Allan, Diana, 160n14, 173n51
allegory, mirror (one-way) as, 23
Almibar: dialogue with other therapists, 70,
71, 102, 106; gift of recordings to author,
81–82; in session, 80–81, 159n6; therapeutic interventions, 72; watching therapy sessions, 48, 50, 59, 77, 78, 91; weekly meetings
with other therapists, 47
always-ness, 161n24
always-never, 84, 85, 104, 108
Amalia, 10–11
American Dream, 58
Anderson, Ben, 51, 52, 153n55, 155n84
Anderson, Chris, 128
anger, 65, 66–67, 68, 155n83
animality, 172n40
anonymous gaze, 44, 45, 159n3
anthropology: context and this book, 138n30,
173n51; human, beyond the, 136n11; polic-
ing within discipline, 23, 24; on ritual, 107
anxiety, 112
apparatus. See *dispositifs*

Arasse, Daniel, 145n73

arbitrariness, fundamental, 20

archives: hypno-, 128; mimetic (Mazzarella), 125

Argentina: author's life in, 8, 9, 22, 112, 113, 114–15, 116–17, 119; cultural context, 138n30, 159n8; economic crisis (2001–2), 9, 49, 60, 62–63, 64–65, 76; protests, 159n8; psychoanalysis and, 9–10, 136nn16–17, 137nn18–19, 137n22; social class, 154n60

armchairs: *dispositifs* and, 97; image of, 79, 103; posture and, 91–92; refrain and, 88; in therapy room, 81, 85, 91, 94

ashes, 31

"ask your therapist!," 65

atmosphere(s): affect and, 51, 55, 59, 69; changes in, 70; couples and, 59, 60, 153n55; cruel optimism as, 60, 70, 74, 96; *dispositifs* and, 96; in therapy, 102

attachments: affect and, 13, 57, 82; algorithms and, 94; children and, 94; cruel optimism and, 58, 59–60, 125, 153n50, 165n73; objects and, 57, 94, 97; to one's own self, 24; styles, 163n53; theory, 94, 135n4, 163n53

attention: as affective process (Brennan), 172n34; living, 63, 64, 65, 67–68, 69; regimes of, 127, 172n35

Aulagner, Piera, 173n44

author's life: in Argentina, 8, 9, 22, 112, 113, 114–15, 116–17, 119; body and embodiment, 131–32; in Buenos Aires, 112; cruel optimism and, 58, 70; cybernetics and, 8; dancing and, 111, 126, 133; Deleuze's words and, 165n74; *dispositifs* and, 126; dreams and, 131; drinking and, 22–23, 115, 151nn34–35, 175n69; father (in death), 125–26, 131; father (in life), 141n27, 167n95, 174n60; hypnosis in, 3, 111–12, 113, 114, 116–17, 119–20, 121, 123, 126, 128, 129, 131–32; marriage (crisis in), 50, 112; mother (in death), 112, 113, 125–26, 131; relationships, 116–17; students, 13, 87, 106, 120

availability, 92, 143n51, 162n39

Badiou, Alain, 144n62

Baird, Haley, 63–64, 68, 154n69, 164n58, 165n67, 168n4, 173n43, 174n60

Barrett, Lisa Feldman, 150n16

Barthes, Roland, 162n33

Bateson, Gregory: on alcoholic and the bottle, 136n10; binary relationships, 30, 143n53, 143n55; cybernetics and, 4, 6, 135n5, 155n73, 155n75; loops, 29, 30, 143n55; mind in work, 66, 144n57, 157n98; reception of work, 4–5; systemic therapy and, 4, 115, 135n5, 155n73; systems in work, 66, 143n56, 144n57, 157n98

Bayesian brain hypothesis, 88, 161n24, 167n86

becoming, 8

Benjamin, Jessica, 33, 41, 144n65

Bentham, Jeremy, 147n84

Bergson, Henri, 156n88

Berlant, Lauren: on attachment, 57, 153nn50–51, 165n73; author's email to (unsent), 58; on the good life, 124; on impacts, 174n56; on impasse, 55; on intimacy, 144n63, 159n3; on (re)turns, 57, 160n9. *See also* cruel optimism (Berlant)

binary relationships, 30, 143n53, 143n55

binge-scrolling, 20–21, 45, 97, 99, 104, 122

binge-watching, 89, 93, 139n3

blankets, 95

Bleichmar, Silvia, 62–63

blueness, 111, 123, 126

body, the: affect and, 51, 52–53; feminine, 27; for Merleau-Ponty, 55, 140n9, 158n2; porosity of, 51, 123; as screen, 146n75; of the therapist, 74; transformation through first, 74; the world and, 53, 55

Bombay, Jean-Philippe, 161n25, 164n65, 166n85, 167n87

Borch-Jacobsen, Mikkel, 157n101, 173nn44–45

brain. *See* default mode network (DMN); neuroscience

breathing, 99, 107, 121

Brenda: breakup (request for), 31–32; dancing, 15; "do you see? do you see?," 32; one-way mirror and, 17, 21, 25, 31, 32, 34, 41, 42, 44, 45, 119, 151n31; other relationships, 15–16

Brennan, Teresa, 63, 66, 67, 154n66, 155n77, 155n83, 172n34

Brooks, David, 175n66

Brotherton, Sean, 136n17

bubble(s): algorithms and, 122–23; cruel op-

timism and, 70; hypno- (Mazzarella), 119, 122; as image, 50, 119–20, 121, 124, 125, 126, 127, 128; love/couple-, 7, 118, 119; nonlinearity of, 128; reading and, 93; refrains and, 105; screens and, 148n100; as space, 118–20, 126, 163n51; subjecthood and, 174n64; in therapy room, 80, 119–20, 121, 126, 127, 129
Buddhism, 168n2
buzz, 77, 98, 106, 109

camera: gaze and, 141n20; patients' awareness of, 12, 43; white noise of, 81, 83. See also eye of the camera
cannibalism, 14, 41
capitalism: love and, 153n44; psychedelic, 128
Caracas, 175n69
Carbone, Mauro, 145n71
Carson, Anne, 171n29
Casetti, Francesco, 148n100
cathexis, 151n31
Catholicism, 157n101
causality, circular, 66
cave, Plato's, 38
CBT (cognitive behavior therapy), 44
Ceberio, Marcelo, 153n53
cell phones, 20–21, 97, 98, 164n64, 165n69
Certeau, Michel de, 139n7, 149n5, 157n101
chairs, 91–92, 105, 163n50. See also armchairs
change, 51, 115, 123, 132
chaos and refrains, 88
cheating, 80
Checkerboard illusion (Adelson), 140n11
chewing, 104, 144n60
children: affect and, 63; attachments and, 94; dreams and, 176n80; the ego and, 25; games, 90, 94–95, 97; identification (psychoanalytically), 24, 27; mirror stage and, 142n33; objects and, 95
Christianity, 112, 168n2
circular causality, 66
Clara, 47–48, 50, 59, 71, 91
classical music, 91
Claudio, 15–16, 17, 18, 31–32, 34, 42
Clough, Patricia, 158n108
cognitive behavior therapy (CBT), 44
Cohen, Lawrence, 160n10

collective effervescence (Durkheim), 75
collective memory, 76
collective transformation, 107
collectivity, 75–76, 127
colonizer and colonized, 67
colors, 126
communication technologies, 137n26
community, witnessing of, 76
complementary relationships, 30
compulsivity, 5, 12, 79, 90, 96, 104, 108
consciousness, 121
constant transformation, 51
constitutive resonance (Mazzarella), 119
contemplation, as term, 145n73
control, 100
Copjec, Joan, 145n66, 146n82, 147n84
cosmology, 14, 19, 107–8, 176n80
countertransference, 72
couples: atmosphere and, 59, 60, 153n55; cheating, 80; cinematic aspects, 144n63; couple-image (Collu), 174n52; future and, 87; heteronormativity and, 56, 152n42; origin stories, 153n46; past relationships before coupling, 16; therapists' views on, 70, 72, 74. See also love; relationships
Couples Therapy (TV show), 138n27
Couture, Daisy, 140n8, 140n12, 155n76, 176n80
crises, 14, 64, 76
Cristina, 7
critical race theory, 27
critique, 13
cruel optimism (Berlant), 57, 153n51, 165n73; as atmosphere, 60, 70, 74, 96; attachment and, 58, 59–60, 125, 153n50, 165n73; author's life and, 58, 70; bubbles and, 70; objects and, 57, 125; present as protecting, 108; as relation, 57; Simona and Enrique's, 59–60, 73, 74
Csordas, Thomas, 162n36
cure, talking, 75
cutting, screens as, 38, 45
cybernetics, 4, 5–6, 155n74; author's experience and, 8; #CyberneticErotics, 23; family therapy and, 137n25, 139n2; in life now, 76; reciprocality in, 154n73; second-order, 137n25, 139n2; systemic therapy and, 135n5, 155n74

Damasio, Antonio, 150nn15–16
dancing: author's life and, 111, 126, 133; being and not being and, 126; Brenda and, 15; digital binges and, 122–23; *eat or be eaten* dance, 41; Gala and Jorge and, 35; interruptions as, 35, 36; oscillations and, 111, 113; present (mythical) and, 90; with reader, 42; repetition and, 96, 107; screens and, 42; swimming and, 111; with the theme, 91, 103, 105; therapy as, 91
data, 40, 128–29, 130, 175n66
dating apps, 153n46
death drive, 14, 90, 96–97, 103, 162n29, 166n80, 166n83
decompositional transformation, 14, 103, 133
default mode network (DMN), 170n23
Deleuze, Gilles: on affect, 51, 150n20; on artists' creation, 150n20; author's life and, 165n74; on bodies affecting other bodies, 51; liberation and capture (double movement of), 139n33, 174n57; on plane of immanence, 129; on refrains, 88, 160n18, 161n22; on repetition, 160n18; on territorialization, 172n41
demons, 168n2
depression, 155n83
Descartes, Rene, 129
desire, 130–31
Desjarlais, Robert, 140n9, 140n14, 143n49, 175n76
dialogues, 37
Di Croce, Nicola, 174n54
difference and repetition, 96, 165n74
diffract abusive gazes, 46
digital *dispositifs*, 97–98
#DigitalEcstasy, 23
digital panopticon, 40
dispositifs, 92–93, 163n40, 163n45; affective, 96; atmospheres and, 96; attachment and, 94, 97; author's life and, 126; digital, 97–98; folded within (being), 104; as game, 163n46; go-to, 104; images and, 124, 125, 126; letting go of, 99; objects as, 94, 96; perception and, 105; repetition as, 107; returning to, 99, 109; unconscious, 124
DMN (default mode network), 170n23
domestic violence, 7
dominance-submission relationships, 30

dopamine hits, 97
Dostaler, Ned, 175n76
draining you, 54, 67
dreams: author's life and, 131; Freud on, 129–30, 156n89, 174n61, 176n80; lucid, 125, 129, 173n46; unconscious and, 130
drinking: activities while, 34; author's life and, 22–23, 115, 151nn34–35, 175n69; Hernan's, 7; plane of immanence and, 129; unconscious and, 175n69. *See also* alcohol
dumpee and dumper, 67–68, 155n80
Dupuis, David, 174n62
Durkheim, Émile, 75, 167n96
dyadic loops, 13, 30, 33, 34, 37, 41, 42
dysmorphia, 26

eating, 30, 31, 39, 41, 147n88, 151nn34–35. *See also* cannibalism
economic crisis (Argentina, 2001–2), 9, 49, 60, 62–63, 64–65, 76
economic labor, 61
ego, the: children and, 25; death drive and, 166n83; dissolution, 99, 157n98; Freud on, 24, 118, 119, 123, 141n25, 171n26; hammering itself, 141n25; identification and, 24, 26, 31, 141n28; loosening grip on, 119; as object, 142n32
Ekman, Paul, 150n20
electricity (concept), 3, 75, 107, 167n96
Eliade, Mircea, 160n12
Elisa, 145n67
Ellenberger, Henri, 171n33
Elsa, 42
emails, 58, 66, 105
Emanuel, 55
emotional labor, 61
energy, 66, 88–89
Enrique: author's reflections on, 67; cruel optimism, 59–60, 61, 73, 74; on fighting in relationship, 49, 59; "I don't know," 55, 63, 69; impasse and, 74; loop stuck in, 65–66, 70, 154n72, 169n10; Micol (therapist) and, 56, 58–59, 71, 72; personal struggles, 49–50, 56, 58, 61–62, 64–65, 68–69, 76, 77, 149n5; Simona's comments in therapy about, 28; therapy sessions, 48, 59, 61, 64, 77
Epstein, Jean, 159n7

Erickson, Milton, 115, 116, 169n9, 169nn11–12, 172n35
eroticism, 171n29
ethnography: defining, 23; hypnosis and, 168n3
Evans-Pritchard, E. E., 40, 147n87
everydayness, 47, 58, 59
evil eyes, 148n94
exhaustion, 47, 63, 64, 68, 69, 99, 113
exorcisms, 74, 157n101
eye of the camera, 159n7; buzzing and, 106; gaze and, 39; man on couch looking into, 11; Nico and Silvia and, 106; Paula looking into, 30, 33, 41; Romina and, 81; screaming at, 32, 36; Silvia and, 86; Simona and Enrique and, 78; Thiago looking into, 2, 41

face, the, 151n37
family, 135n4, 141n27, 145n69
Fanon, Frantz, 26, 67, 155n82
father, 24, 72, 73, 176n80
Favret-Saada, Jeanne, 138n30, 157n105
feedback loops, 3, 4, 5, 29, 30
feeling, structures of, 160n16
femininity, 27, 63, 64, 67
feminist theory, 27, 56
fighting: in relationships, 4, 49, 53, 85–87, 101, 169n12; in therapy, 100, 102, 105–6, 165n78
film theory, 146n82
fish, 31
folding into loops, 13
food: maple syrup, 89, 161n24; milk, 60; pastries, 48; pork poke, 173n43
fort/da game (Freud), 90, 94–95, 97
Foucault, Michel, 40, 147n84, 152n42
framing, 7, 38
free therapy, 9
Freud, Sigmund: on death drive, 103, 166n80; on dreams, 129–30, 156n89, 174n61, 176n80; on ego, 141n25, 171n26; on "good little boy," 98, 162n31; on hypnosis, 118, 119, 123; on identification, 24, 30–31, 141n26; on libido, 151n31; on repetition, 90, 96–97; on transference, 156n91; on uncanny, 159n5; on the unconscious, 173n44
friends who drain you, 54, 67
future, the, 87, 104

Gaia hypothesis, 5
Gala, 34–37, 41
games, 90, 94–95, 97, 163n46
gaslighting, 143n52
gaze(s): use of term, 22; anonymous, 44, 45, 159n3; camera and, 141n20; diffract abusive, 46; as dispositifs, 96; identification and, 26, 28; imagined, 24, 34, 37, 45; of imagined reader, 23; invisible, 44; learning the, 21; loops of, 43; male, 27, 39, 146n82; mirror (one-way) and, 36; of the other, 27, 40; partners seeing each other through the others', 29; power of, 46; prophylactic, 148n94; as protective, 44, 148n96; reciprocality of, 29; in relationships, 45; reparative, 37, 42; scholarship on, 141n21; screens and, 40, 41; social media and, 40–41; subject and, 146n82; transformative, 42; violence of, 26; white, racist, 26
Geertz, Clifford, 135n6, 160n14
gender and affect, 63, 64, 67, 71
Giddens, Anthony, 56, 152n42, 153n45
gifts, 130, 176n77
good life, the (Berlant), 57, 124–25
Google Flu Trends, 175n67
Gori, Yanina, 148n102, 161n22, 168n1, 175n76
go-to cathexes, 13, 68, 97, 100, 104. See also cathexis
governance, 158n108
Graeber, David, 143n56
Greene, Jeremy, 137n26
Gregg, Melissa, 53
Guattari, Félix, 88, 129, 150n20, 160n18, 172n41. See also Deleuze, Gilles

Haley. See Baird, Haley
Haley, Jay, 115, 135n5, 169n9, 169n11
Han, Byung-Chul, 98, 147n84, 163n43, 165n68, 167n91, 168n101, 172n41
Haraway, Donna, 139n7
healing rituals, 75
Hegel, G. W. F., 132, 172n40
Heidegger, Martin, 145n73
Hernan, 7
heteronormativity, 56, 152n42
Heusch, Luc de, 157n101, 170n20
higher power, 5
Hochschild, Arlie, 149n6

Hodgins, Jordan, 140n12
home: being at, 104–5; coming back, 4, 161n21
homeostasis, 166n80
Hugo, 173n43
Huhtamo, Erkki, 145n70, 146n74
humor. *See* jokes
hypnosis, 12, 115, 117, 121–22, 123–24, 169n16,
    170n19; affective attachments and, 13; an-
    imality and, 172n40; author's experiences
    with, 3, 111–12, 113, 114, 116–17, 119–20, 121,
    123, 126, 128, 129, 131–32; brain in, 170n23;
    entering into/inductions, 113–14, 116, 117,
    120, 122, 132, 172n37; ethnography and,
    168n3; Freud on, 118, 119, 123; image work
    and, 14; imagination and, 123; Lacanian
    psychoanalysis vs., 9; loops and, 14, 129;
    love and, 118; phenomena, 121; reorienta-
    tion and, 121; research on, 170n23; resisting,
    169n11; space in, 112, 118; spiritual traditions
    (compared with), 169n6; streets of the city
    and, 114; temporality in, 112

identification, 12, 27; children and, 24; the ego
    and, 24, 26, 31, 141n28; Freud on, 24, 30–31,
    141n26; gaze and, 26, 28; mediation of, 41;
    mirrors and, 27; mirror stage and, 24–25;
    oral phase, 30; projective, 14, 26, 30, 34, 41,
    118, 142n38; reciprocality of, 29; roman-
    tic relationships and, 28; thirdness and, 41;
    with vision, 25
identity, use of term, 164n60
"I don't know," 28, 49–50, 52, 55, 61, 63, 69, 70,
    74, 168n99
Illouz, Eva, 144n63, 152nn42–43, 153n44
image(s), 116; affect and, 124; anthropology
    through (Stevenson), 169n14; couple-image
    (Collu), 174n52; as *dispositifs*, 124, 125, 126;
    of the good life, 124–25; hypnosis and, 114,
    116, 119, 120, 121; image work, 14, 127; for
    Lacan, 142n32; playing with, 123, 125; pro-
    jection of, 145n70; in psychoanalysis, 71;
    for the refrain, 88; self-, 145n66; uncon-
    scious and, 114, 123, 125, 129 (*see also* im-
    age(s): hypnosis and). *See also* mirror stage
imagined gaze, 24, 34, 37, 45
impasse, 50, 55, 61
influencers, 125
infrastructural sovereignty, 92

inspiration, 114
interruptions: as dancing, 35, 36; to loops, 8,
    14, 17, 32, 65, 116, 169n10; reciprocal, 35;
    repetitions and, 6, 32, 102, 106, 144n62,
    169n12; during teaching, 106; during ther-
    apy, 35; transformation through, 107
in the name of what?, 77
invisible gaze, 44
Italian language, 148n95

Jackson, Don, 135n5
James, William, 162n27
Jameson, Fredric, 172n37
jokes, 16, 54
Jorge, 34–37
jouissance, 162n34
Julio, 79–80, 81–82, 91, 92

Kelledy, Lisa, 154n73
Kirmayer, Laurence, 158n105, 170n19
kite, 99
Knight, David, 149n11
knocking, 16, 22, 24, 31, 37, 46
Kohn, Eduardo, 136n8, 136n11, 157n98, 174n63

labor, 61
Lacan, Jacques: desire for, 130–31; hypnosis vs.
    psychoanalytic method of, 9; mirror stage,
    24–25, 95, 142n29, 142nn31–32, 164n54;
    psychoanalysis (Lacanian), 1, 6; screens for,
    39, 140n16; unconscious for, 165n77
language, Italian, 148n95
Laplanche, Jean, 151n31
Latour, Bruno, 146n75
laughter: affect and, 156n87; author's, 31, 65,
    133; author's father, 141n27; author's mom,
    126; author's reactions to, 20; Claudio's, 16;
    Gala's, 37; Wanda's, 65, 101
learning, 156n87
Lefebvre, Henri, 160n18
Lévi-Strauss, Claude, 147n87
liberation phenomenology, 14, 155n82
libido, 30, 41, 151n31
life. *See* good life, the (Berlant)
Lifshitz, Michael, 171n33
likes on social media, 172n41
liminality, 118, 158n106, 170n20

listening, 136n16
Liu, Lydia, 159n5
living attention, 63, 64, 65, 67–68, 69
loops, 3; affective, 53; compulsive, 104; of
   cruel optimism, 59; dyadic, 13, 30, 33, 34,
   37, 41, 42; feedback, 3, 4, 5, 29, 30; folding
   into, 13; of gazes, 43; hypnosis and, 14,
   129; interrupting, 8, 14, 17, 32, 65, 116,
   169n10; as loops, 136n15; relational, 6,
   12, 14; stuck in (being), 65; sustenance
   through, 13; symmetrical, 29–30; in systemic therapy, 65, 169n10; of therapy recordings, 11, 82–83, 89–90, 91, 94; on video
   tapes, 91
love: advice from author, 77; author's experiences with, 108; capitalism and, 153n44; as
   event (Badiou), 144n62; as generative force,
   79; good life and, 57; as habit, 79; heteronormativity, 56, 152n42; hypnosis and, 118;
   relationality of, 56; as return, 79; as ritual,
   109. *See also* couples
Luhrmann, Tanya, 118
Lyons, Brandon, 154n73

male gaze, 27, 39, 146n82
Marcuse, Herbert, 97, 166n83
Maria, 42, 55
Marina, Dr., 8
Marisa, 17, 18, 21, 31, 34, 165n78
Markovic, Jelena, 170n19
marriage, 50
Marsilli-Vargas, Xochitl, 136n16
masculinity and affect, 63, 64, 67
Massumi, Brian, 52, 54, 124, 150n17
Mateo, 10
Mattingly, Cheryl, 144n64
Mauss, Marcel, 176n77
Mazzarella, William, 41, 107, 119, 144n65,
   153n59, 156n90, 156n93, 158n106, 167n98
McCoy, Matthew, 175n76
mediation, 20, 41
memory, 71, 76, 156n88
Merleau-Ponty, Maurice: the body for, 55,
   140n9, 158n2; on darkness of theater,
   145n70; inspiration for, 114; reversibility
   for, 21–22, 25, 140n17; screen for, 39; vision
   for, 19, 20, 21–22, 25, 139n6; on water, 21
Mesmer, Franz, 121, 171n33, 172n40

Métraux, Alfred, 157n101
Meyers, Todd, 159n4
Micol: dialogue with other therapists, 47, 62,
   69–72, 73, 77, 78; Simona and Enrique and,
   48–49, 56, 58–59, 61–62, 68–69, 70–71,
   74, 76; therapy sessions, 48, 61; watching
   therapy sessions, 91
middle class, 154n60
Milena, 165n78
mimesis, 125
Minuchin, Salvador, 145n69
mirror(s): exercises using, 35–36, 44; pocket,
   35–36; social media as, 27; therapy (use
   during), 35–36; visualizations in front of,
   131
mirror, one-way: as allegory, 23; benefit in systemic therapy, 21; experiences watching, 1,
   2, 10–11, 15, 22, 28, 113; gaze and, 36; knocking from the therapy side, 16, 32; lighting (effect on), 19; patients looking at, 36,
   43; patients meeting team behind, 44; reflections in, 17, 18, 34; subject/gaze and,
   146n82; systemic therapy (use in), 3; talking
   through, 17, 30, 31, 32, 33; therapists' relationship with, 42; thirdness and, 33; the
   world (between us) and, 21; Zoom as, 23
mirror stage: children and, 142n33; identification and, 24–25; for Lacan, 24–25, 95,
   142n29, 142nn31–32, 164n54; reenact-
   ments, 34; visibility and, 25
Mitchell, W. J. T., 159n7
modernity, 152n42
monologues, 37
Montreal, 63–64
more of the same-ness, 56, 69
mother, 72, 142n42, 143n43, 161n26
Mulvey, Laura, 39
mushrooms, 174n63
music, listening to, 167n90, 167n95
mysticism, 112
myth, 84, 104, 108

Nancy, Jean-Luc, 132
narcissism, 25, 142n35, 145n66, 153n52
narrative, 152n39
neoliberalism, 62, 91, 154n60
Netflix, 79, 89, 158n108
neuroscience, 51–52, 161n23, 171n33

new moon, 39–40

Ng, Emily, 160n19

Nico, 85–87, 91, 99, 100–103, 105–6, 108

ni inversión ni diversión (no investment and no diversion), 87, 105

Nimr, Ramzi, 149n7

#NoFilter, 27

nonreciprocality, 66, 68

nothingness, 21, 51

notifications, 27, 97–98

"now at least someone can see," 17, 31, 32, 36

objects: attachments and, 57, 94, 97; children and, 95; ego and, 142n32, 171n26; loosening, 168n100; orientation toward (Ahmed), 92–93, 162n38; repetition and, 97; transitional, 95, 108, 128, 167n87

Ogden, Thomas, 144n65

O'Neil, Cathy, 175n67

ontology, 19, 140n9, 143n47, 168n5

opacity, 19, 116, 157n105

openness, 108

open the windows, 14, 77

optical illusions, 20

oscillatory movements, 112–13

oscillatory transformation, 112

other, gaze of, 27, 40

pain, 105

Paltrow, Gwyneth, 174n63

Pandolfo, Stefania, 166n83, 175n74

Panofsky, Erwin, 146n73

panopticon, 40, 147n84

paper, 130

paradoxes, 169n12

paranoia, 43

parental figures, 24. *See also* family; father; mother

past, the, 73

pastries, 48

patience, 132

Paula: arguments with Thiago, 1–2, 32, 33; camera (looking at), 2, 12, 30, 33, 36, 41, 44; "do you see?," 2, 12, 30, 33, 36; failed attempts at therapy, 1; forgetfulness, 143n56; loop stuck in, 29, 30

peer review, 150n21

pep talks: diffract abusive gazes, 46; don't listen to it!, 167n90; get off the chair, 109; just write the email, 153n52; maple syrup, 161n24; red-faced reviewer, 150n21; Scapula shrug, 140n19; send it!, 58; standing desks, 162n37

perception: affect and, 54; for Deleuze, 150n20; *dispositifs* and, 96, 105; gaps filled by, 21; as hallucination, 140n11; imaginary and, 141n17; memory and, 156n88; for Merleau-Ponty, 141n17; of one's own body, 26; predictive, 105; racialized/gendered, 143n48, 155n82, 167n88; uncanny and, 159n5; the world and, 20, 21, 54, 89

personhood, 135n6

perspective, 145n73

phenomenology (Desjarlais), 140n14

phenomenology, 14, 155n82, 181n21. *See also* Merleau-Ponty, Maurice

phenomenon, as term, 19

Phillips, Adam, 141n28

Piasere, Leonardo, 167n94

plane of immanence (Deleuze and Guattari), 129

Plato's cave, 38

pleasure principle (Freud), 90

Plotkin, Mariano, 137n19

Pontalis, Jean-Bertrand, 151n31

posttraumatic stress, 90

posture, 92

Povinelli, Elizabeth, 152n42

power: forms of, 158n108; structural, 23

predictions, 88–89, 167n86

presence: armchair and, 162n34; gifts and, 130; hypnosis and, 114; imagined, 22; one-way mirror and, 11, 76, 138n30; theory and, 145n73; of therapist, 162n34, 165n78; the world and, 127

present, the, 56, 84, 87, 104, 108

preserving energy, 88–89

process, vision as, 20

Professor Z., 22–23, 24, 25, 28, 43, 149n103

projections: projective identification, 14, 26, 30, 34, 41, 118, 142n38; reciprocality of, 29

prophylactic gazes, 148n94

protection: gaze as, 44; screens as protective, 45

protests, 159n8

psychedelics, 125, 127, 128

psychoanalysis: Argentina and, 9–10, 136nn16–17, 137nn18–19, 137n22; author's interest in, 112; collective sessions, 9; projective identification and, 26; psyche in, 71; transference, 72–73, 147n91, 156nn90–91, 156n93. *See also* Freud, Sigmund; Lacan, Jacques

publics, 146n79

queer theory, 56

rain, 16, 31, 77, 114, 133

reading, 54, 93

real, the, 131

realness of being seen, 20

reciprocality and nonreciprocality, 35, 66, 68

recording therapy sessions, 11, 34, 37

recursivity: refrains, 105; returns, 159n9

reflections, 162n34

refraction, 12, 168n3

refrains: always-never, 84, 85; of armchairs, 88; bubbles and, 105; chaos and, 88; go-to, 100; images of, 88; recursive, 105; in relationships, 84, 87; repetition and, 83–84, 87, 88, 99; territories and (Deleuze, Guattari), 160n18

regimes of availability, 92

relationality of love, 56

relational loops, 6, 12, 14

relationships: breaking up, 31–32, 80, 82; complementary, 30; exhaustion, 47; feedback loops in, 65–66; fighting in, 4, 49, 53, 85–87, 101; gaze in, 45; identification and, 28; life cycles within, 85–86; refrains in, 84, 87; themes in, 91. *See also* couples

reparation(s): reparative gaze, 37, 42; reparative reading (Sedgwick), 138n31; thirdness and, 43

repetition(s): affect and, 13, 55, 97; ceremonial, 84; change and, 51, 123; compulsive, 5, 12, 79, 90, 96, 108; cosmology and, 108; dancing and, 96, 107; difference and, 96, 165n74; as *dispositifs*, 107; everyday, 7, 83; for Freud, 90, 96–97; in gambling, 164n62; holding us together, 97, 107; interrupting, 6, 32, 102, 106, 144n62, 169n12; intoxication through, 79; lived, 156n91; loops and,

3, 5, 32; as mother (of skill) (Robbins), 91, 162n32; objects and, 97; of refrains, 83–84, 87, 88, 99; repeating, 6; rhythm and, 85, 94, 117, 118, 160n18; ritual, 99, 107, 108; of scrolling, 122; stability of, 89; state accessed through, 99; of statements in therapy, 36; temporality and, 107; therapeutics of, 43; unconscious, 90

research process for this book, 2, 8

resonance, 119, 171n29

returns, recursive, 159n9

reversibility of vision (Merleau-Ponty), 21–22, 25

Revista Ñ (periodical), 137n23

rhythm, 85, 94, 100, 117, 118, 160n18

Ricoeur, Paul, 152n39

ritual(s): of affect dispossession, 74; cosmology and, 107–8; healing, 74; love as, 109; power of, 167n98; repetition and, 107–8; scholarship on, 170n20; shamanic, 75; in therapy, 108, 157n101

Robbins, Tony, 162n32

Rodrigo, 17

Romina, 79–80, 81–83, 85, 89–90, 91, 92, 159n3

rosaries, 98

Rossi, Ernest, 172n35

Roustang, François, 113–14, 124, 173n47

sadness, 49, 55–56, 65

Saji, Alia Al-, 27, 143nn47–48, 155n82, 160n13, 167n88, 168n5

Sánchez, 34–35, 36–37

Santana, Carlos, 167n95

Sartre, Jean-Paul, 141n22

Scalia, Jeremiah, 173n43

schedules, 98

schizophrenia, 135n5

Schüll, Natasha Dow, 164n62

screen(s): use of term, 38, 43; algorithms and, 45; the body as, 146n75; bubbles and, 148n100; as cutting, 38, 45; dancing and, 42; as form never fully given (Carbone), 145n71; gaze and, 40, 41; as interface, 146n74; for Lacan, 39, 140n16; for Merleau-Ponty, 39; as protective, 45; publics and, 146n79; staring at blank, 23, 98; therapy as, 12; vision and, 145n70; ways of observing, 23, 39–40

Sedgwick, Eve Kosofsky, 138n31, 151n37
seeing: being seen and, 17, 20, 23, 28, 39; "do you see?," 2, 12, 17, 22, 30, 31, 32, 33, 36, 46; partners seeing each other, 28
Seigworth, Gregory, 53
self, the: use of term, 164n60; control over, 121; excess and, 136n10; systems vs., 5; technologies of, 175n69
self-knowledge, 175n75
self-referentiality, 45
self-worth, 25
Seth, Anil, 140n11
"shall we leave it here?," 80, 82, 159n6
shamans, 74, 75, 76, 174n62
shame, 127
Sheiner, Eli, 140n12
shrugging, 141n19
silence, 61, 80
Silverman, Kaja, 39, 141n20, 142n31
Silvia, 85–87, 91, 99, 100–103, 105–6, 108
Simona: cruel optimism, 59–60, 73; Enrique (frustration with), 28, 49, 61–62, 63, 68–69, 76; Enrique (in union with), 59; everydayness and, 55, 56, 58; loop stuck in, 65–66, 70, 154n72, 169n10; Micol (therapist) and, 56, 58–59, 71, 72; one-way mirror and, 44, 64; therapy sessions, 48, 60, 77
singing, 99, 117
situationism, 107
sky, 99
Sloterdijk, Peter, 73, 118, 119, 153nn58–59, 171n30, 174n64
smell, 117
Sobchack, Vivian, 146n74
social, the, 107
social class, 154n60
social media: feeds, 127, 174n61; filters, 27; gaze and, 40–41; likes, 172n41; as mirror, 27; notifications, 27, 97–98. See also TikTok
Society of Psychological Hypnosis, 117
Sofia: lo que viste vs. lo que viviste (what you saw vs. what you lived), 169n8; sessions with author, 111–12, 113, 114–15, 116–17, 119–20, 121, 123, 126, 128, 131–32; space in therapy, 118, 123
Solomonova, Elizaveta, 173n46
Song, Hoon, 147n84
sound, 126

sovereignty, infrastructural, 92
space: between, 66; in hypnotherapy, 112, 118; liminal, 118; occupying, 168n5
spectatorship-exhibitionism relationships, 30
Spinoza, Baruch, 51, 53
spirituality, 118, 133, 168n2, 169n6. See also Christianity; mysticism
Spotify, 89, 105
standing desks, 162n37
Stevenson, Lisa, 124, 136n15, 156n89, 169n14, 173n51
Stewart, Kathleen, 51, 138n31
Stillinger, Leo, 143n49, 160n18, 174n53
Strange Situation Procedure, 94, 135n4, 158n107, 163n53
streets of the city: ambivalence, 159n8; atmospheric impasse, 50; echoes, 32; fighting, 7–8; hypnosis, 114; inaudible noise, 83; protests, 9; selling clothes, 61; wandering, 65
stuckness, 51
students, 13, 87, 106, 120
subaltern subjectivities, 27
subjecthood, 92, 146n82, 167n91, 174n64. See also dispositifs
subjectivity, 27, 96, 124, 155n82, 164n60
Succession (TV show), 173n48
surface, 126, 143n43
surveillance, 40, 45, 147n84
symmetrical loops, 29–30
symptoms, 113
systemic therapy, 2, 43–44, 149n4; author's research on, 8; circular causality in, 4; collectivity and, 75–76; college students (resonances with lives of), 13; complementary interactions, 154n72; cybernetics and, 135n5, 155n74; development of, 135n5; frustration at, 7; influences on, 4–5; loops in, 65, 169n10; as a system, 73, 149n2; as theatrical space, 12. See also visual devices in therapy
systems, the self vs., 5

Taggart, Eric, 94, 136n14, 142n29, 148n93, 164n54
Tai Chi, 31, 133
talking cure, 75
teaching, interruptions for, 106
technologies of the self, 175n69

temporality: always-never, 84; atmospheric stuckness, 51; author's reflections on, 79; discontinuity between sessions, 91; the future, 87, 104; gifts, 89; haunting, 89; in hypnotherapy, 112; keeping a beat, 80, 85; losing track of time, 100; the past, 73; the present, 56, 84, 87, 104, 108; rhythms, 80, 85, 100; social media apps and, 104

tenderness, 31

texting, 15

theatricality, 12, 94

theory: end of, 128; as term, 145n73

therapists: bodies of, 74; cornered by (the feeling of being), 80; in training, 10, 15, 17; views on patients, 70–71, 72

therapy: atmospheres in, 102; author's experiences with, 112, 113; being asked to leave, 1–2, 4, 6; as dancing, 91; discontinuity between sessions, 91; experiences watching, 10–11, 77; fighting in, 100, 102, 105–6, 165n78; free, 9; gaze and, 148n96; interruptions during, 35; paradoxes as technique, 169n12; paying for, 81; recording sessions, 11, 34; rituals in, 108, 157n101; as a screen, 12; transformation and, 46

Thiago: arguments with Paula, 1–2, 30, 32, 33; failed attempts at therapy, 1; forgetfulness, 143n56; gaze, 29; loop stuck in, 29, 30; "now at least someone can see," 17, 31, 32, 36; one-way mirror and, 44; retreat from talking, 30; screaming at camera, 12, 30, 32, 36, 41

thirdness, 33, 144n65; absent third, 162n34; bingeing (third hour of), 45; dyadic relations and, 33, 34, 41; focal point (third), 91; gaze (imagined), 34; inject, 41; reflecting third, 37; reparative, 43; session (third), 80; the third (finding the), 34; wine (third glass of), 23

this time, 57–58

Thompson, Evan, 170n19

TikTok, 27, 99, 104, 149n105, 172n38, 174n61

tissues, 10, 60, 61

Tomkins, Silvan, 5–6, 151n37, 156n87

trance, 122, 123, 168n1, 169n11

transcription, 145n67

transference, 72–73, 147n91, 156nn90–91, 156n93

transformation: anything but, 104; the body (first through), 74; constant, 51; decompositional, 14, 103, 133; forms (between), 120; impossible, 108; oscillatory, 112; surrender and, 144n62; therapeutic, 46; writing and, 133

transformative gaze, 42

transitional objects, 95, 108, 128, 167n87

translation, 135n1

transparency, 19

treatment, valuating effectiveness of, 43–44

Turner, Victor, 158n106, 170n20

twelve-step programs, 5

twoness, 33

uncanny, the, 159n5

unconscious, the: affective exchanges and, 73; algorithms and, 127, 165n77; cybernetics and, 165n77; dreaming and, 129; drinking and, 175n69; hypnosis and, 114–15, 116, 121; knowledge of, 116, 121; work of, 118

unsayable, the, 52

Ushigua, Manari, 174n63

Utah, 87

vacations, 99, 100

Vertov, Dziga, 159n7

Vespignani, Alessandro, 175n66

Vezzetti, Hugo, 137n22

video of therapy (live feed): blue screen, 81, 82, 83, 85, 89, 91, 94, 109; experiences watching, 48, 59, 80, 81; looking in eye of, 81, 86; loops and, 91, 94; talking to, 69; use in therapy, 48

video-recorded sessions: of author's hypnotherapy, 111–12; gifted to author, 81–82

Villa Freud (Buenos Aires), 9

violence, 7, 26

virtual, the, 151n30

Visacovsky, Sergio, 136n17

visibility, 21, 25

vision: binocular rivalry, 140n10; identification with, 25; mediation of, 20; for Merleau-Ponty, 19, 20, 21–22, 25, 139n6; narcissism of, 25; panopticism and, 147n84; positionality of, 143n48; as process, 20; reversibility of (Merleau-Ponty), 21–22, 25; screens and, 146n70; theory and (Heidegger), 145n73; West (primacy in), 19, 139n7 visual devices in therapy, 3, 17–18, 33, 139n2; attention and, 11; decompression through, 33; efficacy of, 44; loops and, 11; mediation of, 12; private and public space blurred through, 10; reversibility of vision and, 21–22. *See also* mirror, one-way; video of therapy (live feed)

vitality, 14, 82

voice, 126

voyeurism, 28, 143n50

walking, 149n5

Wanda: dialogue with other therapists, 47, 101–2, 106, 107, 108; on loops, 65; Nico and Silvia and, 86, 99–101, 102, 105–6, 107, 108; therapy sessions, 86; things said, 65, 67; watching therapy sessions, 48, 50, 78

Warner, Michael, 146n79

water and visibility, 21

Weinstein, Deborah, 135n4

Wengrow, David, 143n56

WhatsApp, 15

whiteness, 26, 143n47

Wiener, Norbert, 155n73

Wiltwyck team, 145n69

windows, 14, 77, 146n73

wine: activities to do while drinking, 34; descriptions of drinking, 22, 23; good night (purchasing for), 4; thrown at wall, 7

Winnicott, Donald, 95, 148n101, 158n107, 161n22, 161n26

witchcraft, 40–41

witnessing of community, 76

women as breadwinners, 62, 65

world, the, 21, 54, 55, 143n47

World War I, 90

writing, 45, 93, 133

Yan, Yunxiang, 152n42

Yapko, Michael, 169n16

Young, Iris Marion, 27

Zeavin, Hannah, 137n26

Zigon, Jarrett, 175n76

Žižek, Slavoj, 143n43

Zoom, 23, 131

Zupančič, Alenka, 166n80

www.ingramcontent.com/pod-product-compliance
Lightning Source LLC
Chambersburg PA
CBHW030328270326
41926CB00010B/1547